746.434 Walters, James.
W
        Crochet workshop

C1

DATE			

Crochet Workshop
James Walters

SIDGWICK & JACKSON
LONDON

Crochet Workshop

James Walters

Full instructions for making the designs
marked CSG 957 are in Coats Sewing
Group Book No. 957 — Crochet Doilies

First published in Great Britain in 1979
by Sidgwick and Jackson Limited

Reprinted 1983

Copyright © 1979 by James Walter

Design: James Walters
Photography: Rex Moreton

ISBN 0 283 98396 5 (cloth)
ISBN 0 283 98408 2 (paper)

Printed and bound in Great Britain by
Collins, Glasgow
for Sidgwick and Jackson Limited
1 Tavistock Chambers, Bloomsbury Way
London WC1A 2SG

Contents

Introduction

Crochet has probably been around for a long time—the hooked stick is such a basic tool that its usefulness for a great variety of purposes must first have occurred to man in the very distant past—but its early history and development are obscure. The basic character, techniques, traditions and styles of the craft which most people would think of as crochet today seem to be derived from the decorative lacework of the thirteenth century, usually associated with nuns, but also carried out by men and boys.

The Victorians took a great interest in crochet—work of great beauty and staggering technical achievement was done by them—and they put it all down on paper. Despite the Irish tradition, however, which they deliberately developed as part of a crash job creation programme following the famine, they did also manage to turn the craft into more of a pastime and identify it firmly with the female, in which condition it has languished until recently.

In the last few years in various parts of the world (although not notably so far in the UK) people of all kinds are not only rediscovering the old craft, but extending it in scope and scale. Its appeal seems to strike at all levels and its potential to explode upon any serious examination. Some reasons for this may be that it is so easy—compared to, say, playing a musical instrument, or even driving a car—that any moderately determined person can soon make beautiful and/or useful, original things without benefit of great knowledge or physical or mental skill. And yet it can be wholly absorbing and fulfilling to sensual, spiritual and intellectual people alike. On the mechanical level the physical work is well known to be supremely therapeutic, and in the age of machines it remains triumphantly a hand craft, a natural activity for those who seek their peace of mind in natural things. Finally in these busy days of economic strain it is no small matter that crochet involves no elaborate equipment and is therefore very cheap and portable.

This book is primarily organized as a logical sequence of study, so that you can start as an absolute beginner and go just as far as you like into the subject. (The index will enable you to treat it as a source of reference later, or for dipping into.) Naturally it is hoped that, regardless of your age, or traditions, mentally you are one of that extremely diverse new generation of interested folk who will set no limits to the extent of their enthusiasm, and

that you will therefore devour it all and eventually produce another book of your own for us all to read. If your intentions are less flamboyant, please take my bullying in good part and on no account feel put down by anything I say!

Whatever your approach, you should be clear about mine as regards the material in this book and the way in which it is presented. I have tried very hard not to prejudge your motives, mould your tastes or pre-empt your creative imagination (without signalling such presumption). This means there are no fully developed or completely worked out parcels of designs, or even ideas, for you merely to regurgitate. The various stitch patterns for instance are never included simply because of their prettiness, but because they each illustrate at least one separate, identifiable basic principle of quality/construction, etc. It also means that you must not look for authoritative reassurance: you must be sure to treat all statements which even hint at dogmatism with great scepticism. There is only one rule: forge your own rules, but only after conscientious experiment and lengthy absorbtion in the subject—and then set yourself to find valuable ways of breaking them!

This is a workshop: there are no discussions about art and no aesthetic value judgements. If your study is going to be fruitful, let it be because you use the information as a set of tools to take the lid off your own creativity.

Most ideas start as tiny grains of sand in an oyster. You work and worry at them, until they grow into complete pearls. They could arise from strictly crochet matters—an exciting yarn, intriguing stitch pattern, a colour combination, a shape—or from related crafts—an effect in knitting, tatting, macramé, weaving—or from further afield—painting, physics, chemistry, biology, astronomy, the landscape. Maybe they are forced out to meet some external need—a wedding, somebody's birthday, a present of a parcel of yarn, the winter/summer coming on—or sparked off by inner emotions.

Apart from looking at and thinking about everything you see (and touch), there are two ways most people find useful for generating ideas and stimulating the imagination: deliberate, programmed, patterned thoughts and the opposite— spontaneous association of unrelated experiences. In the latter case you must look for releasers, which work on you—a good meal, watching aeroplanes take off and land, making love, listening to music, digging the garden, talking to people.

For programmed thinking, try these: study each aspect of the fabric profile (Chapter 3) and all the examples in the book and then: set out to devise alternative stitch patterns with exactly the same characteristics as those you see in the book; discover what combinations of characteristics are not represented in the book and devise patterns to fill in the gaps; think out what characteristics you can discern in crochet which are not even referred to in the book, and make patterns to express them; work through the elements of stitch-making procedure separately and string them together in different ways to make both individual stitches and groups or combinations of stitches which are not even hinted at in the book; think up new stitch-making procedures altogether: take every stitch pattern you know and put it through all the modifications described in the book, then through any others you can think of. Now go out and find every known kind of 'yarn' (and a few more) and try all kinds of stitch patterns with them. Study your various efforts from the point of view of physical weight per given area, comparing yarns, stitch patterns, tension. See how they stretch, drop, behave generally.

Treat this book as a set of questions, not answers. Gradually you will be finding out not only about your craft, but about yourself, and beginning to take a more positive role in directing your own efforts. You will, of course, never be able to stop learning about both. Bear in mind, too, that although there is room in this book to talk about crochet only in isolation, it is a marvellous craft for mixing with others, particularly knitting, macramé, tatting, weaving, leatherwork and general clothes-making, and can be incorporated in most kinds of fine art.

Now you confident ones will already be raring to go, but let me first have a quiet word with the hard nuts—the confirmed non-designers! Do not bother to tell me you cannot design for yourself. I have heard it all before and it is almost never true. 'Not-being-able-to-design' is just a temporary state of mind which blows away as soon as the fresh breeze of common sense touches it.
'OK. So you are convinced you cannot design! Take this yarn . . .'
'Oh, I couldn't make anything out of that. It is such a horrid colour!'
'Good. You have just made the first design decision.'

At its most basic design is only a matter of making a series of fundamental decisions. To start with they may seem so obvious as hardly to count as decisions at all and your reasons for making them may all be negative: 'Not *that* colour . . . not *that* yarn . . . not *that* stitch pattern. *That* style is in terrible taste . . . I would not be seen dead in *that* . . .'

Even the positive elements which creep into your thoughts as you warm to the task may rely heavily at first on copying in some respect: something you are familiar with, something you remember you liked, something you have discovered you would be comfortable in, something you always wanted. Sometimes you may be deliberately trying to copy, but your memory or your understanding lets you down and you have to improvise. This improvisation means that you are designing. Next you may feel: 'That would be nice, if only it were lighter/a different shape/in a different quality yarn/not so see-through . . .' and you are into your own adaptations.

Slavish copying has its value in your early attempts, but quite soon becomes sterile (and, in any case, unnecessary). Fastening onto ideas—your own, or anyone else's—modifying and adapting them to new situations and bringing them together in new combinations, however, has been the mainspring of art, craft and every other natural activity since before Cro-Magnon man. Why not join the crowd?

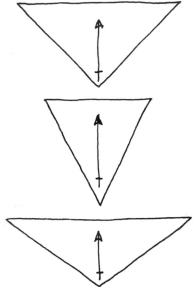

If you are really blocked, pick some simple article of which the final shape and size will not matter very much—say, a triangular shawl—and make it in any medium thickness yarn you like the look of, using basic stitches. Plan it so as to make the whole job as easy for yourself as possible. For instance, in the case of the shawl, think of starting at the narrow end. The work will grow encouragingly quickly at the beginning; you are not committed to how big the thing is going to be—just stop when you fancy, when you become bored, or when the yarn runs out; no seemingly endless base chain to force reluctant stitches into. Your only problem is to make the fabric get regularly wider as you go. Guess how much to increase. So long as you keep the edges moderately straight and increase the same amount at each edge, you may get wider too fast, or too slowly, but neither will be serious. Afterwards you may be able to think of little ways to add personal touches to the garment: try surface crochet, a border, a fringe, etc. (No. I am not going to tell you what stitch to work, or how many!)

As for making something complicated in several separate pieces, if you are at sea in the planning stage, copy the structure of some similar, well-loved article, or a paper pattern if you have one. You will soon learn how to modify this to suit your developing purposes. Above all feed your enthusiasm and ambition with success and learn from everything you do, particularly from your mistakes.

Chapter 1
Basic Technique

The Groundwork

What do you need?

To start with, just a 5.00mm crochet hook and a ball of light coloured double knitting yarn. Of course any hook and any yarn which fits the hook snugly will do, but a fairly large hook and a pale coloured smooth, non-feathery yarn make things easier to begin with. A pair of scissors is handy too. (For more detailed information on hooks and other equipment, see the Appendices at the back of the book.)

Lefthanders

If you read 'left' for 'right' and vice versa, you will be working a perfectly satisfactory mirror-image of what the righthanders are doing. Keep a mirror handy to check the drawings and stitch diagrams. Beware of the terms 'right side' and 'wrong side' of the work (see page 35)—they are the same for you as for righthanders.

Abbreviations

For the sake of brevity basic terms in crochet are abbreviated. In the main text the words will be spelled out in full and, to begin with, the abbreviations will follow in brackets, so that you can pick them up as you go along. When in doubt consult the full list on page 244. Relevant abbreviations are always given at the beginning of commercial pattern instructions, but before long you will know them all by heart anyway.

Diagrams

The diagrams in this book are mostly self-explanatory, but if you have any difficulty understanding the details of stitch diagrams, please refer to page 244. It pays to become familiar with this simple method of annotating crochet as a means of sorting out both other peoples' and your own original stitch patterns at the drawing board stage.

The Action

Crochet means making a succession of loops in a continuous thread with a hook. The right hand holds and works the hook; the left also holds the work and controls the supply of thread from the ball. Before you even pick up the hook, it is best to find out how the left hand works.

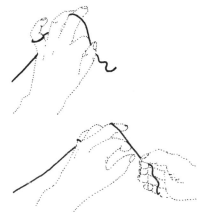

Left hand: Take the end of the thread between forefinger and thumb. Lead it over first and second fingers, under the third and round the little finger.

Allow the fingers to relax and curl up slightly. Make sure that there is plenty of unwound yarn from the ball. Then, releasing forefinger and thumb, pull the short end with the right hand, so that the thread slips continuously through the fingers, but also so that, whenever you like, you can hold and stop the thread running through your third and little fingers by squeezing. Release again, squeeze, release, and so on. When you can do this more or less without the thread constantly jumping off your fingers, stopping your circulation or giving you cramp, try this exercise: tie a small pair of scissors, or something of roughly the same weight, to the end of the yarn, arrange the thread around the left hand as before and repeat the movements.

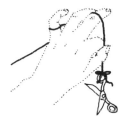

Hold   forefinger and thumb
Relax little finger
Raise middle finger (to ease supply thread
          through third and little fingers).

Hold   third and little fingers
Relax forefinger and thumb
Lower middle finger (as weight pulls thread
          through).

You are simply flexing the left hand so as to make the thread pass in controlled stages from left to right, by stopping first at one side of the hand, then at the other. When you are actually crocheting, it is the working of the hook which takes up the thread. The middle finger is always kept in gentle tension against the loop of thread spanning the back of the hand, not only to ease the thread through, but also so that the hook has something positive to engage and pull against. In practice the flexing movements merge into one continuous action.

Do not spend too much time on the exercise, which is only to give you some idea of what should be happening.

Right hand: Hold the hook at the flattened part of the stem (or about 5cm/2in from the tip) like a pencil between forefinger

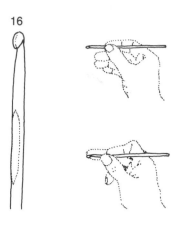

and thumb just so that you can tap the end of the hook with the tip of your middle finger. Crochet movements are very much like writing in the air and just as the tip of a fountain pen must be turned round in a particular way in relation to the paper, if it is to write at all, so must the tip of the hook in crochet normally be turned on its side with the notch or hook facing you. The flattening on the stem not only defines the best place to hold the hook and makes continued holding of it for long periods more comfortable, it also keeps the tip at the best angle preventing 'twiddling', or rolling between the fingers, which should not be necessary for the majority of the movements.

Initial Slip Knot

Crochet starts with a slip knot at the beginning of the yarn which you make like this:

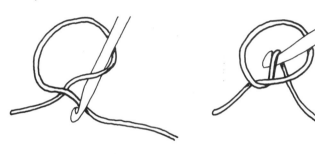

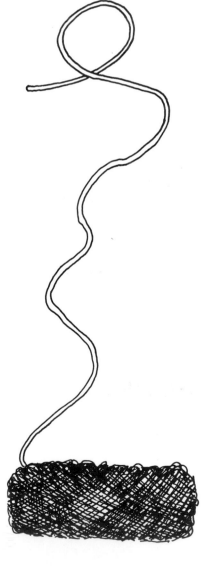

Pull up the short end to tighten the knot itself gently and on the supply thread to slide the knot up to the hook where it should be snug round the wide part of the stem. The slip knot disappears when you remove the hook and tug the short end.

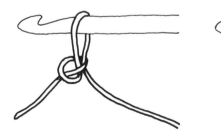

Yarn Round Hook (yrh)

To make all the stitches in crochet the hook has to engage the supply thread, forming a new loop, which is drawn through the previous ones. In different patterns this action may be called 'yarn round hook (yrh)', 'yarn over hook (yoh)', 'wool round hook (wrh)', or 'wool over hook (woh)'. It will be called 'yarn round hook (yrh)' in this book. It means duck the tip of the hook under and round anticlockwise (lefthanders—clockwise) to catch the supply thread. All pattern instructions assume you will take the yarn round the hook in this way, but see page 83 for other ways.

The Stitches

Chain (ch) ○

The chain (ch) is the basis of all crochet stitches (sts) and a series of chains (chs) forms the foundation of most patterns—this is sometimes called the Foundation Chain or Base Chain.

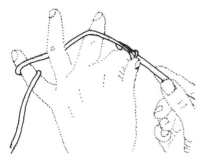 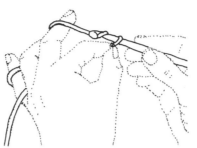 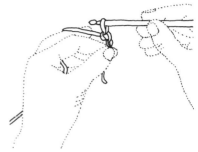

Start with the slip loop. Take the knot in the left hand and arrange the thread round the left hand as before.

Raise left hand middle finger. Yarn round hook (yrh).

Draw thread through loop already on hook. You have made 1 chain (1ch) and there is a single new loop on the hook.

Remembering the original exercise, practise making a length of continuous chains (chs), shifting the left hand position after each one to bring the forefinger and thumb up close to the hook again. If this seems tricky, it may help to drop the righthand middle finger over the loop on the hook whilst you reposition the left hand. Presently you will only have to do this after every 3, 5 or maybe even more chains (chs).

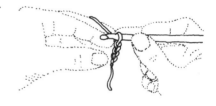

You should aim for an easy and flowing rhythm, producing a stream of neat and even chains (chs). Every so often, try poking the hook into some of the earlier ones. If this proves difficult and the hook will not penetrate, you are working too tightly. This probably means the thread is not easing through the third and little fingers properly at the right moment: this in turn could mean that your control is not yet very good, or that your ball of yarn is stuck. Always make sure that there is some unwound yarn between the ball and left hand.

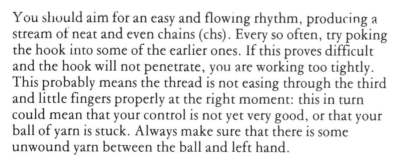

If on the other hand you could easily get two hooks at once into the same chain (ch), you are working too loosely. This probably means that your third and little fingers are not managing to stop the thread sliding through at all, the middle finger is not therefore able to make any tension and the hook is having to fish for the supply thread.

Perfection lies somewhere between. Do not bore yourself trying to achieve it yet, though; move on and learn how to do the other stitches (sts), then, if you still have problems, look at page 22.

You will discover that your length of chains (chs) unravels very smartly if you remove the hook and pull the supply thread. Because of its construction most crochet work unravels in this way right back to the beginning, or to where the last ball was joined in. To prevent this happening, cut the yarn a few centimetres (a couple of inches) away from the hook, draw the cut end through the last loop and tighten gently (see also Fastening Off, page 36).

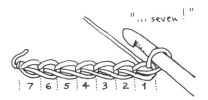

Counting chains: Before you begin any particular piece of crochet, you must know the total number of chains (chs) to be worked (pattern instructions usually tell you; if they do not, see Chapter 3). Count them as you make each one. Do not count the initial slip knot, but count 'one' for the first actual chain (ch) made. When you think you have the right number, to make a check, keep the length of chain (ch) untwisted and count each set of links back to the beginning. Again do not count the loop which is still on the hook, but count 'one' for the first full set of links.

Inserting the hook into the base chain: You will notice that in each chain (ch) there appear to be three threads lying together. In order to make all the stitches (sts) that follow, you have to poke the hook through a previously made chain (ch). Always do this so that there are two threads above the hook and one thread below. Make sure the same side of your base chain is always facing you, otherwise individual chains (chs) will be difficult to identify.

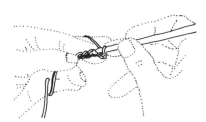

Do not pull the base chain too tight lengthwise. Have your left hand forefinger directly behind the chain (ch) in question, to prevent it moving away from the hook, and to feel the tip of the hook coming through.

If the loop on the hook tends to slip off, drop your right hand middle finger onto it while you are finding the correct place to go in.

Slip Stitch (SS) ⌒

The slip stitch (SS), sometimes called Single Crochet (sc), is like a chain (ch), which is worked after you have poked the hook through another part of the fabric, or into one of your base chains first. For beginners working slip stitches (SSs) directly into a base chain is more difficult than any of the other stitches. Why not leave it until later, or practise it first by making some slip stitches (SSs) into some other piece of fabric altogether, such as the hem of an old sweater? Insert the hook, yarn round hook (yrh), draw the thread through the sweater and through the loop on the hook. That is a slip stitch (SS)—a chain (ch) with some other fabric caught up between the threads. You can make a row of slip stitches (SSs) along the hem of the sweater by repeating these movements.

The slip stitch (SS) is the shallowest stitch (st) in crochet, that is, it adds least bulk to what you have already done. Consequently it is not normally used alone as a fabric stitch (except see Belts, page 196), but as a means of joining the end of a row to the beginning in a circle (see page 30), or manoeuvering the hook from one part of the work to another invisibly without breaking off the yarn, or as a decoration in Surface Crochet (see page 139).

Double Crochet (dc) +

The double crochet is like a slip stitch (SS) with one extra step. The first row of crochet after the base chain—usually called the Foundation or Base Row—is very often worked in double crochet (dc), because it is firm and neat and makes an excellent edging. It is also useful for narrow contrast stripes (see page 147). As a complete fabric, however, it tends to be rather heavy and inflexible—not to say laborious to make—unless it is worked loosely on a large hook or with springy yarn. Double crochet (dc) can also be worked backwards (see page 190) as a decorative edging.

Half Treble (h.tr) T

The half treble (h.tr) is like a double crochet (dc) with one extra preliminary step. It is slightly deeper than the double crochet.

Treble (tr) Ŧ

The treble (tr) is like a half treble, but with one extra step. It is deeper again than the half treble (h.tr) and is the basic, utility stitch. It can be used solidly by itself, or in various combinations and arrangements to form groups, clusters, mesh and openwork effects (see Chapter 3).

Double Treble (d.tr), Triple Treble (t.tr), etc. Ŧ Ŧ

These and all longer stitches (sts) are like trebles (trs) with one more preliminary wrapping of the yarn round the hook before you start and one more step at the end each time. Each makes a deeper stitch (st) than the last. This process can be extended indefinitely to produce as long a stitch (st) as you like. In practice any stitch (st) longer than a triple treble (t.tr) is normally explained fully in pattern instructions, because it does not appear often. If only one such type of long stitch occurs in the pattern, it may be called simply a Long Treble (l.tr).

Slip Stitch (ss) ⌒

Start with a length of base chain — 1 chain (1ch) for each stitch required.

Prepare
Insert hook in chain next to hook.

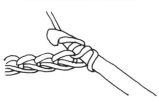

Step 1
Yarn round hook (yrh).

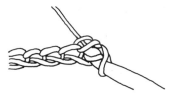

Draw thread straight through chain (ch) and loop on hook. You have made 1 slip stitch (1ss) and there is a single new loop on the hook.

You may need to make two movements out of this. After drawing through the base chain either revolve the hook through 180° and fiddle it through the loop on the hook, or

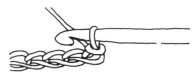

bend the righthand end of the base chain down and round, so that the lefthand forefinger and thumb can grasp this together with the rest of the chain (this becomes easier after you have worked a couple of stitches). Then draw through without revolving the hook.

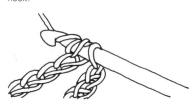

Double Crochet (dc) +

Start with a length of base chain — 1 chain (1ch) for each stitch required plus 1, e.g. 11 chains (11ch) for 10 stitches (10sts).

Prepare
Insert hook in 3rd chain from hook.

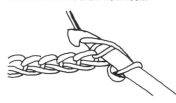

Step 1
Yarn round hook (yrh).

Draw thread through base chain only = 2 loops on hook.

Step 2
Yarn round hook (yrh).

Draw through 2 loops.
You have made 1 double crochet (1dc) and there is a single new loop on the hook.

Half Treble (h.tr) T

Start with a length of base chain = 1 chain (1ch) for each stitch required plus 1, e.g. 11 chains (11ch) for 10 stitches (10sts).

Prepare
Yarn round hook (yrh).

Insert hook in 3rd chain from hook.

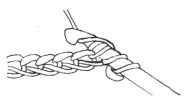

Step 1
Yarn round hook (yrh).

Draw thread through base chain only = 3 loops on hook.

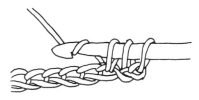

Step 2
Yarn round hook (yrh).

Draw thread through all loops.
You have made 1 half treble (1h.tr) and there is a single new loop on hook.

If the last loop tries to 'run away' take a new grip round the lower part of this and the previous stitch or turning chain and complete the final pull-through with a semi-rotary, semi-levering movement.

Treble (tr) ꝼ

Start with a length of base chain — 1 chain (1ch) for each stitch required plus 2, e.g. 12 chains (12ch) for 10 stitches (10sts).

Prepare
Yarn round hook (yrh).

Insert hook in 4th chain from hook.

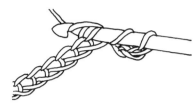

Step 1
Yarn round hook (yrh).

Draw thread through base chain only = 3 loops on hook.

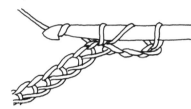

Step 2
Yarn round hook (yrh).

Draw through 2 loops = 2 loops on hook.

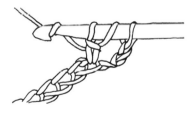

Step 3
Repeat (rep) the last step once.
You have made 1 treble (1tr) and there is a single new loop on the hook.

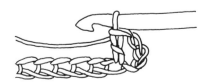

Double Treble (d.tr) ꝼ

Start with a length of base chain — 1 chain (1ch) for each stitch required plus 3, e.g. 13 chains (13ch) for 10 stitches (10sts).

Prepare
Yarn twice round hook (yrh twice).
Insert hook in 5th chain from hook.

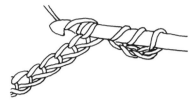

Step 1
Yarn round hook (yrh).
Draw thread through base chain only = 4 loops on hook.

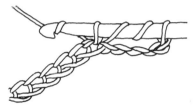

Step 2
Yarn round hook (yrh).
Draw thread through 2 loops = 3 loops on hook.

Step 3
Repeat (rep) step 2 once = 2 loops on hook.

Step 4
Repeat (rep) step 2 again.
You have made 1 double treble (1d.tr) and there is a single new loop on the hook.

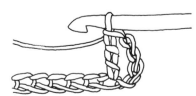

Triple Treble (t.tr) ꝼ

Start with a length of base chain — 1 chain (1ch) for each stitch required plus 4, e.g. 14 chains (14ch) for 10 stitches (10sts).

Prepare
Yarn 3 times round hook (yrh 3 times).
Insert hook in 6th chain from hook.

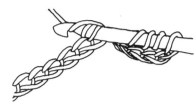

Step 1
Yarn round hook (yrh).
Draw thread through base chain only = 5 loops on hook.

Step 2
Yarn round hook (yrh).
Draw through 2 loops = 4 loops on hook.

Step 3
Repeat (rep) step 2 once = 3 loops on hook.

Step 4
Repeat (rep) step 2 again = 2 loops on hook.

Step 5
Repeat (rep) step 2 again.
You have made 1 triple treble (1t.tr) and there is a single new loop on the hook.

Problems

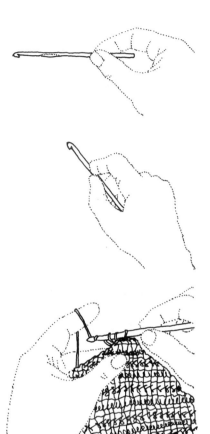

Hands, Hook and Yarn

The position of the hook in the right hand as described and shown in this book is the most logical, efficient and comfortable for the majority of people in the context of relatively small scale work using soft, light yarns. It presupposes that most of the necessary movement will be the responsibility of the right hand—and this is easily obtainable from the articulation of the wrist and fingers in most cases; the elbow remains still and the weight of the arm can be supported on the arm of a chair. Some people ignore the flattened part of the hook, holding it instead at the end. Others prefer to hold the hook altogether more firmly and rigidly, giving the left hand most of the task of providing the movement; they frequently adopt the full hand grip, or one of its variations. When thick, stiff, or heavy yarn or rope is involved, the full hand grip becomes essential. Then the whole right arm is brought into play, since the hand alone is not strong enough to perform the movements.

As far as the left hand is concerned the most usual variation is to hold the work between middle finger and thumb and use the first finger to brace the supply thread. Some dedicated knitters have to hold both hook and supply thread in the right hand and flick the yarn over the hook from that side—which is of course 'quite wrong'! Try and make a reasonable effort to train yourself into the orthodox style, but, if you do not win this particular battle with yourself, do not despair; you may have difficulty finding ways of working certain special things, such as loop stitch (see page 86), but in general there is no clear-cut reason why this technique should not be serviceable.

Even if the supply thread does come through the left hand each individual will find a slightly different way of arranging it. There seem to be as many different, but perfectly effective ways of coping as there are crochet workers. The fact is that to make any sort of useful crochet fabric, over the course of many hours small movements have to be repeated thousands of times, smoothly, regularly, quickly and, if possible, without effort or pain. Inevitably your fingers, rather than theory, will show you how this is to be done.

Making Chains

Drawing through: There should be no effort involved in drawing the supply thread through the loop on the hook. If there is check
1   that the hook is not speared through the thread;
2   that the full part of the stem, not just the narrow part of the

neck, slips easily through the loop before you pick up the
supply thread;
3   that the barb of the hook is at the right angle to the loop.
If the movement is still stiff, the chances are you are applying
far too much tension on the supply thread in your anxiety to
keep it from slipping off the hook, and the hook is engaged in a
tug-of-war with the left hand.

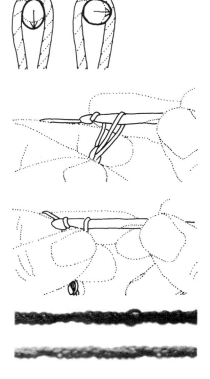

Tight chains: Apart from making the moment of drawing
through difficult, excessive tension in the supply thread will
have the effect of tightening up the *previous* chain loop,
however loose you made it at the time. The treatment:
1   Make a chain (ch), drawing through the loop until it is
obviously much too big.
2   Duck the hook under the supply thread.
3   Drop the tip of the right hand middle finger onto the
threads on the hook to prevent slippage.
4   Shift the left hand grip to pinch together all three threads at
the bottom half of this chain (ch), so that there is no slippage
into or out of the chain as you draw the supply thread through
again and up into another oversize loop.

Uneven chains: Before you develop a fluent technique you must
expect uneven, inconsistent results, but be sure that you always
pick up the supply thread the same way each time: hook under
and round anticlockwise.

The Loops on the Hook
Here are three common problems which can be dealt with
together:
1   the loops on the hook will not stay in place while you try
and insert the hook;
2   by the time the hook has been inserted, the previous stitch
(particularly if this happens to be the turning chain) has become
wrapped round the hook as well as the loops; or
3   the loops collect in the neck of the hook and become so
tight that you can no longer slide the hook through them.
All these problems are the result of too much or too little
tension on the supply thread. You cannot expect your left hand
to do any better for the moment. It will, eventually, after you
have had some extended practice, but in the meantime, after
wrapping the threads round the hook, clamp down the right
hand middle finger, only releasing it after the hook has been
inserted and the next loop pulled through.

Pulling Through the Loops
Greater care and accuracy is needed for pulling through several
sets of loops than for simple chain making. Take care that the
hook is at the most advantageous angle, or you will snag them.

Exert only enough tension on the supply thread to keep it in the hook; if you drag harder, you will be tightening up the very loop you want to pull through. If the loops are generally too tight, stop fighting, relax them and try again. Never just pull doggedly; press the back of the hook gently upwards into the tops of the loops you are drawing through and rock it slightly from side to side, only drawing through as you feel it wants to come. In the case of the longer stitches do not be afraid to shift your left hand grip nearer the hook after each stage.

Making a Simple Fabric

A simple fabric can be made by working one or another of the basic stitches (sts) to and fro in rows (linear), or round and round a central point (circular). From the second row onwards this means inserting the hook under just the top two loops, which lie over each stitch (st) of the previous row. Sometimes for special pattern effects you must insert the hook into only one of the top two loops, or between the stitches, or even into more distant parts of the fabric altogether. If you are following someone else's pattern, it is assumed you will always work under those top two loops, unless you are specifically instructed otherwise.

In this chapter the working examples are all in treble (tr), because this is easier to see and to work, but the other stitches all work according to the same principles. The beginner should try out all of them, starting with treble (tr), then going backwards through half treble (h.tr) to double crochet (dc). The abbreviated jargon in italics accompanying the general explanations, which go with the working examples, is the kind of thing you should expect to see in pattern instructions.

Turning Chain (T.ch)

You may have noticed that the single loop left on the hook after completing the last chain (ch) of the base chain becomes the top of the first stitch (also, for that matter, that the loop left on the hook at the completion of any stitch always becomes the top of the next one, or the lower part of the turning chain, if that follows). Consequently you have to miss 2, 3, 4 etc. chains (chs) before inserting the hook and, when you have completed the first stitch (st), these missed chains (chs) stand up alongside it at

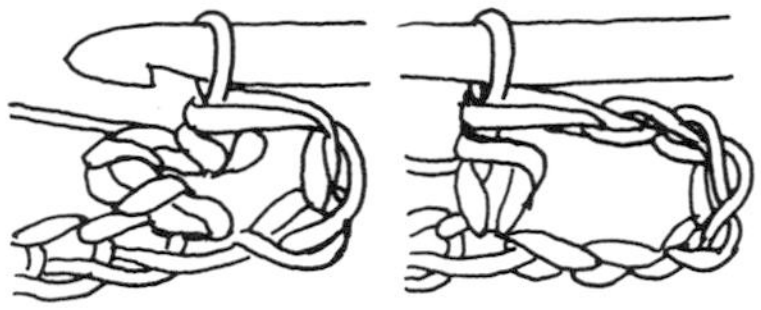

right angles to the base chain. Naturally the longer that first stitch is, the more chains (chs) have to be missed to give it room. Too few and the stitch (st) will have to bend over; too many and the column of missed chains (chs) will have to do so.

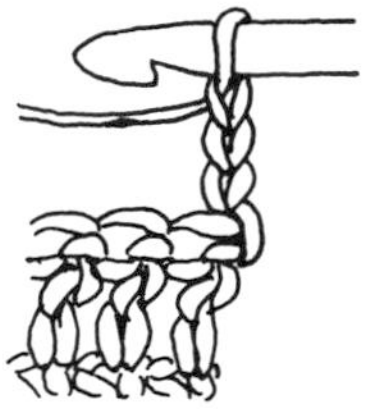

When you have worked a complete row and before you can start the next, you must again work some chains (chs)—the actual number depending upon the height of stitch (st) you are about to use—to bring the hook up to a suitable height. This is called the turning chain. Pattern instructions always specify into which chain (ch) of the base chain you should work the first stitch (st) and also the number of chains (chs) to work for turning. The usual scheme is noted below, but it does vary.

Whenever you turn the work, always make a habit of doing so in the same direction. Otherwise the turning chain will be twisted in a different way each time and will be difficult to recognize when you come back over it at the end of the next row. Most people find the best way is to turn the work as though it were the page of a book—the top of the turning chain then seems to be turned most sympathetically towards you, when you come to work into it later. Other people find this increases the gap between the turning chain and the next stitch and so you may need to experiment.

Type of Stitch	Work 1st stitch	Turning Chain
Slip Stitch (SS) ⌃	Next chain to hook	0
Double Crochet (dc) +	3rd chain from hook	1 chain (ch)
Half Treble (h.tr) T	3rd chain from hook	2 chains (chs)
Treble (tr) ⫪	4th chain from hook	3 chains (chs)
Double Treble (d.tr) ⫪	5th chain from hook	4 chains (chs)
Triple Treble (t.tr) ⫪	6th chain from hook	5 chains (chs)

When you are experienced you may find your own personal tension requires an adjustment to this scheme.

There are two ways of regarding the turning chain (t.ch):
1 simply as a method of raising the hook to a suitable height to commence the next row—Simple Turning Chain; or
2 both as a method of raising the hook and as a stitch (st) in its own right—Turning Chain-as-Stitch.
It is important to understand the difference between these two treatments and to decide which is best for you.

The simple turning chain: This turning chain (t.ch) does not count as a stitch (st). You must be careful to ignore it when counting your stitches and avoid working any stitches (sts) into the top of it, when you come to the end of each row. The illustration shows how to work it step by step in treble (tr) and what it looks like. Compare this with the next illustration.

Treble Fabric
Simple Turning Chain

If you repeat row 2, you will be working the correct basic fabric with straight edges.

Rep row 2 for straight patt.

Make a slip loop, then 13 chains (13ch).

Row 1: Starting into the 4th chain from hook, work 1 treble into each chain to the end. You have 10 stitches, because you are not counting the turning chain (the turned up part of the base chain). Work 3 chains and turn the work ready for the next row.

1tr in 4th ch from hook, 1tr in each ch to end, 3ch to turn = 10sts.

Row 2: Work 1 treble into the top of the last stitch in the previous row and then into each of the other stitches to the end, but not into the top of the turning chain. Work 3 chains and turn the work.

1tr into each st to end, 3ch to turn.

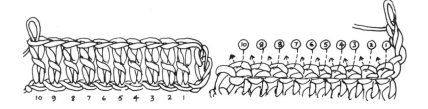

Treble Fabric
Turning Chain-as-Stitch

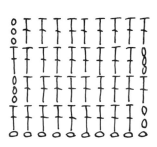

If you repeat row 2 you will be working the correct basic fabric with straight edges.

Rep row 2 for straight patt.

Make a slip loop, then 12 chains (12ch).

Row 1: Starting into the 4th chain from hook work one treble into each chain to the end. You have 10 stitches, because you are counting the turning chain (the turned up part of the base chain). Turn the work ready for the next row.

1tr in 4th ch from hook, 1tr in each ch to end, turn = 10sts.

Row 2: Work 3 chains to count as the first treble. Missing the top of the last stitch in the previous row, work 1 treble into the next and each stitch to the end of the row, including into the top of the turning chain (turned up part of the base chain). Turn the work.

3ch as 1tr, miss first st, 1tr in each st to end, turn.

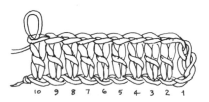

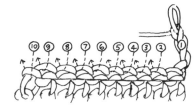

The turning chain-as-stitch: This turning chain counts as a stitch. You must include it when counting your stitches and work a stitch into the top of it at the end of a row. The illustration shows how to work it step by step in treble (tr) and what it looks like. Compare this with the previous illustration.

The same principles can be applied to any of the other stitches. Remember to insert the first stitch into a chain that is the appropriate number from the hook and thereafter to modify the length of your turning chain to the particular stitch. Most authorities seem to favour the simple turning chain treatment for double crochet (dc) and turning chain-as-stitch treatment for all the longer stitches (sts)—probably because the single turning chain (t.ch) can be easy to miss altogether and a little difficult to work into. The only problem with this dual approach is inconsistency. If your pattern calls for alternate rows in, say, double (dc) and treble (tr) crochet, strange things can happen.

As you work you reckon to count the stitches always after the treble (tr) rows, because this is easier; but although you still seem to have the correct number, the fabric is creeping to the left! You become confused and eventually sufficiently demoralized perhaps to try and surreptitiously work a few extra stitches on the right to stop the edge fading away and missing a few on the left. You hope to be able to pull and press the whole thing into shape at the end, if the worst comes to the worst. Clearly in order to work a piece of fabric with consistent edges and the same number of stitches (sts) in each row, without unwittingly increasing or decreasing (usually called 'working straight'), you must adopt one or the other treatment right from the start and stick to it for each row. For the sake of clarity in this book we shall use only turning chain-as-stitch from now on unless otherwise indicated.

Working in rows without turning: Sometimes it is desirable to work each row in the same direction without turning. To do this you must fasten off the yarn at the end of each row and rejoin at the beginning again. This is a tedious way of working, but may be necessary to obtain the desired texture or pattern.

You are naturally always working into the fronts of the stitches (sts) this time. They look different; the two loops slant downwards towards you, so the angle of the hook going in needs to be modified. Since there is no turning involved, the turning chain (t.ch) may be called the starting chain (st.ch) in some patterns, but both terms amount to the same thing.

To see what double crochet (dc), half treble (h.tr) treble (tr) and double treble (d.tr), etc. look like when worked always in the same direction, see pages 134 and 135.

Treble Fabric
worked without turning

Make a slip loop, then 12 chains (12ch).

Row 1: Starting into the 4th chain from hook work 1 treble into each chain to the end. You have 10 stitches. Fasten off but do not turn the work.

Lay the new short end over the top of the previous row of stitches and encase it (this saves time darning in later) as you work one treble into each stitch to the end. Fasten off, but do not turn.

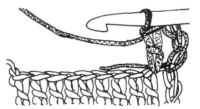

Row 2: (and every alternate row): Insert the hook into the top chain of the starting chain (turned up part of the base chain) and join the supply thread in again (see page 36) as you make 3 chains (3ch) to count as the first treble. Beware: it is easy to confuse this with the 2 loops which complete the first proper treble in the previous row.

Row 3 (and every alternate row): Join the supply thread into the top of the first proper treble in the previous row and work two trebles into the last stitch

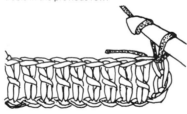

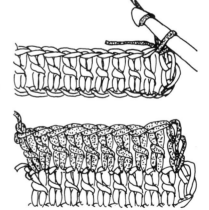

Alternative Base Chains
Although they are hardly ever asked for in pattern instructions double and treble chains are an extremely useful part of the repertoire for linear work. They are really a succession of double crochet (dc) and treble (tr) stitches (sts) respectively worked into each other's sides, and look like an ordinary base chain plus a row of stitches (sts) made simultaneously. They are generally a more immediate and accurate indicator of what your eventual tension will be (see page 55); they are more flexible than simple base chains and do not have that tendency to twiddle up. They are much simpler to work into and the place to insert the hook is much easier to see.

Make a slip loop and 2 chains.

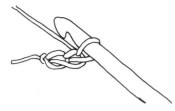

Insert hook into the 2nd chain from hook (the first chain made) and work 1 double crochet (1dc).

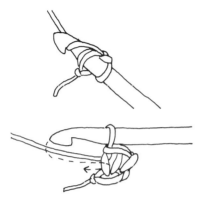

Insert hook into the single lefthand thread forming the previous double crochet and work 1 double crochet (1dc).

Repeat the last sequence as required.

Double Chain

Make a slip loop and 3 chains.

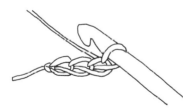

Yarn round hook. Insert hook into the 3rd chain from hook (the first chain made) and work 1 treble (1tr).

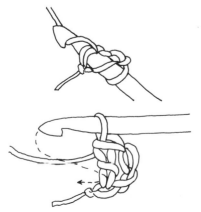

Going into the single lefthand thread at the bottom of the previous treble work 1 treble (1tr).

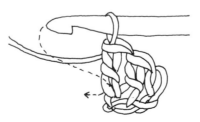

Repeat the last sequence as required.

Treble Chain

Circular Fabric

Triangles, squares, hexagons and many other different shapes apart from true circles can be made on a circular basis, that is, starting with a central ring and working round and round. Whatever the actual shape, it follows from simple geometry that, if the fabric is eventually to lie flat, you must work more stitches with each successive row, by working more than one stitch into the same place at intervals. It is obviously important how many more you work: too many, and your work will begin to undulate around the edges; not enough and it will bend up into a cup shape. If you are following pattern instructions you do not need to know how to organize this, because they all give specific details.

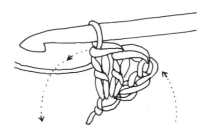

Starting a circle: The most usual way to start is to make a short length of base chain and join this into a ring with a slip stitch (SS) into the first chain made.

This ring can be any length, but should be only 3 or 4 chains long if you do not want an actual hole in the centre of your fabric.

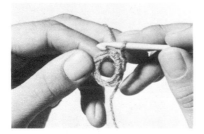

Alternatively two or three turns of the supply thread can be taken round the thumb to serve as your ring. Afterwards the end can be pulled up tight and secured.

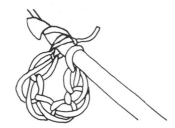

However there is nothing against working into a single chain at the end of a short base row.

If you have a curtain ring, you can join directly into that (see page 36).

There are two methods of constructing circular work:
In Rounds—the end of each row (usually called a round in
circular work) is joined up to its own beginning to form a ring
and a new starting chain is worked to take the hook up to the
right height for the next row. You have the option (pattern
instructions permitting) of turning the work, or not, at the end
of each round, and therefore of working into the fronts or backs
of stitches.

In Spirals—at the end of the first round, up to which point all
the stitches have been worked into the ring, you simply carry on
round and round by going into the tops of the previous stitches.
When the basic stitch is treble (tr) or larger it is possible to taper
the beginning and end of the spiral by using graduated, shorter
stitches. Otherwise there will be a step effect. Your single,
continuous round will always be worked with the same side of
the fabric facing you.

It is easy to make a spiral by mistake, when you should be
making separate rings. Beginners often find their chief
stumbling block is being unable to identify the beginning of
each round and, after that, finding the right loops to join up to.
There is no short cut: you must think clearly, work methodically
and learn the correct 'look' of the thing. Decide what you think
is right, try it, see presently if you are gaining or losing a stitch
each round; learn from this to adjust your procedure, try again,
and so on (see also page 32).

With spirals it is useful to mark the beginning of the first
'round' with a safety pin or piece of contrasting thread, so you
know when you have completed each circuit.

The illustrations show three characteristic fabrics made in the
circular format. See if you can make them simply by looking at
the master stitch diagrams. If not, consult the full supporting
verbal instructions and drawings. The square is often used to
make patchwork garments and other articles (see page 151). In
this case a half square—divided along the diagonal—can be
extremely useful. If you plan to make each motif in one colour,
remember that the half square can be made without breaking
off the yarn only by turning at the end of each row. To make
both half and full squares match, therefore, you are obliged to
turn between each round during the full square as well.

Circle

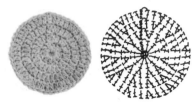

These instructions assume you will be working each round with the right side facing and with the same yarn, but you could turn between rounds (for a different effect) and/or use different colours.

Make 4 chains and join them up into a ring by working a slip stitch into the first chain.

Make 4ch, SS to first ch to form ring.

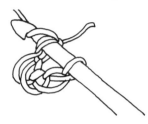

Round 1: Work 3 chains to count as the first treble, then 11 trebles into the ring inserting the hook through the central hole, not into the individual chains.

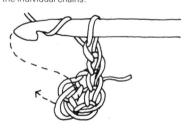

It will probably seem as though there is not enough room for all the stitches and you may inadvertently trap the first 3 chains of the round, or even work some of your trebles into it, instead of into the ring. Before any of this happens, pull the stitches back round the ring against the starting chain to make room.

Insert the hook into the top (3rd) chain of the starting chain and work a slip stitch to join the round. Do not turn the work. You have 12 stitches, counting the starting chain.

3ch as 1tr, 11trs into ring, SS to join = 12sts.

Round 2: Work 3 chains to count as first treble, then 1 treble into the top of the previous starting chain, i.e. where the present one seems to have come from. You have 2 stitches coming out of 1 stitch.

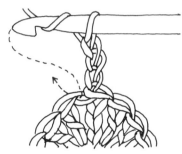

Now work 2 trebles into every stitch right round the circle.

Insert the hook into the top (3rd) chain of the starting chain and work a slip stitch to join the round. Do not turn the work. You have 24 stitches, counting the starting chain.

3ch as 1tr, 1tr in same place, 2trs in each st to end, SS to join.

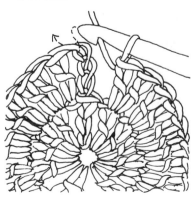

Round 3: Work 3 chains to count as first treble and 1 treble into the top of the previous starting chain, making 2 stitches.

Now work one treble into the next stitch and 2 trebles into the next. Repeat this all the way round, ending with the single treble into the last stitch.

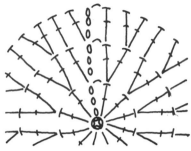

Join with a slip stitch as usual. Do not turn. You have 36 stitches.

3ch as 1tr, 1tr in same place, (1tr in next st, 2trs in next st) 11 times, 1tr in last st, SS to join.

Round 4: Work 3 chains to count as first treble and 1 treble into the top of the previous starting chain.

Now work 1 treble into each of the next 2 stitches and 2 trebles into the third and repeat that all the way round, ending with single trebles into each of the last 2 stitches.

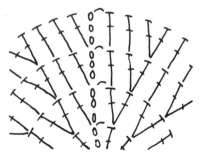

Join with a slip stitch as usual. Do not turn. You have 48 stitches.

3ch as 1tr, 1tr in same place, (1tr in each of next 2sts, 2trs in next st) 11 times, 1tr in each of last 2sts, SS to join.

To continue, work one more single treble between the pairs of trebles each round, so as always to increase by 12 stitches.

Granny Square

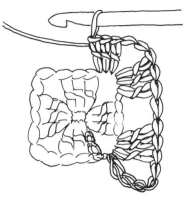
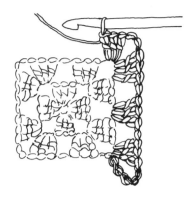

These instructions assume you will be working each round with the right side facing but see the notes in the main text (page 31) about turning — particularly if your project involves some 'half' squares.

If you are making multicoloured squares with a different colour for each round, fasten off after the first (joining) slip stitch (see page 36) and join your next colour afresh into the corner 2 chain space immediately following.

Make 4 chains and join them up into a ring by working a slip stitch into the first chain.

Make 4ch, SS to first ch to form ring.

Round 1: Work 5 chains to count as 1 treble and a 2 chain space. Doing the trebles into the centre of the ring go round the circle like this: 3 trebles, 2 chains, 3 trebles, 2 chains, 3 trebles, 2 chains, 2 trebles. Insert the hook into the 3rd chain of the 5 starting chains and work a slip stitch to join. Work another slip stitch into the next chain.

5ch as 1tr and 2ch.sp, * into ring work (3trs, 2ch), rep from * twice, 2trs into ring, SS to 3rd of 5ch, SS into next ch.

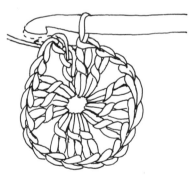

Round 2: Work 5 chains to count as 1 treble and a 2 chain space. Now work 3 trebles under the single chain space before the next group of trebles. Work 1 chain, miss 3 trebles and then under the next 2 chain space work 3 trebles, 2 chains, 3 trebles (always insert the hook underneath the chains as a whole, not into particular threads).

Repeat all of that last sentence under the next 2 chain space and again under the next one.

Work 1 chain, miss 3 trebles, then work 2 trebles under the place where the starting chain emerges.

Insert the hook in the 3rd chain of the 5 starting chains and work a slip stitch to join. Work another slip stitch into the next chain.

5ch as 1tr and 2 ch.sp, 3trs in next ch.sp * 1 ch, miss 3trs, in next 2ch.sp work (3trs, 2ch, 3trs), rep from * twice, 1ch, miss 3trs, in next ch.sp work 2trs, SS to 3rd of 5ch, SS into next ch.

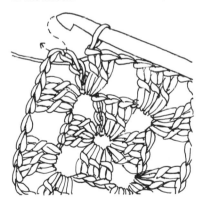

Round 3: Work 5 chains, then 3 trebles under the next chain space. Work 1 chain, miss 3 trebles, then work 3 trebles under the next chain space. Work 1 chain, miss 3 trebles then, under the next 2 chain space, work 3 trebles, 2 chains, 3 trebles.

Repeat all of the last two sentences as far as the next 2 chain space and again as far as the next one.

Work 1 chain, miss 3 trebles, then work 3 trebles under the next chain space. Work 1 chain miss 3 trebles, then work 2 trebles under the place where the starting chain emerges. Join with a slip stitch into the 3rd chain of the 5 starting chains as usual and another slip stitch into the next chain.

5ch as 1tr and 2 ch.sp, 3trs into next ch.sp, * 1ch, miss 3trs, 3trs in next ch.sp, 1ch, miss 3trs, (3trs, 2ch, 3trs) in next 2ch.sp, rep from * twice, 1ch, miss 3trs, 2trs in next ch.sp, SS to 3rd of 5ch, SS into next ch.

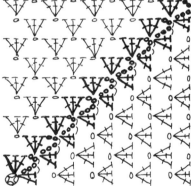

Already the square is shaping up clearly and can go on for ever. Remember that there must always be 2 groups of trebles (with 2 chains between) in each of the four corners. The starting chain takes the place of the last treble of the righthand group in its particular corner, which is why you end each round with 2 trebles only. The gaps between all the other groups along the sides of the square are only 1 chain.

Half Granny Square

Procedures: If you are working every row in the same direction, join the yarn for each new row into the 4th chain of the previous starting chain and fasten off after the last stitch at the end of the row. If you are working continuously to and fro, simply turn the work at the end of each row, but remember to join in any new colour during the last stage of the final double treble (see page 37).

Make the starting ring as for the full square.

Row 1: Work 5 chains to count as 1 double treble and 1 chain space. Into the ring work: 3 trebles, 2 chains, 3 trebles, 1 chain, 1 double treble.

5ch as 1d.tr and 1 ch sp, into ring work 3trs, 2ch, 3trs, 1ch, 1d.tr.

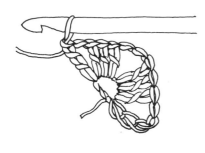

Row 2: Work 5 chains as 1 double treble and a 1 chain space, under the first chain space before the group of 3 trebles work 3 trebles, then work 1 chain, miss the group and under the 2 chain space work 3 trebles, 2 chains, 3 trebles.

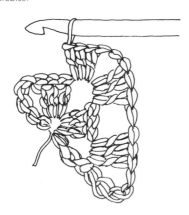

Work 1 chain, miss the next group, then under the chain between that group and the last double treble (or turning chain) work 3 trebles, 1 chain and, to finish, 1 double treble in the double treble (or 4th chain of the turning chain).

5ch, 3trs in next ch.sp, 1ch, (3trs, 2ch, 3trs) in next 2ch.sp, 1ch, 3trs in next ch.sp, 1ch, 1d.tr in d.tr (or 4th ch of t.ch).

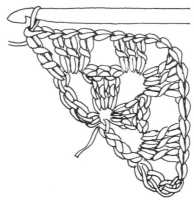

Every row thereafter: Work 5 chains to start and 3 trebles under the first chain before the first group. Along the first side of the half square always work 1 chain, miss the next group, then work 3 trebles under the next chain, 1 chain, and so on until you reach the corner in the middle of the row.

Under this corner 2 chain space always work 3 trebles, 2 chains, 3 trebles, then continue along the second side of the half square as for the first side, finishing with 1 chain, miss the last group, 3 trebles under the chain between the last group and the double treble (or turning chain), 1 chain, 1 double treble into the last double treble (or 4th chain of the turning chain).

*5ch, * 3trs in next ch.sp, 1ch, miss 3trs ** rep from * to ** to corner, in 2ch.sp at corner work (3trs, 2ch, 3trs, 1ch), rep from * to ** to last st, ending 1d.tr in last st (or 4th ch of t.ch).*

Spiral

Make 2 chains.

Round 1: Into the first chain made (2nd from hook) work 2 double crochets, 2 half trebles, 8 trebles. There are 12 stitches in the round. Mark the first double crochet with contrasting thread to indicate the beginning of the round

Into 2nd ch. from hook work 2dc, 2h.tr, 8tr.

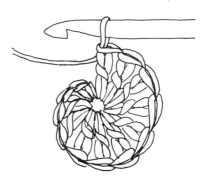

Round 2: Work 2 trebles into each of the next 12 stitches. You have 24 stitches.

(2trs into next st.) 12 times.

Round 3: Work 2 trebles into the next stitch and 1 treble into the next stitch. Repeat all of the last sentence 11 more times. You have 36 stitches.

(2trs into next st, 1tr into next st) 12 times.

Round 4: Work 2 trebles into the next stitch and 1 treble into each of the next 2 stitches. Repeat all of that last sentence 11 more times. You have 48 stitches.

(2trs into next st, 1 tr into each of next 2sts) 12 times.

Again you can carry on for ever, working more single trebles between the pairs each time round. When you want to stop work a few half trebles, double crochets and finally a slip stitch to finish without a step.

General Information about Fabric Making

Right and Wrong Side (RS and WS): Most stitch patterns have a 'right' side—which is eventually the outside, or side which you will see—and a 'wrong' side—the inside, or side which you will not see. Although the two sides may not always look particularly different, the concept of right and wrong side may still be very important and should on no account be ignored. When the procedure is to turn at the end of each row, most patterns specify the first right side row (not necessarily the first row worked). This means that the side of the work facing you as you work that row is the right side of the fabric. From then on every second row will also be worked with the right side facing. If the procedure is to work every row/round in the same direction, the same side of the work will always be facing you and this will normally be the right side.

The easiest way to re-establish afterwards which side is which, if this is not obvious, when you are working in rows, is to lay the fabric out with the original base chain at the bottom and the short end of thread from the slip knot at the bottom left. The side facing is now the same as when you worked the first row. You can assume this to be the right side, unless your original design or instructions tell you differently.

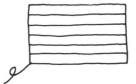

Front and Back: These terms naturally denote different aspects of objects, but, as in standard usage, they may be used in different ways: to identify permanently a particular part, irrespective of how the object may move or the viewer move around it, e.g. the sections of fabric, which are to become the Front and Back of a garment; to refer temporarily to the surface turned towards (front) or away from you (back) as you view it at the moment, i.e. as soon as you turn the work, what was the front becomes the back and vice versa. Although the sense is usually clear from the context, pattern instructions generally use capital initial letters, e.g. 'Front' 'Back', to emphasize the permanent meaning and small letters throughout for the temporary one. Whatever the sense 'front' and 'back' are *not* synonymous with 'right side' and 'wrong side'.

Left and Right: Take care with the terms 'left' and 'right', which like 'front' and 'back' can either refer to the left and right of something as you view it at the moment, or define for all time a piece of fabric destined to be a particular section of a garment. A conventional thumbnail sketch of the two front parts of, say, a waistcoat, with the right sides showing will depict the Left Front on the right and the Right Front on the left of the picture as you view it. The term 'right edge' of a piece of fabric, when unqualified, normally means the righthand edge as you view it, when the right side of the work is facing you.

Fastening off: Whenever you have to stop work in the middle and fasten off temporarily it is wise either to slip a safety pin or stitch holder through the last loop on the hook, or pull the loop through far enough for you to be able to tie a loose knot with it round the supply thread.

To fasten off permanently after the last stitch has been completed (unless this is a slip stitch) take the yarn round the hook and pull through once more. Cut the yarn about 5cm (2in) away from the hook, or further, if the thread is required for sewing a seam (see Making Up page 226). Draw the short end right through and tighten gently.

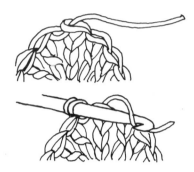

If the last stitch worked is a slip stitch, for instance at the completion of a circle, do not take the yarn round the hook again but simply cut the yarn and pull through the short end directly. Then insert the hook from back to front through the place where the slip stitch was worked (not through the last loop of the slip stitch itself) and withdraw the short end to the back again. Tighten gently. If the short end is now on the right side (RS), insert the hook from the front through an adjacent stitch and withdraw the short end to this side once more.

Joining in: When crochet starts without its own base chain of any kind, but is worked directly onto some existing fabric, the working thread has to be 'joined in'. This may be: when a curtain ring is used as the basis for circular work, for an edging, when the pattern requires you to break off and made a fresh start in another place, when you wish to join pieces of fabric with a crochet seam, or for surface crochet.

Joining In

First Method
Insert hook to make next stitch.

Drape new yarn over hook and draw through.

Work starting/turning chain as required using both strands of new yarn for the first chain.

If possible (see page 38) lay the short end along the top of the next few stitches and work over it as you go.

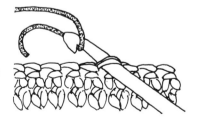

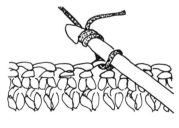

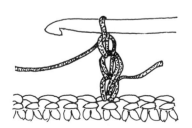

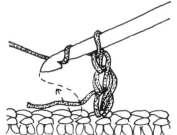

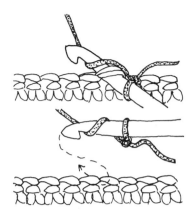

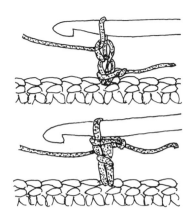

Second Method
Make a slip loop on hook.

Slip stitch into required position.

Work starting/turning chain as usual.

Third Method
Make a slip loop on hook.

Stop this from rotating around the hook with the right hand middle finger, or by holding onto the short end, and work an ordinary stitch as required.

Changing yarn: The term 'join in' may also refer to a different situation: when a changeover is required from one thread to another during a continuous sequence. This may be: when the ball happens to run out, when an unacceptable spinning blemish or knot appears (you cut out the affected section), or when another colour is called for. Most authorities urge you to make changeovers in the first two situations at the edges of the work. It is worth bearing this in mind, but given that you cannot foresee knots, that the price of materials is high and the tendency in design is towards seamless garments with long individual rows, it is more practical to concentrate on perfecting a neat and quick way of changing, whenever you happen to have to.

Colour and general purpose changeover: the method illustrated, which involves changing over while making a stitch, works for all occasions and for all stitches except the chain and the slip stitch.

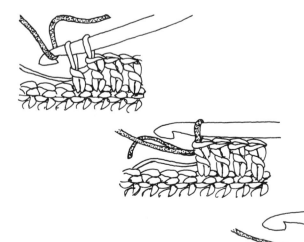

General Changeover

Whatever stitch is in progress work normally until you have only one step to go. This will mean you have only 2 loops left on the hook, except with half treble, when there are 3 loops.

Drop the old yarn. Double the end of the new yarn over to make a simple loop, pick this up and pull through to complete the stitch.

Lead the short ends of both yarns to the front, or back, whichever is the wrong side of the work. Hold them there with the fingers of the left hand while you take up the new thread and continue.

It is not wise ever to try and change whilst making chains, although it can be done. At a slip stitch, for instance at the close of a round in circular work, when the next round needs to be a different colour, it is better to fasten off the old yarn and join in the fresh thread separately (as for 'joining in').

The 'colour' method is essential, when you want to swap from one colour to another without breaking off; this applies particularly to Jacquard work. Even in the case of simple horizontal stripes, you will remember that the loop on the hook after the last stitch in a row has been completed will become part of the turning chain (or first stitch) of the next row, and must therefore be the colour of that next row.

Every time you break off a thread, or join in a completely new one there are short ends to deal with. If you have not worked them in as you crocheted, they will have to be darned in individually into the wrong side of the fabric afterwards (see below). After hours of work, when the crochet proper is done, it can be daunting to find just how many such ends there are and how much more work is still required. So it's as well to see if there are ways of working over them as you go.

Working over ends: How far you feel it is acceptable to work over ends, rather than darn them in—indeed whether you think it is worth bothering with them at all—is a personal matter. In openwork patterns or over any parts of a fabric, which are not completely solid, working over short ends is unlikely to be satisfactory, because the fabric does not mask them (this is the main disadvantage with the popular multicoloured 'granny' squares). In solid patterns the stitches will mask short ends of the same colour thread, but only during right side (RS) rows.

If you happen to be on a wrong side (WS) row when the break comes, change as for general purposes, leading the short ends to the front, then work over them on the next row.

Splicing ends: some knitters favour splicing the ends for changeovers in the same colour. This method is fiddly (even for a handspinner!) and time-consuming and, in crochet, less satisfactory than the other methods, even when well done, but it is described here in case it appeals to anyone.

Splicing Ends

Untwist the ends of the new and old yarn for a short distance. Cut away half the strands of each, overlay the ends and twist up together until they hold. Work gently until you are past the join. Snip off any stray ends later.

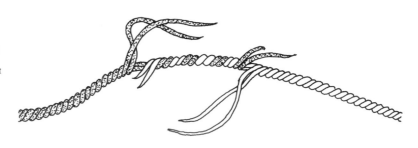

Some people darn one end through the other for a
short distance with a needle. This, too, involves stopping and
fiddling with no improvement in the finished result.

Bear in mind that, when you are changing yarn just for the sake
of the colour pattern, it may not be necessary physically to break
off the threads temporarily not in use. Instead they may be led
loosely up the side of the work (linear) until they are joined in
again. Afterwards, however, it may be necessary to oversew the
edges, before making up, to hold the threads in place.

Simple Shaping

Once you are quite sure and confident about working straight
i.e. so that you always have the same number of stitches in each
row each worked into the right place, your edges are even,
parallel with each other and at right angles to the rows, you can
begin to make your work deliberately wider (increase) or
narrower (decrease) in a controlled way at one or both edges. For
practice it is a good plan to shape one edge at a time, keeping
the other straight, so that you do not forget how to do it and can
prove to yourself that the shaping is not a fluke.

Increasing
Simple increasing is a matter of working more than one stitch
into the same place at the beginning or end of the row.

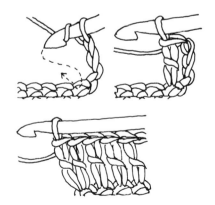

To increase one stitch (1st) at the beginning of a row, work the
first proper stitch into the very first stitch—this is the one you
normally miss—so that there are now two stitches (2sts) in all,
counting the turning chain, coming out of the first stitch.

To increase one stitch (1st) at the end of a row work two stitches
(2sts), instead of the usual one, into the top of the turning
chain, which counts as the last stitch in the row.

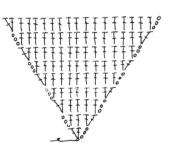

The example shows this process at work in a treble fabric.

A shallower rate of increase can be achieved by increasing only every 2nd, 3rd, 10th, row, etc, and working the intervening ones straight.

To increase two stitches (2sts) at each end of a row in treble and upwards work two stitches (2sts) into the first stitch—making three stitches (3sts) in all counting the turning chain—and three stitches (3sts) into the top of the turning chain at the end.

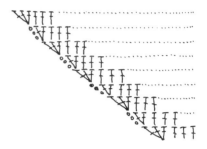

This procedure is not entirely satisfactory in double crochet, or half treble for more than a few rows at a time, because these stitches are so short; it may be preferable to try the general method of increasing below.

General Increasing: in order to increase more than two stitches at one edge it is not practical to go on working more and more stitches into the same place. Extra chains must be worked—extensions to the original base chain as it were. If the increase is to occur at the beginning of the row, this is easy enough; if at the end, you have to remember to take special measures.

General Increasing

To increase at the beginning of a row work extra chains calculated as follows:
The usual turning chain, plus the number of extra stitches minus one, e.g. to increase 5 stitches in treble: 3 (for treble turning chain) + 5 − 1 = 7 chains.

Now work across the extra chains as you would into a base chain (first treble into the 4th chain from the hook, 1 treble into each of the chains), then across the old stitches normally.

To increase at the end of a row; just before you reach the end, leave the main working thread temporarily, take another ball of the same yarn, make a slip loop, work the same number of chains as extra stitches required, slip stitch into the top of the turning chain and fasten off.

Resume working the main fabric and go across the extra chains as well.

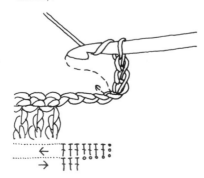
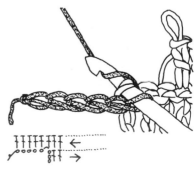

If you can remember to do so, you may prefer to fasten off at the end of the last row but one before the increase, turn, make a new slip knot in the same thread, work the same number of chains as extra stitches required, then continue normally across the fabric. When you come back to this edge again, the extra chains will already be there.

If you dislike fastening off, work the usual turning chain plus the number of extra stitches required minus one. Slip stitch back across the extra chains one by one, miss the first stitch in the main fabric (the early part of your long turning chain counts for this) and continue as from the second stitch normally.

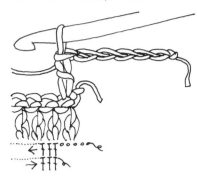 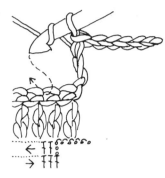

Both methods of increasing may need to be combined.

 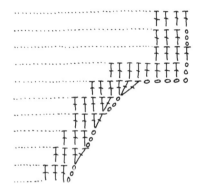

Some people prefer to keep their edges symmetrical and maintain a single edge stitch as a kind of selvedge. This looks elegant and attractive in diagram, but it is not very satisfactory in practice.

 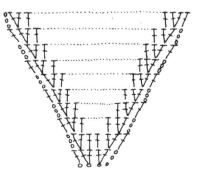

Decreasing

The most straightforward way to decrease is just not to work one, or more stitches at the beginning, or end of a row. At the end this means stopping and turning before you reach the end; at the beginning, working slip stitches across one more stitch than you need to eliminate, and only then working the usual turning chain which serves as the new edge stitch and carrying on from there. See also 'tunisian finishing', page 83. This method leaves a step effect, which becomes more marked the longer the basic stitch used, and may not be at all desirable. So long as you need decrease only one or two stitches at a time, a better finish can be obtained by working stitches together so that they merge at the top.

Working stitches together: The principles of working stitches together should be thoroughly understood and mastered, because they are crucial not only to shaping, but to the formation of many clusters and pattern effects (see Chapter 3).

Working Stitches Together

To join 2 stitches together

Work the first stitch normally up to the last stage, omitting the last 'pull through'. This is sometimes called *'leave the last loop of stitch on hook'*.

Notice that with the exception of half treble (which will have 3 loops left) there will always be 2 loops left on the hook at this stage, however long or short the whole stitch.

Work the next stitch normally up to exactly the same point. If the first stitch confuses you, mask it out with the lefthand thumb.

Notice that with the exception of half treble (which will have 5 loops left) there will always be 3 loops left on the hook at this stage.

Take the yarn round the hook once more and draw through all the loops. This is sometimes called *'close all loops together'*. You are completing the last stage of both stitches in one movement and so joining them at the top.

There will always be only 1 loop remaining on the hook.

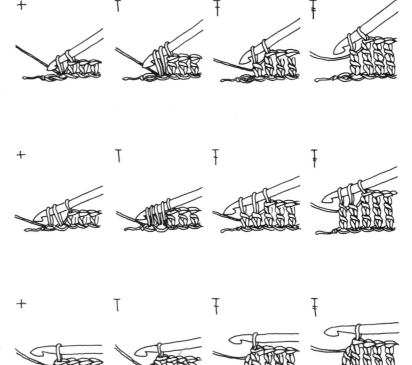

Half Treble—special note: because of the extra loops, joined half trebles make a very bulky cluster. Whereas this may be appropriate for special textured effects, it is out of place in simple fabrics. A better result is obtained by working the second stitch as a double crochet, i.e. without the preliminary 'yarn round hook'.

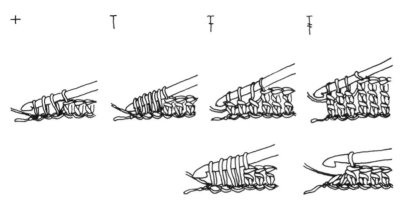

To join 3 stitches together

It is not usually practical in simple edge shaping to attempt to join 3 double crochet or half treble stitches together, but this is the technique.

Work as for joining 2 stitches together, but, before ending, work a third one as well.

Except for half treble (which will have 7 loops left) there will be 4 loops on the hook.

To make a less bulky cluster in half treble, work both the second and third parts as double crochet.

To decrease one stitch (1st) at the beginning of a row miss the first stitch (the turning chain counts for this), go into the 2nd and 3rd and work these together.

To decrease one stitch (1st) at the end work the last two stitches together, remembering that the last one goes into the top of the turning chain.

The example shows this process at work in a treble fabric:

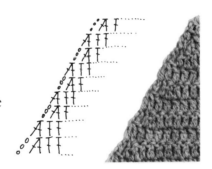

A shallower rate of decrease can be achieved by decreasing only every 2nd, 3rd, 10th, etc. row and working the intervening rows straight.

To decrease two stitches (2sts) at the beginning of a row in treble and upwards miss the first stitch, go into the 2nd, 3rd and 4th and work these three together.

To decrease two stitches (2sts) at the end in treble and upwards work the last three stitches together, remembering that the last of these goes into the top of the turning chain.

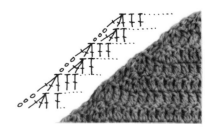

This procedure is not entirely satisfactory in double crochet or half treble; you may prefer to use the original step method.

It is important to learn to recognize the look of the top of a cluster of stitches which have been joined together, so that you will know where you are when you come to work into the top of it later. Although there are still only two loops lying on top of the cluster, there are some more threads than usual immediately underneath waiting to confuse you. The turning chain, which precedes a cluster, may also not look quite its usual self either.

When you are counting your stitches, however many are joined into a cluster, the whole lot counts as 'one' stitch.

General decreasing: To decrease more than two stitches at a time the original step method is required again—possibly in combination with the 'together' method as well.

The angle of increase/decrease naturally depends upon the number of stitches added/subtracted in each row and the depth of stitch being used.

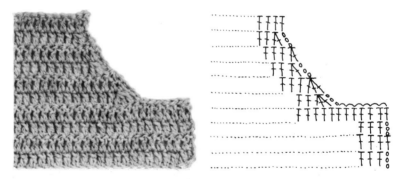

Problems

Linear Fabrics
Working straight, increasing, decreasing: Most beginners find little difficulty in understanding actually how to make the various stitches and, however clumsy the movements feel at first, the fingers soon begin to cope. But although 'how' may be easy, 'where' often takes longer to establish.

When you are in full swing the two loops on top of each consecutive stitch are usually fairly obvious and, when you are working to and fro, the hook seems not too reluctant to slip under them. The problems occur at the beginnings and ends of the rows. If this is how it is for you, pick up your hook and yarn and follow me:

Make six chains (6ch), work one treble (1tr) into the fourth chain (4th ch) from the hook and one treble (1tr) into each of the last two chains (2ch). Your row has four stitches (4 sts). You are going to continue to make a fabric all in treble for the moment, because the stitch itself is not difficult and is long enough to see properly.

Turn the work (like opening a book, or in your own way, but always stick to the same way). Work the turning chain, i.e. three chains (3ch) loosely. Now . . . which is the first stitch? If you cannot puzzle it out, turn back and undo the turning chain to where you were when the last stitch in the first row was just completed. Now you can identify the two loops on top of that last stitch. Slip a piece of contrasting thread under them, turn again and re-work the turning chain loosely. The thread in the last (now first) stitch marks the spot. Learn to identify it from this side, distinguishing it from the various threads forming the turning chain.

You are working straight at this edge for the moment, so you miss the first (marked) stitch. Count 'one' for the turning chain, work one treble (1tr) into the second stitch (2nd st) and count 'two', one treble (1tr) into the third stitch (3rd st) and count 'three'. There are supposed to be only four stitches in the row. 'Three' tells you right away that there must be one more to do and, if you have made no mistake so far, one more place for it to go. And you know that that place must be the top of the turning chain immediately next door to where the third stitch went.

You obviously cannot spend all your life relying on counting every stitch in every row just so you know when you should have come to the end (although this is a worthwhile habit to develop for your crochet, it can be bad news for your sanity); you must learn instead to recognize the tops of the last few stitches in a row and the turning chain in particular, so that you can tell at a glance, and without a frisson of doubt, when there are still 3, 2, 1 stitches to go. Do not strain the fabric south-west and north-east, as that will make the whole turning chain disappear.

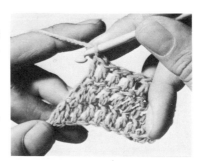

Complete the row: yarn round the hook, insert the hook into the top chain of the turning chain—two threads above the hook and one below. Easier said than done? Until you are fluent and relaxed that top chain is likely to be the tightest thing in the fabric after the initial slip knot; you will appreciate it when it begins to loosen up. The temptations are: to pick up one thread only, or to go into the next chain down, because it is usually much looser, or to poke the hook between the second-last stitch and the turning chain without picking up any individual loops at all. These must be resisted, because they all make the edge of the work unsatisfactory in different ways.

Carry on working in trebles straight with four stitches (4 sts) in the row until you are absolutely sure of yourself.

Now begin to increase one stitch (1st) only every row, but at one edge only, starting at the end of the next row like this:
First Increase Row: Work to the end exactly as for another straight row, check that you have the four stitches (4 sts), then work a second treble into exactly the same place as the last stitch. Count 'five' and turn.
Second Increase Row: Work the turning chain loosely. Count 'one' for this. Then work one treble (1 tr) into the first stitch—the place you normally miss—and count 'two'. Work to the end of the row normally. You should end up counting 'six' after the last stitch into the top of the turning chain.

Repeat both increase rows in turn twice more (or until you are quite sure again). You have ten stitches (10 sts).

inc.(2)
inc.(1)

Now begin to decrease one stitch (1st) only every row at the same edge as has been increasing before like this:
First Decrease Row: Work as for a straight row until two stitches (2 sts) remain unworked—you should have counted up to 'eight'. Now work these last two together like this:

Yarn round the hook, insert the hook into the second-last stitch, yarn round the hook, pull the loop through the fabric, yarn round the hook, pull through two loops—there are now two loops on the hook. Yarn round the hook, insert the hook into the last stitch, i.e. the top of the turning chain, yarn round the hook, pull the loop through the fabric, yarn round the hook, pull through two loops—there are now three loops on the hook. Yarn round the hook, pull through all three loops. Count 'nine'. (All clusters of stitches worked together only count as one stitch.) Turn.

Second Decrease Row: Work the turning chain loosely—count 'one'. Miss the first stitch. This looks slightly different now, because it is the top of that last cluster. Go into the second and third stitches and work them together in the same way—count 'two'. Work to the end of the row normally. You should end up counting 'eight' after the last stitch into the top of the turning chain.

Repeat both decrease rows in turn twice more. You have four stitches again. Do not break off but change over to half treble and go through the whole straight-increase-decrease programme again. (Remember your decrease clusters will be less bulky if you omit the 'yarn round hook' before the second of the two stitches.) Then change to double crochet and repeat the programme again. You should be so familiar with the procedure now that the fact that you can hardly see what you are doing at the ends of the rows does not put you off. You can work by feel, plus what you know must be right. Finally prove your progress to yourself by going back to treble, double treble and triple treble, this time increasing and decreasing two stitches instead of one with no further help from me!

Step decreasing: When slip stitching across the first few stitches of a row, it is not strictly necessary to slip stitch into the first stitch before working the turning chain—you would slowly be going nowhere. In fact you can easily go straight into the second stitch (to decrease one stitch) and on into the next, etc. Pattern instructions, however, normally tell you how far to go by saying how many slip stitches to make, or how many stitches to slip stitch across. This usually means going into the first one.

Circular Fabrics

The prevailing problem as usual (apart from working the increases correctly—a matter of concentration) is recognizing the starting/turning chain every round, particularly in double crochet, and picking the right loops to insert the hook for the joining slip stitch. Use the method of counting all the stitches all the way round as you go, to educate your eye into recognizing when you have done enough. Otherwise you can easily be fooled into working an extra stitch at the end of the round—the way the starting chain leans away and the loops below it open up is too inviting. Persevere. Check. You know how many stitches you should have. You know how many you have got. That does not leave much doubt about the kind of mistake you can have made. Try it again.

Granny square and half square general progress checking: You may be working the individual stitches and joining up the rounds/rows correctly and yet the shape seems somehow to be 'wonky'. Check that you have one chain between the groups along the sides and two chains between the corner pairs, then take an overall look.

Mask off each quarter section with your hands in turn and run your eye over it: there should be one group in row 1, two groups in row 2, three in row 3, etc.

Again, mask off the corner pairs of groups which run diagonally into one another: they may have wandered off to one side, or you may have missed out one of a pair.

General Problems

Some unevenness or rough appearance is inevitable until you develop a rhythm, but check for actual mistakes. Apart from the edges, which you look at carefully and separately, are all the stitches worked into two loops? The top two loops? Not between stitches? Not splitting the yarn? None missed out? No two-into-one in mid row?

Perfectionists will worry that the edges of their work, even when correctly made, do not look quite so neat as the main body of the fabric. The simple turning chain procedure creates little bumps and the Turning-Chain-as-Stitch wider than usual gaps between the turning chain and next stitch, particularly in half treble; increasing and decreasing induces little bends in the line of the rows. You should not expect to be able to eliminate these defects entirely, but take comfort from the fact that a raw edge is hardly ever left in crochet—it normally disappears into a seam, or under an edging or fringe. The join in circular work must usually remain exposed, however, and when this is a nuisance, it is worth experimenting to find your own best method of disguising it (see page 112).

Tension: When you follow other people's pattern instructions you must work to the same tension, i.e. number of stitches/rows per given measure, as they did. We are not yet concerned about that, but you may already be anxious to know whether your early efforts are generally too loose or too tight, or worried at their inconsistency. You may ambitiously have started a circular lace doily and found that it will not remotely lie flat (as it always does in the photographs). For the moment simply stop worrying. Tension is not even worth discussing until you have put in many hours of regular crochet and settled into your own rhythm. After that, inconsistency is usually the result of infrequent practice or normal emotional changes and has to be lived with. You will find in any case that no cotton lacework will ever lie flat until carefully pressed.

Chapter 2
Reading Pattern Instructions

General Approach

Anyone who has mastered the basic procedures is ready to start making something. Some people have absolutely no inclination to copy another person's work; some find the business of following a text in traditional crochet jargon too uncongenial. Others like to crochet with handspun or other idiosyncratic yarns, and so they cannot use commercial pattern instructions directly. It is a pity to reject these altogether, because they constitute more or less the only crochet literature there is—a careful collection becomes the basis of a useful stitch pattern dictionary and study of them may well provide the only form of crochet design education and experience you can get, however restricted it may be.

Conversely, less adventurous spirits, who have learned to believe they are not clever or imaginative enough to think out anything for themselves, will tend to cling to the printed word. They, in turn, might reflect that sometimes it can be much more difficult to follow someone else's directions than to devise your own from scratch. In any case the main object of most pattern instructions is to sell yarn, or magazines. This restricts the range, character and complexity of the work represented in them in ways which have nothing to do with the desirability of the designs to you as an individual.

In the first place every design must appeal not just to you, but to a large number of other people. Therefore in style they must be predominantly classic, traditional, or at least safe and non-controversial. In terms of fashion they must follow, not lead the way. Technically they must not go beyond the capacity of the relative beginner. For economic reasons the text must occupy no more than a limited space on the printed page. These considerations may never bother you, but they do keep more things out of print than you might imagine. What you find at the tip of the iceberg may be quite enough, but if not, you can always do something about it yourself.

Choosing a pattern

Given time you can expect to be able to make anything you fancy. As an absolute beginner, however, unless you start with very specific views, or if your reserves of tenacity are known to be low you may wish to pick out something easy. Remember, though, that the most important consideration is always that you should want very much to see the particular finished article in your hands.

If your main inclination is towards the fine work like crochet lace, you will go for that right away. It is more difficult to cope with physically and the patterns are generally much more elaborate and lengthy, but your special enthusiasm will pull you through the turgid early moments. Otherwise try something requiring yarn at least of double knitting thickness and a 4.00mm hook, avoiding fancy yarns with nubs, slubs or bouclæ effects, or feathery yarns such as mohair, or slippery yarns, because of the physical difficulty of handling them. If you feel you will need a palpable sense of achievement early on, or if you intend to travel about on buses and trains as you work, try a patchwork fabric; the first complete motif will take only a few minutes; you will not need to refer to the instructions again and you will never have to carry too much material around with you. (The day of reckoning comes at the end, when you have to join all the pieces and darn in the ends!)

Choose something with a simple, regular shape and a one- or two-row repeat pattern, so that you will very quickly get to know what you are doing without having to think or consult the instructions very often. This will allow your fingers to settle down to a rhythm and develop regular tension. Above all pick an article which does not have to fit a particular person exactly or will be just as useful if it does not finish up the intended size. Ask yourself whether you feel up to coping with buttons, zips, pockets, collars, etc. on your first attempts.

The Preamble

Materials

Yarn: The instructions will tell you what sort of yarn to buy and how much. If the recommended yarn has an obvious special character which attracted you to the design in the first place, there is no point in using anything else. Apart from that you can of course use any yarn you like, when you have the experience to judge what is involved, but until then it is not wise to do so. The recommendation is rather more than just salesmanship on the part of the manufacturer; all yarns are different. Even those nominally of the same quality e.g. double knitting, can vary considerably between the brands. If you choose a different one, you are less likely to achieve the right tension straight away, you cannot be sure of the final effect, visually, or in performance, and you no longer know how much yarn to buy.

Different people will use different amounts of yarn, even though they are working the same article to the same tension. The recommended amounts are based on average requirements and you have no alternative but to assume you are average in this until experience proves otherwise. Consider seriously the warning to buy enough to complete the article in one batch. Dye lots do vary. Although this will not matter in a multicoloured or eccentric article, if you are making, for instance, a conventional item of clothing in one main shade, the chances are you will regard the whole thing as ruined if there is an arbitrary 'tidemark' running round it. Allow extra if you know you will want to make the article longer, or wider. Some patterns help you work out how much you will need, otherwise you have to make an intelligent guess. Be careful in the case of shapes like skirts, which get wider as they go down; a single ball may do 7 to 10cm (3 or 4 in) all round at the top, but barely 2cm at the bottom (1 in). Keep your ball bands, which note the dye lot number; in an emergency you may be lucky enough to find some more of the same.

Hook: Your attitude to suggested hook sizes must be quite flexible. When the designer works out a pattern, he establishes the tension he wants, then tells you what hook was used to obtain it. Almost everyone's natural tension, however, is different and you may easily need a different hook to achieve the same tension. Consequently, if you are taking up crochet at all seriously, it is essential to have a complete set of all the available sizes of hook from, say, 7.00mm down to 2.00mm for clothes and on down to the smallest size for micro crochet. You can then make fabrics with the same yarn slightly tighter or looser automatically, without modifying the control of your hands whilst working. Remember it is the specified tension you must imitate, not the particular hook size recommended.

Other notions: Most patterns list special oddments you will need, such as zips, buttons, elastic, etc, but not what they regard as standard equipment, such as a wool needle for sewing seams. You may need matching sewing thread for some things, although the main yarn itself, split up into its separate plies if very thick, is normally used for basic seams.

Size/Measurements

Patterns are usually presented in a number of different sizes simultaneously. The convention is to place all the information for the smallest size first, followed, usually in brackets, by that relating to the others in ascending order. Under the heading 'Measurements' the sizes to which the rest of the instructions refer are spelled out in this way. These may be denoted by some form of standard coding in the case of clothes, otherwise by actual measurements. Again in the case of clothes, unless otherwise indicated, the figures will refer to the size of person the garment is intended to fit and will include what the designer feels to be adequate ease, or extra width, to provide appropriate fit or make the fabric hang correctly. Occasionally there will be a thumbnail sketch noting all the main dimensions of a garment. Otherwise some will be listed and others may emerge from the text. If you think you are going to have to modify any of them to fit a particular person, see Modifying/Adapting below.

The main body of the text, with all the different figures for different sizes included, can be confusing to read. If you are not expecting to use your copy for more than one size, it is worth going through the whole text putting rings round the figures and references to your size, or crossing out all the others completely. Do not do this, however, until you have definitely established your tension (see below).

Abbreviations

All the abbreviations used in the main text will be listed at the beginning. You will probably be used to them, but check. Make sure whether the pattern has crossed the Atlantic; the terms used on both sides for the basic stitches are the same, but their meaning is different (see page 244).

In addition to the abbreviations for common words and phrases and for the basic stitches, certain symbols, usually capital letters, are used to distinguish the colours of yarn. M may denote the main shade and C, or Con, the contrast shade. Where there is more than one contrast shade, these may be termed 1st, 2nd, 3rd, etc. C. When there are many colours of more or less equal status they may be called simply A, B, C, D, etc. Or, if the point of the colour arrangement is that one or more should be dark shades and others correspondingly light shades, they may be indicated D1, D2, D3, and L1, L2, L3, etc. Make sure you do not confuse these capitals with others, such as F for front, B for back, RS for right side, WS for wrong side, SS for slip stitch, etc.

There are certain words in crochet which have a general meaning:

Group (Gp)   Several stitches worked into the same place so that they appear to fan out from the bottom.

Cluster (Cl)   The upside-down version of group, i.e. several stitches usually started in different places but joined together at the top, so that they appear to fan out downwards from the top. (Stitches both started in the same place and also joined at the top usually go under the general title of Clusters.)

In particular patterns, however, these terms and their abbreviations may be used to denote a specific formation of group or cluster and a full explanation will be given as to how to work them, either in the preamble or in the main text. The exact procedure for making any fancy stitches—puffs, bobbles, raised stitches (see Chapter 3)—will also be described. In the case of clusters the explantion may often say 'Leaving last loop of each stitch on hook, work . . . ending yarn round hook (yrh), pull through all loops', or '. . . close all loops to end'. This is a reference to the procedure for joining stitches shown on page 42, when the last step of each stitch is left unworked until the end.

The unwary beginner is apt to read the abbreviation 'gp' (group) as 'gap' and so fatally misconstruc the instructions. The word 'gap' is not used in crochet; the concept is covered, either by use of the word 'space' (sp), when one or more chains have been worked deliberately instead of vertical stitches to form a palpable gap with a chain bridge spanning it, or by the instruction to work 'between stitches', where, although there may be some physical gap in practice, the vertical stitches have all been worked consecutively and there is no true space. When in doubt, there is no question of working into a 'gap' with no true space, unless you are specifically instructed to work 'between stitches'. E.g. '. . . 3 trs in centre of next gp, 1ch, 1tr in next sp, 1ch, miss 1tr, 1tr in next sp, 1ch, 3trs in centre of next gp, . . .'.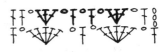

When 'group' is abbreviated as 'gr', this confusion does not arise.

Tension (Gauge)

Except when you have deliberately chosen a pattern which can happily be any size, the most important single factor in following someone else's instructions successfully is tension, i.e. the number of stitches and rows which occur over a given measure. Accordingly your instructions state the tension obtained by the designer (with a suggested hook size) and usually advise you to make a test piece before you start the real work. For some deep psychological reason most normal people regard this as a frustrating chore and a waste of time in a busy world, although even a flimsy grasp of the realities reveals that the exact opposite is the case. A crochet pattern is not a fixed, physical thing, like a paper pattern for dress-making, but only a formula for stringing a series of stitches together, and it cannot work out the way you and the designer have in mind unless those stitches are the right size.

Thanks, Ma!

Making tension samples is not just for novices, but something the sensible expert *always* does. Your more experienced neighbours may be found lightly boasting that they never bother to do this, 'but it always works out all right!' What they actually mean is that small discrepancies are easy to gloss over and forget, or that the garment conveniently fits another member of the family, or simply that they are lucky. But crochet does take a lot of time, and who has so much of that to waste that they can afford to let luck enter into it?

The test piece: Using the suggested hook size and the actual yarn for the article, set about making a piece of the actual stitch pattern to which the tension specification refers (see Pattern below). Within reason the larger the test piece, the more realistic will be your measurements. Formerly pattern instructions expressed tension over the smallest practical measure (1 in), but a test piece so narrow is quite useless. More recently 10cm (4 in) has become more usual and this is the minimum width over which it is useful to measure tension. The test piece itself needs to be rather wider than this, say 15cm (6 in), so that the edges, which are deceptive, can be comfortably excluded. As a rough guide a base row of 25 to 35 stitches should be adequate for simple patterns in basic stitches. In lacy patterns, where the tension is expressed not in stitches but in groups, or repeats of the pattern, the piece must be, say, 4 or 5 repeats wide, so that you can measure, say, 3 or 4 of them. In circular work tension may be defined either by the overall dimensions of the piece after so many rounds have been worked (so, if all is well at that stage, you can continue and make your test into the actual article), or as so many stitches in a given measure, as though the article were linear. In this case make a simple linear test piece in the stitch stated. You have to assume that if your tension is correct here, it will also be correct in the article itself.

The tension in your base chain and first few rows will not usually be representative of your real working tension. Continue the test piece until this settles down—normally by the time the piece has become a square—or at least until the edges have become straight and parallel for a few centimetres. Without stretching it artificially, lay the piece down flat, pinning it if necessary. Mark off in the middle the number of stitches the specification says you should have over at least 10cm (4 in) by slipping pins in between the appropriate stitches and measure carefully. If your pins are too close together, you have been working too tightly and should make another piece with a size larger hook. If they are too far apart, try again with a size smaller hook. If things are close, try measuring at different places in the piece. Take it up and work a little more, if you are not sure.

Let us see how much difference slight variations in the test piece can make to the final article. Suppose we are making a sweater in a solid treble pattern, which must measure 91cm (36 in) all round under the arms. Let us say the tension stated in the instructions is 4sts = 1 in. The total number of stitches at that point, with front and back added together is 144. Our tension turns out to be slightly tight, actually $4\frac{1}{4}$ stitches over the inch, but hardly enough to notice over such a small span. Luckily we are measuring over 10cm (4 in) and can see clearly that there are 17 instead of 16 stitches within the measure. Can this make much difference? In effect we shall be one stitch short every 10cm (4 in), or 9 stitches short all round. 9 stitches measures over 5cm (2 in), so in this case our sweater will be under 86cm (34 in)—smaller even than the next size down made correctly.

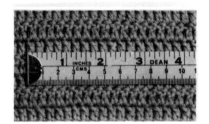

If you are good at arithmetic, or have a pocket calculator, it is easy to work out from your test measurement what size your article would be: take the size you are aiming at, e.g. 91cm (36 in) bust/chest, multiply by the number of stitches you should have in the measure (16) and then divide by the number of stitches you actually have (17).

Failing that, bear in mind as a rough guideline, that the difference between any two consecutive standard adult bust sizes, e.g. 81cm (32 in), 87cm (34 in), 91cm (36 in), 97cm (38 in), is around $\frac{1}{16}$th to $\frac{1}{18}$th (the smaller the sizes, the bigger the difference), so, if your tension sample is too tight, or too loose by one whole stitch in 16, 17, or 18, your article will be approximately one size smaller or larger than you intended.

We should be able to get nearer to the correct tension by trying again with a size larger hook, but what if, this time, our work is slightly too loose? After all the sizes of hook are not infinitely variable. Depending on the nature of the garment and the person for whom it is intended, we may be able to decide that it will be satisfactory to make it a little larger or smaller than one of the standard sizes. (How many people are actually standard?). Or we may be able to modify the pattern simply (see below).

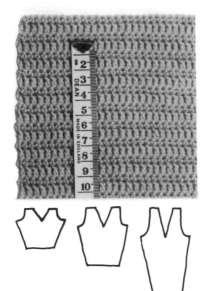

Stitch (horizontal) tension is the most important aspect of tension and you must experiment until this is correct first. Some patterns, however, also quote a measurement for row depth (vertical) as well. Measure this in the same way. Suppose that although your stitch tension is now correct, your row depth is not: how can you modify the latter without affecting the former? Certainly substitution of a different hook will not work. If there is a substantial discrepancy—more than 10%— check that you really have been working the correct stitch. If in fact nothing basic has gone wrong, you will simply have to accept that there is nothing you can do about it physically. It is a mistake to try to alter the height of your individual stitches as you work, because you can never sustain the effort consistently in the long hours ahead. Instead do some detective work to see if it matters or if modifications can be made to the pattern.

We seem to have made quite a meal of this whole matter of tension so far. Is it really such a performance? Most of the time—no. The great thing is to make your test piece—you probably need to do this to make sure you have the stitch pattern sorted out anyway—so that you know where you stand and the major mistakes are ruled out. For instance, you may be mistakenly using an old number 4 hook (ISR 6.00mm) instead of a 4.00mm. Most patterns are simple enough; the chances are that vertical tension will not matter, even if it is quoted, and common sense will get you over any problems.

Serious students will discover, however, that in certain types of complicated pattern tension in both directions can be extremely critical and at the same time difficult to obtain. The fact that no acknowledgement is made of this potential difficulty far less any advice offered, should not persuade you either that no difficulty exists or that you must be stupid or incompetent. The fact is that it is both uneconomic and bad business psychologically to own up to problem areas, so, in the minds of the producers of the instructions, you are tacitly assumed to have joined the ranks of the experts merely by choosing to follow such a pattern and are deemed to have already acquired all the experience and knowledge you need on these occasions.

It must be said, however, that the tension you establish in the test piece, even if it is of reasonable size, may not be reproduced in the larger pattern pieces later, particularly if you have not yet done many regular hours of crochet. This is one of the main reasons for not attempting an article of critical size at the beginning. If this happens to you, treat it as a common fact of life to come to terms with. Discover how your personal tension changes with your moods, the amount of crochet you do and the size of the fabric you are working on. Let this knowledge help your decisions when you are measuring your test pieces, but do not give up making them.

The Pattern

Sometimes the instructions for the main pattern will be given separately in the preamble. Otherwise they will be in the main text. The pattern proper may not begin immediately; first there may be one or more special rows—called base or foundation rows—which are not repeated, but which make a firm edge or a suitable basis for building the particular pattern.

In the case of simple patterns consisting of one or other of the basic stitches repeated, there is no problem in identifying what to do and your test piece can be any width you like. When the pattern is complex you must follow the instructions carefully, stitch by stitch. To understand and interpret what is said, you must be familiar with the various stylistic conventions discussed below. To make the pattern pieces themselves the designer will of course tell you how many stitches you need in the base chain or row so that the repeats of the pattern will work out exactly. To make your smaller test piece, simply work far more stitches than you know will make an adequate width and then pursue the first pattern row as far as you can before the base chain or row runs out. Be careful to end that row at the same point in the repeat sequence as the instructions say, or the information for the next row will not make sense. Then build up your test piece over those stitches.

If your pattern has a marked, built-in decrease at each edge as in the case of a triangular shawl, make the base row of your test piece at least twice as wide as you otherwise would.

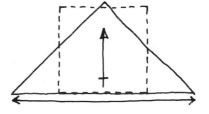

The more rows which have to be worked before the pattern repeats, or the more complicated the pattern is in general, the more important it is to continue the test piece until you are quite certain you are working it correctly. When there is any doubt, draw the stitches in diagram form on paper as roughly as you like. It is far quicker to sort things out with a few strokes of the pen than with the hook and yarn (see How to Sketch Stitch Patterns, page 114).

Certain types of pattern, such as Filet Lace and Jacquard colour work, are given partly in the form of charts. To understand these see page 159.

Language

For the preliminary discussions of certain terms see general information about fabric making, page 35 and Abbreviations, page 34.

The pattern unfolds as a series of instructions as to how to treat each stitch in the previous row, or base chain. '*1dc in 3rd ch from hook, 1dc in next and each ch to end.*'

Unless and until otherwise stated you are expected to assume:

1   You work from right to left (righthanders).
2   You work into each consecutive stitch.
3   You insert the hook under the top 2 loops only of the appropriate stitch (except see working into chains). The text says 'in', or 'into': '*1tr into next st, . . .*'
4   You continue with the same thread in the same direction.

The occasions on which you need to work 'backwards' from left to right are rare, but unless a pattern is completely solid, you will often have to pass over stitches leaving them unworked. The text will say 'miss' or 'skip', and specify exactly what is to be missed: '*1ch, miss 1ch, 1tr in next tr*' or '*3ch, miss 1ch, 3trs and 1ch, 5trs in next tr*'.

Sometimes, however, when the instruction would be quite clear without such complete, negative information, it may be contracted or left out: '*miss next gr, 1gr in next ch.sp*'—contracted. '*5ch, 1dc in centre ch of next loop*'—left out.

When a series of stitches has already been given a collective name, such as 'shell' (see Repetition below), an instruction to work into such a named feature usually implies automatically missing the first and last few stitches of the group: '*1 Shell in next V.gr, 1 V.gr in centre tr of next shell*'. NB Shell = 5 trs, V.gr = 1tr, 3ch, 1tr. Or '*1ch, miss 1ch, 1 gr in centre sp of next gr, 1ch, miss 1ch, 1tr in next tr*'. NB Gr = 3d.trs, 3ch, 3d.trs.

"*1ch., miss 1tr., 1 Bobble in next tr., 1ch., miss 1tr., 1 Shell in centre sp. of next Shell, 1tr. in next ch, 1tr.in Bobble, 1tr. in next ch, 1 Shell in centre sp. of next Shell, rep from * . . ."

NB. Shell = 1ch., 1d.tr, (1ch, 1tr.) twice, 1ch., 1d.tr., 1ch.

When you have read the passage on Repetition/Collective Names below, come back to the next example and study it carefully. Note, for instance, that there are two chains either side of the bobble—the outer ones being part of the shells on either side—and that the first of the 3 treble block goes into the 'next' chain, meaning next after the chain which concludes the shell. The example is slightly unrealistic. Crochet patterns are not intended as puzzles, but sometimes they cannot help it. It does alert you, however, to the necessity of doing exactly what you read.

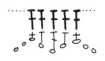

Sometimes when a variety of different stitches is used and you come to work over them again, they are not specified by their individual names, but referred to generally as 'stitches'. Instead of '*1tr in next dc, 1tr in next h.tr, 1tr in next tr, 1tr in next h.tr, 1tr in next dc*' read: '*1tr in each of next 5sts*'.

You must remember that, in all essential respects, a chain is just as much a stitch as any of the more substantial vertical ones: '*1tr in each st to end*'.

However, to be on the safe side most designers would express this example as follows: '*1tr in next ch.sp, 1tr in each of next 5sts, rep from ***'.

Working into chains: There are two standard ways of working into chains: insert the hook either into them properly, picking up 2 loops as you are accustomed to do into the base chain, or underneath the whole collection of threads. The latter method is much quicker, but not always appropriate. The instructions will usually help you decide. Here is a precise instruction to work properly into a particular chain and you must do so, otherwise the double crochet may wander up or down the chain loop and destroy the pattern configuration: '*5ch, 1dc in centre ch of next 5ch loop*'.

Here there are so many stitches going into the loop that there will be no spare room for them to slide around. In any case how do you work 13 stitches over 5 evenly? So you always insert the hook under the whole loop, as you would into the starting ring of a circular fabric: '*13d.trs into (or over) next 5ch loop*'.

In this case it would be possible, but fiddly, to work a whole 3 treble group properly into the chain, but it would make no essential improvement to the behaviour or performance of the fabric, so insert the hook under: '*3tr.gr into next ch.sp*'. Other variations regarding insertion of the hook will be spelled out.

Turning: Do not turn the work unless instructed to do so. Sometimes you may have to do this several times during one row; sometimes you may never have to, even at the end of a row, particularly in circular work.

Most patterns always state how many chains to make for turning or starting a row. As soon as you are confident and know what you are doing, you can easily modify these to suit your own tension. It is not always obvious, however, in solid patterns, whether the turning chain is regarded by the designer as a stitch or not. If there is no clear statement in the preamble, look at how the main text is worded: '*3ch as first tr, miss 1st st, 1tr in next and each st ending 1tr in t.ch, turn*'. Here it is absolutely clear that the turning chain is to count as one stitch. Logically patterns in which the turning chain is not to count often put it at the end, rather than the beginning of the row, but unfortunately this is not invariable: '*1tr in each st to end, 3ch, turn.*' If the wording is ambiguous, stand by to expect the turning chain not to count as a stitch in solid double crochet or half treble patterns, but to do so in treble and upward. When the instructions quote the number of stitches you should have in the row, this can help you decide. The most important thing is to settle what treatment you are going to apply and then stick to it. Next it helps to deduce what the designer had in mind, so you do not get lost when shaping occurs. In openwork patterns it is essential to follow exactly what is said, because the turning chain may have to fulfill different functions.

Punctuation and word order: Were you ever asked to punctuate the following statement, so as to make sense of it? *'Jones where Brown had had had had had had had had had had the examiner's approval.'* Whether or not you know the answer (page 246), you will be reminded how vital punctuation can be to establish meaning and how necessary it is to take account of it when reading. In crochet commas separate each individual phrase, but, to make any sense of the text, you must identify complete clauses. In many cases full stops are still found after each abbreviation and these must not be confused with commas or full stops at the ends of genuine sentences. Remember that the information you require from each clause is: what type of stitch to work; how many of them; what, if anything, to miss on the way; where to work it (them). And remember that a clause cannot begin, or end, without a comma.

Playing around with commas in your mind changes the clause structure and so the meaning: compare '. . . 3trs., in next ch.sp. work 3trs., 2ch., 3trs., in next tr. work 1 P.st., . . .' with '. . ., 3trs. in next ch.sp., work 3 trs., 2ch., 3trs., in next tr., work 1 P.st. . . .'.

Changing the word order within a clause may not: compare '. . ., work 3trs., 2ch., 3trs. in next ch.sp., . . .' with '. . ., in next ch.sp. work 3trs., 2ch., 3trs., . . .', or '3ch' with 'Ch.3'.

Sometimes the commas separating the phrases within a clause may accidentally be read as signalling the end of the clause prematurely: '. . ., in next 2 ch.sp. work 3trs., 2ch., 3trs., 1tr. in next tr., . . .' It makes no sense to say '3trs., 1tr. in next tr.,' and the text would have said '4trs. in next tr.,'.

To make clearer what groups of phrases are to be taken together into one clause, some patterns insert the word 'and' before the last of the set: *'in next ch.sp. work 3trs., 2ch. and 3trs., 1tr in next tr.,'* or they introduce brackets: *'in next ch.sp. work (3trs., 2ch., 3trs.), 1tr. in next tr.,'*

Or: *'1tr. in next tr., 3ch., miss (3trs., 2ch., 3trs.), 1tr. in next tr.,'*

Or: *'(3tr., 2ch., 3tr.) all in next 2ch.sp.,'*

When chains are worked and stitches are missed
simultaneously, the instructions to work the chains usually
precede the instructions to miss: '*4ch., miss 4ch., 1tr. in each of
next 5trs.,*' or '*1ch., miss next 3trs., 2ch. and 3trs., 5trs. in next
tr.,*'

Repetition: Most fabric patterns rely heavily on repetition, but
to keep its appearance in the actual text to a minimum various
devices are used.

Collective names: A main feature of the pattern may be a
collection or sequence of stitches forming a group, cluster, or
picot. This will be spelled out exactly the first time it occurs,
christened on the spot with a collective name and thereafter
referred to by that name alone. The convention is usually to
follow the original explanation by a dash and the words '*called
XXX*' or '*XXX made*', although this may sometimes be
defined by reference to asterisks in the text (see below): '*in next
st. work 1dc., 3ch., 1dc.—called Picot*'

'*. . . leaving last loop of each stitch on hook work 1d.tr. in each
of next 5sts., ending yrh., pull through all loops—Cluster
made*'

The actual name may be simply: 'group', 'cluster', 'picot', etc,
or, if there is more than one such feature, more distinctively
'petal', 'leaf', 'blackberry', 'bobble', or whatever seems to fit
the case most graphically. After a couple of repetitions you will
probably have memorized the special feature, but be absolutely
sure you are repeating exactly, and only, those directions
referred to in the original description. Suppose you have a picot
like this: '*3ch., 1dc in 3rd.ch. from hook—picot made*' and
suppose you have to make one immediately after the turning
chain, the instructions will say: '*3ch., 1 Picot . . .*' In the heat
of the moment you may be inclined to count the 3 turning
chains as the 3 chains at the start of the picot, whereas you must
actually work 6 chains—3 turning chains plus 3 chains for the
picot—and then work the double crochet into the 3rd chain
from the hook.

Brackets: When a short sequence of stitches is to be repeated,
perhaps several times, it is often enclosed in brackets. Then the
total number of times it is to be repeated consecutively is
usually indicated afterwards: '*(1ch., miss 1ch., 1tr. in next tr.) 5
times*'.

In the case of circular work, when the number of repetitions in
the round has been clearly established, this may be contracted
to: '*in next ch.sp. work (3trs., 2ch., 3trs.) all round*'.

Brackets alone do not automatically imply repetition. They may also be used to collect phrases which are to be taken together, or to indicate alternative sizes. There is no confusion in practice between these uses, but to differentiate them, sometimes both square and curved brackets are used.

Be sure to understand that '*(1tr. in next st.) twice*' means '1tr into the next stitch and then another tr. into the next stitch *after that*', not '2trs in next stitch'.

Asterisks, Symbols: When a long sequence of stitches has to be repeated, an asterisk—*—or comparable symbol may be inserted at the beginning and the instruction to repeat at the end: '*4ch. as 1tr. and 1 ch.sp., miss 1ch., *1tr. in each of next 2sts., 1ch., miss one st., 1tr in each of next 3sts., 1ch., miss one st., 1tr in each of next 4sts., 1ch., miss one st., 1tr. in each of next 5sts., 1ch., miss one st., rep from * . . .*'. If the instructions do not say how many times to repeat, simply go on doing so as far as you can, but watch the following points:

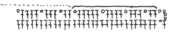

1   '*. . ., rep from * to end,*' In this case you should end up exactly completing a repeat sequence into the last stitch in the row. If you do not have enough stitches, or some left, do not stop prematurely, or start another sequence; there is something wrong with your work so far. Was there the wrong number of stitches in the previous row? Have you worked the present sequences correctly?

2   '*. . ., rep from * to last st., . . .*' This time your complete sequence should end when there is one stitch remaining unworked. ('*. . . to last 5sts., . . .*' means there should be 5 stitches remaining, etc.) Unless you are decreasing the instructions will then go on to say how to deal with that last stitch.

If the instructions do say how many times to repeat, e.g. '*. . ., rep from * 11 times, . . .*' this means 11 *more* times, i.e. 12 times altogether.

Sometimes the pattern requires you to work the first part of an established sequence to end the row. In this case a second symbol or double asterisk may be inserted in the text: '** . . . ** . . ., rep from * to last X sts and from * to ** again*' or '*rep from * X times and from * to ** again.*'

Sometimes a row ends with all but the last detail of the repeat sequence: '*. . ., rep from * omitting 1dc at end of last rep., . . .*'. Sometimes a sequence must be repeated in reverse order: '*. . ., rep from * to * in reverse order, . . .*'. Sometimes a long sequence which is to be given a collective name, is defined by asterisks: '*from * to ** is called 1 Branch.*'

As patterns become more complicated and there are repeats, or partial repeats, within repeats within repeats within repeats, the whole text may become peppered with all manner of symbols and brackets. Take things phrase by phrase. Do literally what is said. If you are working correctly the entire prescribed operation will come to completion at the appropriate place without your having to add or subtract any stitches.

Increase/decrease: Instructions may tell you to increase or decrease, but not how to do so (if the stitch pattern is basic), in which case you pick your favourite method: *'Inc one st at each end of next and every 4th row 6 times'*. This means 7 lots of increasing altogether and by the end you will have 14 more stitches in your fabric.

The number of times you increase or decrease may depend upon the number of stitches you have to start with: *'Dec one st at each end of next and every alt row until 4sts remain'*.

Shaping may be different at each edge and instructions may be extremely condensed:
'Dec one st at Neck edge every row 14 times and at the same time dec one st every alt row at Armhole edge. Cont to dec at Armhole edge and work Neck edge straight until 2sts remain.'
You may find it worthwhile before you start such a passage to make your own crib sheet in the margin or on a separate piece of paper, consisting of a rough sketch with the numbers of the rows and the numbers of stitches. Check and tick off as you go.

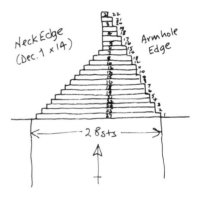

If you are presented with no precise instructions for shaping and do not know how to proceed, consult Chapter 5. When the designer does feel it necessary to spell out the mechanics for increasing and decreasing, the best texts signal this clearly:
'Next Row (Inc): . . .' or *'Inc one st at each end of next and every alt row 6 times as folls: 3ch, 1tr in 1st st—inc made—1tr in each st ending 2trs in t.ch—inc made—turn'*. Unfortunately this is not always the case. So beware: you may merely find you are increasing, or decreasing, and be left to discover this and hope it is intentional. When this happens do not continue blindly; make sure the shaping is compatible with the findings of your general detective work (see Coming to Grips with the Pattern, below).

Divide: The instruction to 'divide' means that, whereas so far you have always been working right across every row, from now on you must expect to work over only some of the stitches. Eventually you will rejoin the yarn and work over some (or all) of the remainder, and so on. This happens in the case of, say, the front of a pullover, or the top parts of a jacket, of which the body is made in one piece. The text may read: *'Divide for Neck . . . (instructions for first half) . . . Return to last*

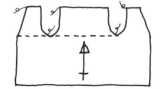

complete row worked, miss X sts and rejoin yarn into next st . . .'; or *'Divide for Right Front, Back and Left Front . . . (instructions for Right Front) . . ., etc.'*

Coming to Grips with the Pattern

Armed with the instructions and the necessary materials most people's natural inclination is to rush home and plunge headlong into the adventure. But what price this very valuable initial enthusiasm, if you find presently that the whole thing has gone mysteriously wrong? Work on the tension/stitch pattern test piece will often save a great deal of anguish, but before starting the pattern pieces, flip through the whole text briefly to get an overall impression of what it involves. See what they say and what they do not say. Your most precious asset is the growing conviction that you are going to make a success of the job, and this comes from knowing exactly what you are going to do, tackling potential problems head on and eliminating uncertainty.

Establish what pieces of the main fabric there are and what shape they are to become. If you have no diagrams or photographs apart from the cover picture, you will have to do some detective work amongst the text. Is a piece linear, or circular? If circular, is it supposed to lie flat, or become cup-shaped? Is it a tube? If so, is it made as a tube, or as one or more flat pieces sewn up afterwards? If linear, is it made upwards, downwards, or sideways in relation to the finished article? Or first upwards, then downwards? There used to be an almost invariable convention that most things—garments to fit the upper part of the body in particular—were worked upwards from the bottom. You were supposed to know this and so, even now, usually no mention is made of the general direction of working, unless the architecture is unconventional.

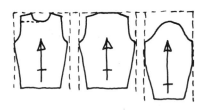

Is it a regular, continuous shape, or do the edges dart in, or out, or curve and straighten, for instance at set-in armholes? If so, are both edges symmetrical, e.g. the back of a sweater? Or asymmetrical, e.g. the front of a jacket, or cardigan? In these cases it is well worthwhile drawing a thumbnail outline of the piece roughly in proportion and with the changes in shape roughly in the right relationships as revealed by the text. On page 177 there are some drawings, which will help you to know what to expect. If the pattern is complicated, or if you are not told in so many words whether the fabric increases/decreases or not, work through the text carefully, drawing a stitch sketch, until this becomes clear.

Are there full instructions for shaping both halves of a garment which are identical, except that the shaping is reversed? If not it can save time in the end to note down on a sketch of the second half the reversed shaping details, so that you do not have to compute mentally on a row by row basis as you work. The characteristic text in this situation may read: *'Right Front: As for Left Front reversing shaping'*. When subsequent pieces have to match the first piece and the shaping of this was linked to the length of the fabric at given points, it is wise to note down how many rows had been worked when the shaping began, or ended, so that you are not in doubt later. The text may read: *'When work measures X cm, shape armhole as follows . . .'* or *'Dec one st at each end of every 4th row until work measures X cm.'* Despite slight differences in vertical tension, it is almost always vital to make pieces which are supposed to match each other the same number of rows, rather than strictly to the same depth against the tape measure. Otherwise you will not be able to match row for row at the seams and the grain of the fabric will be disrupted.

Measuring: A set of thumbnail sketches of all the pieces is particularly useful if you are planning to modify any of the dimensions. On these you can establish where to put in/ take away length and/ or width. First let us be clear how to check measurements. For this at least one straight edge is useful in addition to your tape measure. Lay the fabric flat and, regardless of any edge shaping, always measure vertical dimensions absolutely vertically, i.e. at right angles to the lines of the rows.

Similarly, horizontal measurements must be made parallel to the lines of the rows.

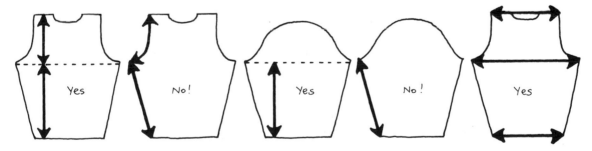

Modifying: You may need to modify some of the dimensions, either because the wearer of the garment is a different size, or because your tension is not quite the same as the designer's. When the stitch pattern is plain and basic, this should be easy.

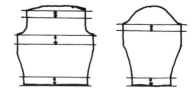

Always modify vertical dimensions in places where there is no edge shaping in progress, so that the horizontal dimensions are not changed at the same time.

Remember to distribute modifications to horizontal dimensions equally: half to a front and half to a back; a quarter to each half of a front, etc.

From the armhole shaping upwards the stitches you add or subtract may affect the overall width of the shoulders, or the details of the armhole/neck/shoulder shaping, depending upon how you choose to distribute them.

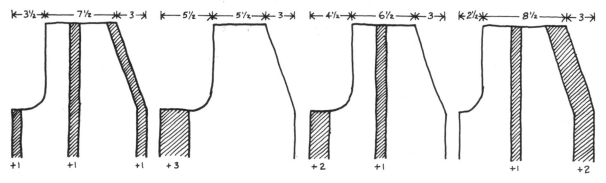

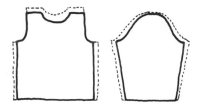

Modifications to any one piece have to be mirrored on any adjacent pieces, e.g. armhole shaping on the main parts must match the top section of a sleeve.

If the depth of the armhole is changed in the main parts, so must the depth of a sleeve top.

The implications of whatever modifications you are able to make should be fully noted on the pattern, or your drawings, before you start, e.g. the numbers of stitches you should now have in various sections at various moments; or the new vertical measurements to which you are working.

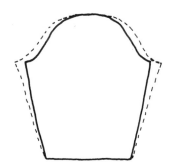

Patterns with several stitches or several rows in a repeat sequence can only be modified simply by the addition or subtraction of whole repeat sequences, which may rule them out for you. On the whole, elaborate or complicated stitch patterns make this kind of modification too difficult to bother with. You would be better off re-designing from scratch. Certainly any modifications to the rate of increasing or decreasing, even in plain patterns, will involve you in some arithmetic and render the instructions more or less useless to you.

Reducing the size of a circular article may be only a matter of stopping at a suitable point. Extending it, other than by working more loosely, or with thicker material, however, will almost always involve both arithmetic and invention.

Adapting: Adaptations can range widely in scope and complexity:
1 Additional embellishments: extra colour, fancy seams and trimmings, surface crochet.
2 Structural alterations: dividing a front into halves (and vice versa), adding/subtracting sleeves, collars, hoods, pockets, turning a dress into a separate skirt or blouse (and vice versa).

3 Modifications to the stitch pattern: the introduction of a panel of contrasting stitches into a plain fabric.

All manner of ideas from here and there may be combined into a patchwork. There is no need to regard any printed pattern as sacrosanct. Any which does the basic working out for you and yet provides scope for the personal adaptations you fancy, is fair game. There are no set principles to tell you what is possible and/or effective—only your own specific analysis of the idea and instinct.

Consider adaptations of scale as well as of form and decoration, such as turning half a lace doily into a semicircular shawl in 4 Ply or double knitting yarn with a compatible hook. The whole process of making adaptations constitutes an admirable preliminary design education and a useful half-way stage to becoming your own designer.

Problems

The beginner usually has far less confidence, but a much greater capacity for blind optimism than the expert. He knows there will be problems and mistakes, but hopes both will somehow go away, provided he does not look too closely at the work. He should realize, however, that the expert is not someone who never makes mistakes, but who has developed a sixth sense for when and where they have occurred and the necessary understanding to put them right. In order to develop this expertise quickly, you should think about everything you do, acquire an awareness of likely problem areas and of your own particular foibles, and work up a routine checking procedure which becomes automatic.

Base chain: Unless you do mostly very lacy work regularly, you will not get much practice in the normal course of events at working extended lengths of chain. Consequently, if you have always had the problem that the tension in your chains is out of proportion to that in the rest of your work, this may not automatically improve with time. If your base chains are always too tight (but your general tension regular) you may solve the problem by using a larger hook for the base chain only. If, however, your basic technique for making a chain includes tightening up the previous one (see page 23), there will be no great improvement however large a hook you use, and you may have to take time out to acquire a really serviceable chain-making technique. Try also making a double instead of a single chain, when circumstances permit (see page 29).

If your chains are too loose, use a smaller hook for the base chain and change to the correct one to work the first row.

When the required base chain is very long, it is always tedious and exacting to count accurately, either as you make it or afterwards (particularly if the yarn is very dark, or a mixed pepper and salt colour). Count as well as you can as you go; then, either make a generous number of extra chains, which you can easily undo afterwards, or make the initial slip knot with an extra long tail; with this it will be easy to add chains backwards onto the original row, if required.

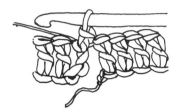

Even if the work is tubular, it may be safer not to join a long base chain into a circle right away. Instead work what you reckon to be a few extra chains, *turn* and work the first row as a straightforward linear row. (You may have to think a bit about where to work the first stitch, since you have no separate turning chain as such.) At the end of it, when you are completely sure all is well and the row is not twisted, join it up into a circle with a slip stitch in the usual way. It is an easy matter to join the base chain as well with the extra tail at the beginning of the yarn, or the extra material of the superfluous chains.

Tension: If your tension is simply erratic, practise as much as you can for longer periods at a time.

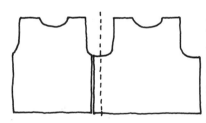

If, despite working a satisfactory test piece you find your first piece of fabric is too narrow or too wide, rather than unravel it all and start again, consider if you cannot make the next piece wider or narrower to compensate. For instance within reason the front and back of, say, a sweater can be different widths, so long as you can still 'fiddle' the armhole shaping. Remember then that the sleeve seam will not align with the side seam any more and will have to be sewn separately.

Joining round in circular work: (see page 32).

Keeping edges straight, etc. in linear work: (see page 44).

Distinguishing the right and wrong side of a fabric: (see page 35).

Solid patterns with 2 stitch or 2 row repeat sequences: It is very easy, if your mind ever wanders for a split second, to get either the stitches or the rows out of phase. You may never see this until (horrors) the very end, unless you make a point of checking regularly with the work at arm's length in a good light (see page 166).

Openwork patterns: These are best checked against a dark background, or against the light.

Splitting yarn, hook inserted in wrong places: If this occurs frequently, even when you are not working with a difficult yarn, make sure you have a strong enough light to work by. Dark yarns require far more light than pale ones. Perhaps you should have your eyes checked, too.

Circular not lying flat: Naturally you must be sure you are working correctly, but be prepared for fine cotton lacework not to lie neat and flat until it has been comprehensively pressed.

Routine Checking

Apart from keeping a weather eye on the general and your own individual problem areas, these are the things to check constantly:

Number of stitches, or repeat features in the row: If the instructions do not always say how many you should have at a particular point, work it out for yourself. It is extremely useful, provided it does not finally result in madness, to develop an automatic, semi-mindless ability to count anything and everything as you do it. When the habit has become irreversible and reliable, it can often be a sound indicator of whether or not you have made a mistake. Always know on every row how many stitches you are expecting to have.

Number of rows worked: It is not always easy, until your eye becomes experienced, to count rows at a glance. Study the fabric until you can.

In addition to the constant, running check going on in your mind, there are certain crucial moments, when it is time to have a formal, thorough check:
1   At the end of the first row—the springboard for the whole piece.
2   At the end of the first repeat sequence of rows.
3   After any increase/decrease row.
4   When any new shaping phase is about to start/has just finished.
5   Just before fastening off and rejoining the yarn elsewhere.
6   Upon completion of each piece, before ends are darned in.
7   After blocking, but before pressing.

Mistakes

Do not be too quick to assume that your instructions are at fault. Certainly both printers and designers manage to make mistakes from time to time, but not as often as you might believe. When they do, it is usually very obvious. If you always believe the worst of them whenever you find a passage mildly perplexing, and go your own way, a situation can easily develop where you are obliged to redesign most of the article on a piecemeal basis.

When you find a mistake in your work, do not rush to unravel it until you are quite sure you have understood the nature of and reason for the mistake—until, in fact, there is no more you can usefully learn from it. If you are not already obsessed by the perfectionist ethic, you may discover that there is no substantial practical or aesthetic reason to correct the mistake at all and you can happily carry on, simply taking note of it.

Beginners' Project

Use any yarn with any hook which fits it; forget about tension and measurements and try this project. It makes use of all the basic stitches and the type of language you can expect to find in pattern instructions. It starts in the middle and is made in rounds which get slightly more complicated towards the outside. Use the stitch diagram as a second source of reference, if you are not clear about the meaning of the text.

The piece in the lower photograph contains 20 deliberate mistakes. How many can you find? (Answers: page 246.)

Make 6ch and join into a ring with SS.

Round 1: (1dc into ring, 9ch) 8 times, SS to first dc = 8 chain loops.

Round 2: SS into each of next 5ch, 7ch, *1h.tr in 5th ch of next loop, 5ch, rep from * 7 times, SS to 2nd ch of st.ch.

Round 3: 3ch, 2trs in same place as last SS, *5ch, miss 5ch, 3trs in the loop which closes next h.tr, rep from * 6 times, 5ch, miss 5ch, SS to top of st.ch, SS into next tr.

Round 4: 3ch, 2trs in same place as last SS, *3ch, miss 1tr and 1ch, tr 3 tog over next 3ch, 3ch, miss 1ch and 1 tr,** 3trs in next tr, rep from * 6 times, and from * to ** again, SS to top of st.ch, SS into next tr.

Round 5: 4ch, 2d.trs in same place as last SS, *5ch, miss 1tr, leaving last loop of each st on hook work 1d.tr in next ch.loop, miss next cl, 1d.tr in next ch.loop = 3 loops on hook, yrh, pull through all loops, 5ch, miss 1tr,** 3d.trs in next tr, rep from * 6 times and from * to ** again, SS to top of st.ch, SS into next tr.

Round 6: 5ch, 2T.trs in same place as last SS, *5ch, miss 1d.tr, 5ch and 1 cl, 1T.tr in next ch.loop, 3ch, going behind last T.tr work 1T.tr in missed ch.loop, 5ch, miss 1d.tr** 3T.trs in next d.tr, rep from * 6 times and from * to ** again, SS to top of st.ch, SS into next d.tr.

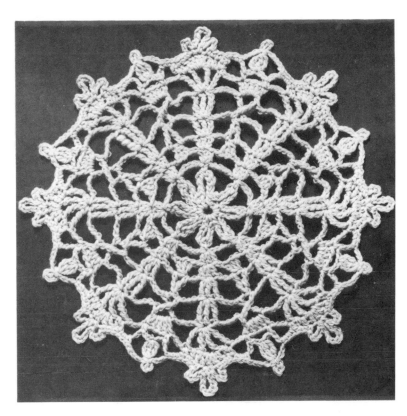

Round 7: 7ch, 1T.tr, (1ch, 1T.tr) twice all in same place as last SS, *3ch, miss 1T.tr, 5ch and 1T.tr, 5trs in next 3ch loop, 3ch, miss 1T.tr, 5ch and 1T.tr,** in next T.tr work 1T.tr (1ch, 1T.tr) 3 times, rep from * 6 times and from * to ** again, SS to 6th ch of st.ch.

Round 8: 1ch, *1h.tr in next ch, 1tr in next T.tr, 3trs in next ch, 1tr in next T.tr, 1h.tr in next ch, 1dc in next T.tr, 5ch, miss 3ch, 1dc in next tr, 5ch, miss 3trs, 1dc in next tr, 5ch, miss 3ch,** 1dc in next T.tr, rep from * 6 times and from * to ** again, SS to st.ch, SS into next h.tr.

Round 9: 1ch, *(1dc into next st) twice, 5ch, (1dc, 9ch, 1dc) in next st, 5ch, 1dc in each of next 3sts, miss next dc, 3dc in next 5ch loop, 4ch, in centre ch of next 5ch loop work d.tr 3 tog, 5ch, SS into top of cl just made, 4ch, 3dc in next 5ch loop, miss next dc** 1dc in next h.tr, rep from * 6 times and from * to ** again, SS to st.ch. Fasten off.

Incorrect

Chapter 3
More Technique

Definitions

Basic Fabric Structure

As we have already seen there are two main ways of making continuous crochet fabrics: by working to and fro from edge to edge (linear) and by working round and round (circular). Each format has different properties and responds to different principles of construction.

Linear format: Any shape (usually vaguely rectangular) which starts from and builds up along one side of a line, by working to and fro. The rows may all be worked in the same direction, but to work without breaking off the yarn involves turning the work at the end of each row, so bringing each face of the fabric to the front on alternate rows.

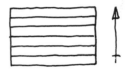

In order to work continuously it is not necessary by definition to add or subtract any stitches. The base line is usually a length of chain (single, double, or treble—see page 17), but may equally be the edge of some other fabric (crochet, or anything else). That line however need not be straight.

The edges of the work need not be straight, or parallel.

This is the general purpose way of making crochet fabric. Any basic shape is possible, though predominantly circular ones are awkward.

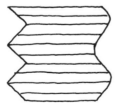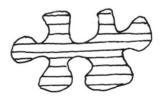

Circular format: Any shape (usually vaguely circular) or segment of such a shape, which starts from and builds up around a ring, or central point, or line (ovals), by working round and round, either in complete rings—concentric, or eccentric—when the last stitch in the round joins to the first, or in spirals, which make long, continuous rounds. To work

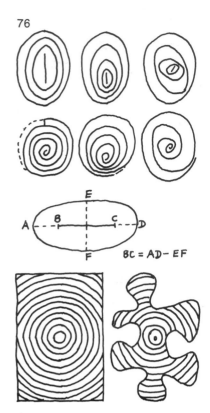

without breaking off the yarn involves keeping the same face of a spiral fabric always to the front. With the ring, provided it is complete, either face can be turned to the front each round.

In order to work continuously it is necessary by definition to add a certain number of stitches each round.

The starting point will normally be a short length of chain joined into a ring with a slip stitch. This could also be a ring of some other fabric (string, curtain ring, etc.), or a couple of turns of the supply thread taken round the thumb and pulled tight afterwards (see page 30). The starting line for an oval will need to be the difference between the longest and shortest diameters of the final shape.

Again any shape is possible, though predominantly rectangular ones, other than squares, are awkward. All the shapes can also be made from the outside inwards, though this is rarely more convenient and is usually only done to fill a hole. In fact there are relatively few articles for which a large circular made fabric is preferable to the linear variety. The outstanding value of the circular format is its ability to render the attractive range of pattern devices which derive from the circle.

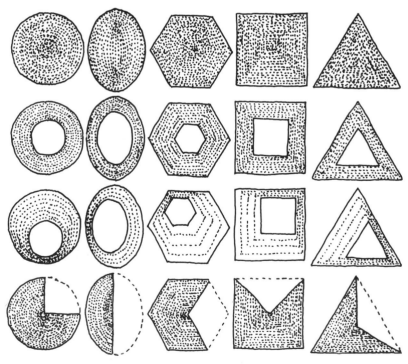

Far from being entirely separate states, however, the linear and circular formats represent opposite sides of a continuum, in the middle of which are cylinders and cones.

Imagine a flat rectangle, roll it round and join edge to edge. You have a straight tube. Indeed you could have joined the base chain into a circle in the first place and subsequently each row in turn, so that the thing would always have been a tube. Such a construction has some of the characteristics of the linear format and some of the circular. Whereas it must be basically linear, it could be worked in rings, or spiral, and the same face could be kept to the front each round.

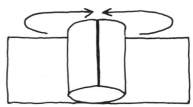

Should you, in the course of making a tube, add or subtract stitches on some regular basis, the shape would become a cone. A very squat cone is no more and no less than a circle which cannot lie flat (or part of a circle stood up so that its edges will meet).

Finally there is little difference between a small portion taken from the outside of a large circle and a piece of simple linear construction.

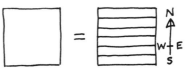

Axis and general direction of working: Whenever you see an outline diagram in this book representing a piece of crochet made in the linear format, you are to understand that, unless otherwise indicated, the lower edge represents the base line, the rows run east-west and the general direction of working (i.e. in which the work grows) is upwards. In other words north-south is said to be the axis and north the general direction of working. Every linear construction has two major axes, north-south and east-west, and, in each case, two possible general directions of working. (These features are indicated by the arrow with barred tail.)

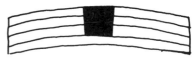

Likewise normally you are to understand from an outline circle that the centre represents the starting point, the rows run around the circle and the general direction of working is outwards. In other words the 'axis' is in-out.

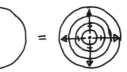

Clearly the general direction of working could also be inwards, but this would be indicated.

There is also an alternative 'axis': circular. And this could be worked in either of two directions, clockwise, or anticlockwise. A circular fabric made in this way is not now of circular, but of linear construction.

Constitution
There are two main ways of making a usable fabric:
One Piece—a whole section of fabric (not necessarily the whole article); consists of one piece made continuously.

Patchwork—a whole section of fabric, or some part of it; consists of smaller, separately made pieces joined together. When the individual pieces have their own independent formal pattern, they are normally called motifs. Usually it is the circular format which lends itself to the making of motifs, but linear ones can be used as well. In the nature of things it is difficult to control the overall size of a patchwork fabric and to engineer more than rudimentary shaping unless the pieces are extremely small, so the technique is usually reserved for simple articles, where these matters will not be critical.

Reversibility

Some stitch patterns (with odd-numbered row repeat sequences) are 'the same' on both sides and are therefore reversible, although when an article consists of more than one piece of reversible fabric it is normally advisable to establish a right side (see page 35) and join the pieces accordingly. Other patterns are inherently one-sided (non-reversible), that is, they present two different faces, of which only one can be regarded as the effective right side.

Weight/Density

Vertical stitches may be worked regularly and consecutively on a one for one basis (solid), or spaces may be introduced (open).

Surface

Crochet stitches are never really smooth, but we use that word to mean as smooth as they can be, i.e. formed of orthodox, basic stitches worked under two loops. There is always an obvious grain, more or less pronounced depending on the pattern, and plenty of opportunity for knobbles, bobbles, ridges, loops and other devices for breaking up the continuity of the surface (textured).

Consistency

A fabric may be designed to lie flat over its whole area (flat) or so that, although the fabric in general will lie on a flat surface, parts will be permanently wrinkled, ruched or puckered in some way. The term 'ruched' is used when the puckering is horizontal, i.e. gathered, and 'crumpled', when it is vertical.

Pattern

The word 'pattern' itself has to cover many shades of meaning and shifts of emphasis, even within the limits of this subject. A 'pattern' may be a design of a whole article, including specification of all the various pieces, their shapes and how they fit together, a set of instructions for assembling it, or merely the leaflet containing these. The 'pattern' of a specific piece of fabric may refer to all the elements together of the work sequence required to make it. These could be: individual stitch-making procedure, the configuration of the stitches (stitch pattern), or any changes of colour (colour pattern). On the other hand the 'pattern' of an otherwise plain background fabric would refer particularly to any decorative or ornamental parts. Let us use the word 'patterning' in this context.

Words used in reference to pattern: Low key: when the patterning element is very slight, or less important than the overall impression; High key: when this element is strong, or predominates. Although almost every stitch pattern can be subjected to whatever colour scheme you wish, some are at their best, or at least quite valid in one colour (monochrome) and others are quite pointless, or even cease to exist, when worked in a single colour (multi-coloured).

Repeat Elements

One of the main characteristics of conventional crochet fabrics is repetition, the repeat elements being stitches or groups of stitches, rows or sets of rows, and colour. It is useful to be able to establish the underlying order of such repetitions in given stitch patterns algebraically. Each separate element is given a single small letter, which represents it in our analysis. Now we can highlight and ponder the significance of the sequence itself, without getting bogged down with actual stitch details.

It is important to make a distinction between two different aspects of repetition: *visual*, what it looks like when done, and *practical*, what you have to do to make it look that way. The notation in this book always refers to the visual, whenever there is any ambiguity. In this example, for instance, every row is clearly 'the same' as you look at it and think about it and the stitch group repeat sequence is always (a.b.c.) read from right to left. It looks straightforward and the notation reflects this. But now assume you are making it. If you do not break off the yarn, but turn the work between rows, every second row will mean working the groups in reverse order—(c.b.a.).

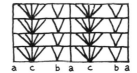

In this example the grouping of the first row has been shifted across to make an equally obvious 2 row repeat and yet, actually to make it working to and fro, you must do exactly the same things every row.

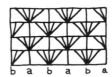

On the other hand if you make the same fabric wider, or narrower, so that alternate rows both begin and end on group 'a'—the single stitch—adjacent rows will be different in practical terms. Common sense shows you that you have not

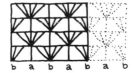

changed the essential stitch pattern and, since it is this the notation seeks to represent, it would be the same for both examples.

Row Construction

To describe the construction of an individual row briefly, we refer to what happens to its top edge, irrespective of whether this matches the bottom.

Straight: straight! Not necessarily parallel to anything. (NB. To 'work straight' means to work in the basic pattern, without any net increase or decrease in the total number of stitches. In the linear format the edges of the fabric will therefore remain straight, as the fabric grows neither wider, nor narrower, but only longer. In the circular format the fabric continues flat, or in the established three-dimensional shape.)

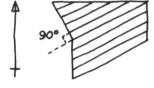

Oblique: straight, but not at right angles to the general direction of working; may however still be at right angles to the edge, if there is any 'shaping'.

Curved: when the whole row makes a single, continuous curve.

Zig-zag: when the row changes direction repeatedly in short straight sections.

Wavy: when the row changes direction repeatedly in short curves.

The amount of zig-zag, or wave, may be constant, or variable.

Zig-zags and waves are symmetrical. If you draw a line through their centres of gravity, upward and downward deviations are mirror images of each other. When deviations are all upward, or all downward, we have arches and scoops respectively. There is not always a real difference between the two; what you call them depends upon how you see them.

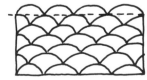

Parallel: not to be confused with straight. It means that the top edge remains equidistant from the top edge of the previous row, with or without deviations, and normally implies using the same depth of stitch throughout, except when straight lines change direction at an acute angle, in which case it may be necessary to work longer stitches into the very corners.

Non-parallel: opposite of parallel. A straight row will be non-parallel when it follows a curved, wavy, oblique, or zig-zag row.

  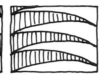

Continuous: a row running from edge to edge, or round its complete circle without interruption.

Interrupted: opposite of continuous. There are two types of interruption:
1   Short segments of a row only are worked at a time, probably with separate supply threads, so as to overlap or interweave with previous segments;
2   Several abbreviated rows are worked back and forth over just a part of the full row, before work proceeds to the next segment. This is necessary either to leave vertical slots in the fabric, or to set up a stitch or colour pattern device normally only obtainable from the circular format, or patchwork.

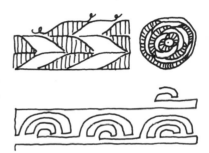

Summary

So far we have sorted out a few concepts, but have not attempted any practical details. Even so it is worth noting that the concepts alone furnish us with a very informative way of identifying roughly any crochet fabric. Try ticking off the characteristics of any you know against the profile checklist. The last part is not a scientific exercise; simply put a blob somewhere along the line between the two extremes. If you pick a fabric with several different pattern ingredients, make a compound profile, turning the blobs into O's marked M (for main pattern) and S (for secondary pattern), or simply 1, 2, 3.

If you find all this too clinical or boring, forget it. But if you ever want to devise your own original patterns, or perhaps adapt ones you already know, or even want to be able to remember and identify patterns you have only a brief moment to inspect, this analysis can be invaluable.

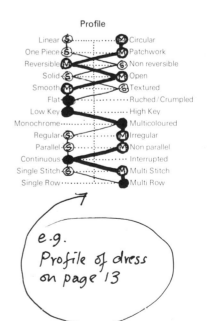

Variations on Basic Stitches

Basic stitches can be made into interesting or useful variations, by modifying just one or more of their steps. Photographs of fabrics made by using most of these techniques are shown in Fabric Profile (pages 119 to 128).

Group 1

(a) Half stitches: In standard crochet the half treble is the only acknowledged 'half' stitch, but there is a half stitch lurking between every consecutive pair of standard stitches. Think of the half treble as something which started out as a treble, but which you shortened by one step by drawing through the last three loops all at once. It has the same preparation as a treble, but the same number of steps as a double crochet. Apply this to any stitch, for example the double treble: *(Yrh) twice, insert hook, yrh, pull through, yrh, pull through 2 loops = 3 loops on hook, yrh, pull through 3 loops.* There is the same preparation of loops as for a double treble, but the same number of steps as for a treble. The result is halfway between the two. In the longer stitches the 'pull through 3 loops' need not be left to last. In simple crochet this procedure is of doubtful value and is ignored, because it overcomplicates the beginner's problems and printed instructions. It can, however, be useful to have in your stitch-making repertoire.

(b) Alternative standard stitches: From the half treble upwards, when you have more than one loop on the hook most of the time, you can draw through more or less loops than the usual two at one step, then compensate at another so completing the stitch in the standard number of steps.

Example 1: Half Treble: *Yrh, insert hook, yrh, draw through the stitch and * next loop on the hook = 2 loops on hook, yrh, draw through 2 loops.*

Example 2: Treble: *Yrh, insert hook, yrh, draw through the stitch and * next loop on the hook = 2 loops on hook, yrh, draw through 1 loop only = 2 loops on hook, yrh, draw through 2 loops.* Try twiddling the hook through 360° (clockwise) at * in these examples.

There are endless variations, particularly with the longer stitches, but these hardly ever seem preferable to the standard ones. They tend to be shorter than standard stitches and affect the fabric grain slightly. Alternative half trebles and trebles have a more pronounced lean than usual, providing a herringbone grain in solid fabrics.

(c) Tunisian finishing: In conventional crochet the hook always finishes up directly above the last stitch or chain loop to be completed. The usual way to move the hook conveniently to another place in the fabric without adding substantially to it is to work discreetly in slip stitch, or to break off the yarn and rejoin. When you want to work, say, a group or sequence of vertical stitches and yet have the hook sitting above the first of these immediately afterwards, for instance for step decreasing (see page 42), special groups (see page 128), or some into-the-side groups (see below), provided there are no chain stitches involved in the sequence, there is another way:

Work all the stitches in question up to the last stage, i.e. leaving the last loop of each on the hook, as though you were planning to join them all together at the top. Then continue: *Yrh, draw through 2 loops, repeat from * until one loop only remains on the hook.*

The structure of the stitches is modified at the top—the two characteristic loops have disappeared—but it is still possible to find somewhere to insert the hook, should you wish to work over them later.

(d) Yarn round hook clockwise: In general, after you have reached the stage in any stitch of inserting the hook into the fabric, from then on it does not matter whether you pick up the supply thread by ducking the hook under anticlockwise, or over clockwise. The way you make the preliminary wrappings, however, does make a difference. Beyond the treble this difference ceases to have any great visual significance in the fabric, but half treble and treble, worked 'hook over' for the first 'yarn round', do provide a worthwhile variation in grain.

Group 2: Inserting the Hook

Most of these modifications do not alter the stitch, but, if repeated, change the look and quality of the fabric.

(a) Insert under one loop only either front loop (nearest you) or back loop. This increases texture, but also flexibility and looseness and makes a fabric weaker and more apt to drop.

(b) Insert under three loops: This gives much greater strength firmness and smoothness. Each stitch takes longer to work and the fabric grows more slowly.

(c) Insert between stitches: This opens up the fabric slightly. Stitches may be quicker to work.

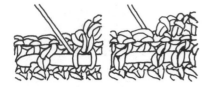

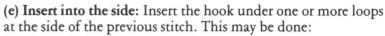

(d) Insert behind the stem ('round the post'). Insert the hook from right to left in and out again behind the stem of a stitch, either in one of the previous rows, or earlier in the current row. This can be done at the front or back of the work. Stitches worked in this way are thrown into relief (raised).

(e) Insert into the side: Insert the hook under one or more loops at the side of the previous stitch. This may be done:
1   To make double, or treble chain (see page 29).
2   As a technique for increasing.
3   As a means of making certain solid shapes in openwork and alternative solid fabrics.
4   To join the longer vertical stitches to each other down their sides, so that the fabric is less penetrable, or for special effects (see page 127).

General technique for into-the-side stitches: The procedure follows the same principles as starting a new row, so you may need to work a 'starting chain'. Anyway treat the stem of the previous stitch (temporarily) as a base chain, i.e. insert the hook through the stem, picking up one, or two threads at the lefthand side (or go right round the stem).

Naturally any of the techniques described below for making individual fancy stitches, such as puffs, bobbles, spikes, can be introduced here to make interesting patterns, or special features.

To join stitches together at the side: In the example double treble is being worked, but the same procedure can be applied to any of the longer stitches. In this case the appearance of the fabric is changed greatly.

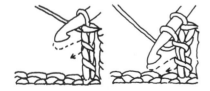

*Insert hook into side of previous stitch just below top (sometimes called 2nd loop, or 2nd stitch), picking up one thread only on lefthand side. *Yrh, pull loop through*.*

*Insert hook into next side loop down and repeat from * to * = 3 loops on hook.* These loops now take over the function of the usual preliminary wrappings of a normal double treble.

Insert hook into next stitch and complete 1 d. tr.

In the circular (tubular) format the last stitch in the round must be joined both to the previous stitch and to the righthand side of the starting chain, otherwise there will be an unwelcome slot in the fabric. To do this, prepare as usual, insert the hook into the ring (or last stitch in the round), yrh, pull loop through, *insert hook through (lowest) side loop of starting chain, yrh, pull through 3 loops, repeat from * into the next side loop up, and again into the top loop.

(f) Insert into the previous stitch: Work from left to right, but otherwise complete each stitch normally. The direction of working makes the stitches twist. This effect is usually used as an edging in double crochet (see page 190).

(g) Insert into any stitch further up the row or any previous stitch. Stitches need not be worked in their obviously consecutive order (see Groups/Clusters, 'X' shapes and Crossed Stitches pages 125, 126).

Group 3: Extending Loops
At one or another stage in making a stitch a loop may be pulled through and extended.

(a) Extended chain loop (Solomon's Knot): *Pull up loop on hook as required, yrh, pull loop through forming loose chain stitch.*

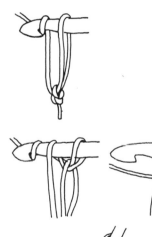

Insert hook under back loop of ch and work 1dc to 'lock' loose chain.

The classic use of this technique is in Solomon's Knot pattern (see page 123), but it can often make a pleasant alternative to a chain loop (a series of small conventional chain stitches).

(b) Extended first loop (spike): Insert the hook anywhere in the fabric, except in the normal place, either into or between or round the stem, directly below or to one side of the current stitch, for example double crochet spike:

Insert hook, yrh, pull loop through and up to height of current row loosely = 2 loops on hook.

Insert hook in next st normally, yrh, pull loop through = 3 loops on hook.

Yrh, pull through 3 loops.

This technique can provide some texture in monochrome patterns, but can be quite dramatic when it is used in more than one colour (see page 145).

(c) Loop (fur) stitch: This is really a double crochet with its middle loop pulled out and is always worked on the wrong side, so that the loop, which is formed at the back of the work, projects on the right side.

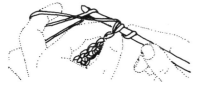

Insert hook. Extend lefthand middle finger to form a loop. Yarn round both threads of this loop.

Pull through = 3 loops on hook.

Yarn round supply thread. Pull through 3 loops. Remove finger from loop.

Beware! The stitch looks just as authentic if you pick up only the lower thread of the extended loop, but then the loop will not be 'locked' and a whole fabric made in this way will gradually pull right apart as the surplus yarn in the loops is drawn back into the fabric and redistributed.

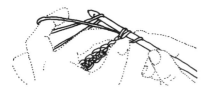

Alternative method: Insert hook and extend lefthand middle finger to form loop.

Take hook over to right of thread between work and finger, and pick up supply thread between finger and ball.

Pull back round and through = 2 loops on hook.

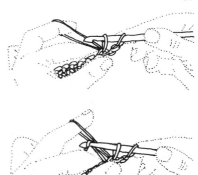

Keeping hook now to left of loop threads, pick up supply thread and pull through to complete.

At first it may seem difficult to make repeated loops of the same length, but this generally comes with practice. However you may find that either your usual hand hold or the technique itself needs modifying to enable you to do it at all. It can be useful to develop the routine of passing the finished loop off the lefthand middle finger and clasping it out of the way against the back of the work with a spare finger of the right hand. You could also try working over a ruler—sliding it through as you go—and, to make very long loops, it may be necessary to prepare a strip of card. This tends to be slow and awkward at the best of times, however, so it helps to cover the raw edges of the card with something smooth to reduce friction. If you work the stitch correctly it is safe to cut the loops one by one to make a fur effect (see page 138).

(d) Extended first loop (puff): Another way of extending the first loop, when you are working the deeper stitches, especially treble, is to insert the hook normally and then pull up the first loop to the full height of your last stitch, for example treble puff:

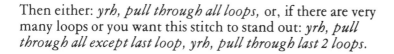

* Yrh, insert hook, yrh, pull loop through and up to height of previous treble, repeat from * as many times as required in same place—say 4 or 5 times.

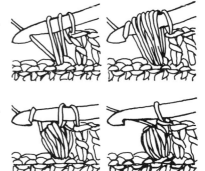

Then either: *yrh, pull through all loops,* or, if there are very many loops or you want this stitch to stand out: *yrh, pull through all except last loop, yrh, pull through last 2 loops.*

This creates a bunching of the threads into a puff which stands out mainly towards the back of the work. Consequently the technique is most often used on wrong side rows, so that the projection is on the right side.

Each insertion of the hook may equally well be in a different place—turning the puff into more of a spray—and it is not necessary always to work *yrh* before each insertion. It is always important, however, to draw up the threads each time generously, so there is no difficulty finally drawing the hook through them and so the main fabric is not distorted.

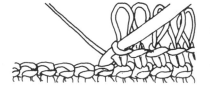

(e) Extended last loop: After working, say, a normal double crochet, **pull up loop on hook as required. Remove hook and reinsert down through top loop, or in side of last dc, picking up single lefthand thread. Yrh, pull loop through.*

Work another normal stitch in the next position. Repeat from * and 'lock' the last loop with a Solomon's Knot (see Group 3: a). Turn and work a row of ordinary stitches into the tops of the loops. These loops are not locked, nor are they even stable until a subsequent row is worked across their tops. The whole effect of this technique and the design thinking behind its use is very similar to that of Hairpin Crochet (see page 212).

Very short extended loops can make an attractive edge (Lace or Purl Picots). To be sure of making loops of equal length insert a pencil, ruler, or strip of card through them as you go.

Group 4: Miscellaneous

(a) Bobble: This is normally worked on the wrong side. The principle is to work several stitches into the same place, joining them all at the top—so that there is too much material horizontally in the middle of the cluster to lie flat—and to choose a longer stitch than the ones used in the rest of the row on either side—so that there is likewise too much material vertically to lie flat. The whole cluster is then forced to stand out in a bobble. The example here is based on a treble occurring in a row of double crochet, but it does work with other combinations.

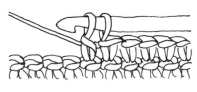

* Yrh, insert hook in next stitch, yrh, pull loop through, yrh, pull through 2 loops = 2 loops on hook.

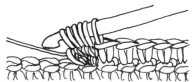

Repeat from * in same place, say, 4 times = 6 loops on hook.

Yrh, finish as for puff stitch.

(b) Popcorn: This alternative to the bobble is made by first working a group of completely finished standard stitches into one stitch, then, before continuing, you remove the hook from the last loop, insert through the top of the first stitch in the group, pick up the loop just vacated and pull this through so as to close up the top of the group and push it out on the right side.

(c) Bullion stitch: You will probably find this impossible without an old-fashioned hook with a tapered barrel:

Yrh as many times as required, say, 5 to 10 times. Insert hook, yrh, draw loop through, yrh, draw through all loops (you may have to grip the wrapped threads), or: *draw through all except last 2 loops, yrh, draw through last 2 loops.*

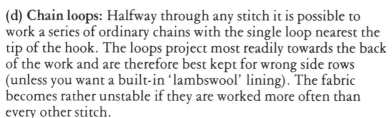
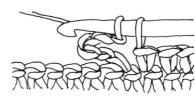

(d) Chain loops: Halfway through any stitch it is possible to work a series of ordinary chains with the single loop nearest the tip of the hook. The loops project most readily towards the back of the work and are therefore best kept for wrong side rows (unless you want a built-in 'lambswool' lining). The fabric becomes rather unstable if they are worked more often than every other stitch.

Many more variations can be made by compounding the variable elements: puff plus round-the-stem, puff plus spike, for example. The techniques which are in general use and which can be found in pattern leaflets, etc. are those which have been found over a period of time to work well in a wide range of fabrics, to be relatively easily described and demonstrated, understood and learned, and not to interrupt the flow too drastically. There are naturally many more, which you can discover with the aid of your own keen interest, some time and an uninhibited approach.

Basic Grid Structure

Solid Rectangular Grids (Linear)

Description: Straight parallel rows at right angles to the general direction of working. Group 1—all rows equal depth (same denomination of stitch). Group 2—rows of variable depth.

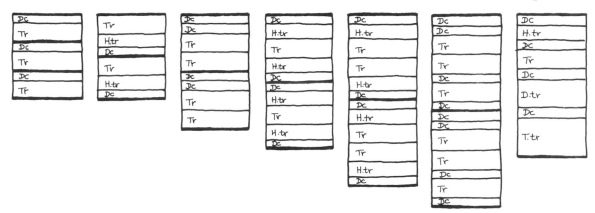

Fabric: Work one stitch and only one consecutively into every stitch of the previous row (counting the turning chain always as one stitch). Each row always has the same number of stitches, except when shaping occurs. Group 2 only: change denomination of stitch from row to row as required.

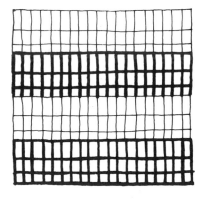

Unless you break the yarn, even numbered row repeats will be non-reversible, because the even rows will always face one side of the fabric and the odd numbered ones the other. In odd-numbered row repeats each row will face the other way each time it occurs and so the fabric will technically be reversible. An odd-numbered row repeat sequence must be performed twice before a true repeat starts again; each sequence becomes a single, wide band, of which we see first one side, then the other. The overall effect is much the same as that of a single row repeat, only on a larger scale.

In some fabrics which consist of a single, large picture or design, not even two rows will be alike. In general, though, if a fabric has repeat sequences at all, it is not very practical, except in the case of extremely fine work, to make the row sequences more than 6 or 8 rows, because the resulting patterns will be on too large a scale for anything except crochet wallpaper. One of the main values in solid patterns of high and particularly odd-numbered row repeat sequences is in making multicoloured stripe patterns, which have an easy-to-remember repeat 'formula', but which, visually, 'never' actually repeat (see page 148).

Solid Oblique Grids (Linear)

Description: Straight, parallel rows running at any angle other than 90° to the general direction of working. Group 1—all rows equal depth. Group 2—rows of variable depth.

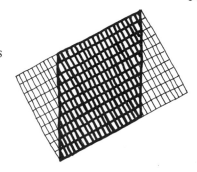

Fabric: As for rectangular grid patterns, except that you must increase at one edge and decrease the same amount at the other to preserve the status quo.

These grids are simply rectangular ones which have become tilted as a result of the additions and subtractions at the edges. The angle obtained depends upon the depth of stitch used and the number of stitches added/subtracted. This varies from individual to individual and with the overall scale of the work but here is a rough guide to the angles obtainable from Group 1 patterns:

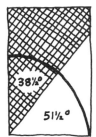 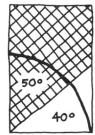 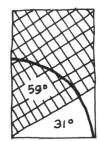 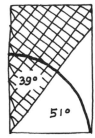 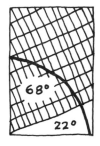 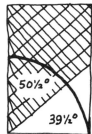

Shallower angles can be obtained by increasing/decreasing one stitch only every 2nd, 3rd, 4th, etc. rows. To plan an angle in advance work a perfectly rectangular test piece in the appropriate pattern and place a ruler, or straight edge, on it to represent the new edge. The number of stitches which has to be subtracted (and added on the other edge) should then be read off over as large a span of rows as possible for accuracy, then averaged out evenly over the rows. E.g. 15 stitches over 9 rows = 5 stitches over 3 rows. Therefore increase/decrease Row 1: 2sts, Row 2: 2sts, Row 3: 1st, etc.

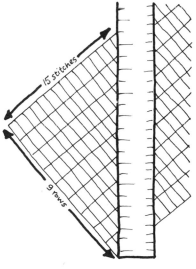

Perhaps the most useful, but also the most elusive, angle to obtain is 45°, because this enables you to make square shapes on the oblique grid. But this is not strictly possible, unless the configuration of stitches of the basic rectangular grid itself works out in exact squares (see page 117).

Group 2 patterns: when the row depth varies it is next to impossible to avoid a ragged edge to the grid. This may not matter at all, provided the raggedness is consistent. If it does, weigh this against the desirability of having variable row depth, or an oblique grid at all.

Solid Rectangular Zig-Zag Grids (Linear)

Description: Zig-zag parallel rows. A straight line connecting alternate nodes of the same row (points where the direction changes) runs at 90° to the general direction of working. Group 1—all rows equal depth. Group 2—rows of variable depth.

Fabric: As for straight, rectangular, grids, except that it is necessary to increase / decrease at each edge and at several points along each row to create changes in direction and preserve the status quo. The numbers of stitches added and subtracted during the course of each whole row must cancel each other out. Simple zig-zags are formed by spacing the nodes evenly and complex ones by spacing them differently.

These zig-zag grids are just like several, thin, oblique grids with alternating bias placed side by side and the angles obtainable are subject to the same principles. There are three ways to treat the nodes:

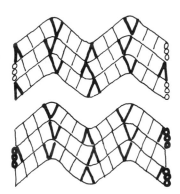

Floating node: If you add / subtract only one stitch at the nodes (to obtain a shallow zig-zag), from the 2nd row onwards you have a decision to make: into which of the two stitches at the peaks do you work the next increase? Over which two stitches in the valleys do you work the decrease? You could work between stitches, but we disregard that here, because it alters the quality of the fabric, and is not a 'basic' strategy. The true choice is between working your increases into the first of the previous pair and decreases to end on the previous cluster—called 'going early'—and your increases into the second of the previous pair and decreases to start on the previous cluster—called 'going late'. It does not matter at all which you do, so long as you are consistent. If you are working to and fro, always go either 'early' or 'late' every row.

If you are working each row in the same direction, make one row all 'early' and the next all 'late'. In this way the nodes hop left and right either side of an imaginary central line, which is parallel to the general direction of working—hence 'floating'. Look closely at the ends of the rows in the examples. In theory to keep the same number of stitches in each row, you must decrease / increase half a stitch at each edge each row. Since this is not possible, you actually decrease / increase a whole stitch every alternate row. When the plan is to go early, this comes at the end, and, when it is to go late, at the beginning of the row.

Some form of floating node must be used whenever an odd number of stitches has to be added / subtracted, but when that number is more than one, the whole situation imposes such a burden on the concentration of the person making the fabric, that the designer is best advised to avoid the device.

Single Node: If you add/subtract 2 stitches, i.e. 3sts into one/3sts.tog, per row at each node, the floating question does not arise, because there is always a central stitch at the peaks and a central cluster in the valleys. Also it is necessary to decrease/increase one whole stitch every row at each edge, which is straightforward. Arbitrary adoption of the floating node principle here would cause some distortion in the fabric.

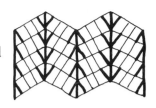

Split Node: At a split node the increases/decreases are engineered over two consecutive stitches. The previous example could have been planned in that way, but the main use, apart from the slight difference in grain it affords, is to relieve congestion when a larger (even) number of stitches has to be added/subtracted at each node.

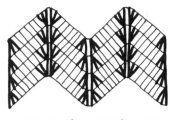

Planning zig-zags: To plan the angles and distance between nodes make a straight rectangular test piece in the required stitch and yarn, place a ruler on this to represent the new grid edge and another one parallel to the first to represent the next line of nodes. Now read off the number of stitches between nodes and the number of stitches to be added/subtracted at the edges. The number which has to be added/subtracted at the nodes then has to be twice that last figure.

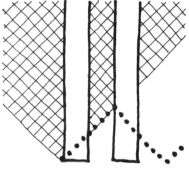

The new plan can now be drawn up. The span between the nodes in the example is 8 stitches, the decrease at the edges is 1 stitch per row and the increase/decrease at the nodes 2 stitches. This can be given the single, or split, node treatment.

In practice angles more than 315° over the peaks (less than 45° in the valleys) usually involve distortion of the fabric.

It may be advisable to work a longer stitch than usual at the centre of a node (see 'Squareness' page 117).

Group 2 zig-zag patterns have the same problems as group 2 oblique grids, but more so. At the nodes some distortion is inevitable—not necessarily enough to matter. Variable zig-zags follow all the same principles as constant ones.

Solid Oblique Zig-zag Grids (Linear)
Description: Zig-zag parallel rows. A straight line connecting alternate nodes in the same row runs at any angle other than 90° to the general direction of working. Group 1—all rows equal depth. Group 2—rows of variable depth.

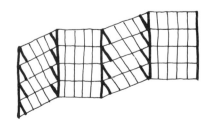

Fabric: As for rectangular zig-zag grids, except that there may or may not be any decreasing/increasing at either or both edges, depending upon whether these occur at peak or valley nodes. In order to keep the lines of the nodes parallel to the general direction of working, the floating node principle must be adopted, regardless of how many stitches need to be added/subtracted. If the rows are worked to and fro, the nodes must be worked early and late on alternate rows. By virtue of the biased floating node, the grid combines some of the features of both rectangular and oblique grids.

Solid Wavy/Curved Grids (Linear)

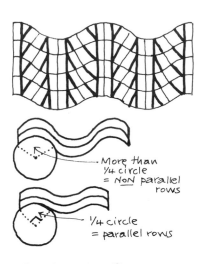

Waves and curves (large, single waves) are only zig-zags with deliberately rounded corners, that is, with the extra material in the nodes spread out evenly sideways along the 'straight' sections. Wave/curve grids come in the same categories and operate according to all the same general principles as zig-zag grids. The various lengths and depths of waves obtainable with different stitch denominations and frequency of nodes are only to be discovered through experiment, but, if a single wave section, however large or small in scale, amounts to more than one quarter of a circle, the rows will cease to be parallel and you must use stitches of different depths in the same row (see Non-parallel, page 113), or you must be content with a single row fabric, e.g. a border.

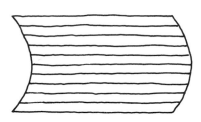

Alternative axis—curved grids: When the curve falls on the other axis, there are two main forms of grid:
1 A simple, shaped variation of the rectangular grid. All the rows, or complete row repeat sequences, are parallel and only the edges of the grid are curved.
2 Graduated stitch depths generate non-parallel rows with a left- or right-handed bias and thus the curvature of the grid (the rows represent the radii of a circle). This form is largely theoretical and of limited practical value. It can only be constructed by trial and error; there is a limit to the permissible difference between the lengths of the shortest and longest stitches included (which imposes limits of scale) and there is an inevitable difference in fabric density from one side to the other.

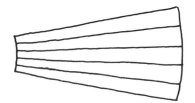

Solid Arched/Scooped Grids (Linear)
Simple and complex arches and scoops are made by alternating zig-zag and wave techniques.

Solid Concentric Grids (Circular)

Description: Concentric parallel rounds. Group 1—all rounds equal depth. Group 2—rounds of variable depth.

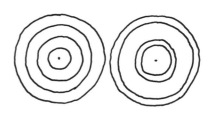

Starting: See page 30 for basic information on the various methods.

Centre point: If a chain ring is used this needs to be large enough to accommodate all the stitches of the first round, but without leaving a hole afterwards—say 3 chains for up to 10 stitches, then 4 chains.

Central ring: If this is a ring of chains, it should have a number of chains compatible with the fabric you are planning (see below). If it is a solid, e.g. curtain ring, you should plan a fabric round it which is compatible with its size.

Fabric: The circumference of a circle is directly related to the radius. If you double the radius, you double the circumference. In crochet terms this means that the number of stitches needed to complete the first round (the circumference) depends upon the depth of the stitch used (the radius). If you go on to work a 2nd, 3rd and 4th round with the same stitch (a Group 1 pattern), you are exactly doubling, trebling and quadrupling the original radius. At the same time you must therefore double, treble and quadruple, etc. the number of stitches in the round. This may sound complicated, but it means that you add exactly the same number of stitches every round and this number is exactly the same as the total number of stitches in the first round. Regardless of what that number may be, there is a simple, mechanical formula, which will do it for you:

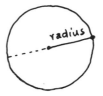

To find the circumference:
1. Measure radius.
2. Multiply by 2. (= diameter)
3. Multiply by 3 (or, more accurately, by π – 3.14)

Round 2: work 2sts into every stitch
Round 3: work 2sts into every 2nd stitch, otherwise one to one
Round 4: work 2sts into every 3rd stitch, otherwise one to one
Round 5: work 2sts into every 4th stitch, otherwise one to one

Furthermore there is next to nothing which you have to remember in order to apply the formula anywhere, anytime, if you think of it in this way:
Count up each stitch to yourself as you work until you have completed the increase, then start at 'one' again; you will find that the number you reach in each sequence is the same as that of the round you are working. For instance Round 5: count out 'One, two, three, four and *five*. One, two, three, four and *five* . . .' All you must remember is to work the last two stitches of your sequence into the same place (to effect the increase). Then, even if you have left a particular piece of work halfway through a row in a drawer untouched for months, as soon as you resume, provided you can count rounds accurately, you will know instantly where you are and how to carry on.

How many stitches in round 1? If the stitches you make are of average proportions, these numbers will serve for solid patterns (openwork patterns need more stitches, because chain stitches are narrower than vertical ones):

Double crochet	5 or 6
Half treble	8
Treble	11 or 12
Double treble	15 or 16

If not, work out your own scheme like this:

Make a solid linear test piece more than 10 stitches by 10 rows. Measure the depth of 10 rows (much more accurate than measuring one row). Multiply by 6.28 (2π), or multiply by 44 and divide by 7. Divide the answer by the measured width of 10 stitches. Go to the next whole number up.

Now all this is strictly mathematical stuff and we do not need to be entirely bound by it, because crochet stitches are flexible, but it does establish an ultimately inescapable fact about operating the circular format, which distinguishes it from linear work: in order to work a flat fabric it is necessary to increase the number of stitches in each round and this by a particular, regular amount. If you start with and/or increase by too few stitches the fabric will bend into a cone or cup shape and if you start with and/or increase by too many stitches you will end up with an undulating surface.

Practical formulae: In practice whatever way you begin it is impossible to make the centre a single minute point, because the bases of the stitches will squash up only so far. The central point amounts in fact to a small ring and the initial radius is slightly greater than the depth of one round. Accordingly you may find it better to start with one, or two extra stitches. But you must remember that increasing each round by the basic formula will result in slightly too much fabric eventually. If and when this happens, it is better to work a round with no increase at all (make a note of it, so that the formula keeps in step) rather than tamper with the procedure of a particular round and so throw the basic formula permanently out of gear.

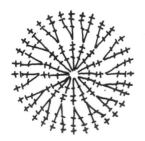

Group 2 patterns: Clearly Group 2 patterns do not work according to the formula at all and it is wise to avoid them altogether, except in cases where you find a particular combination which works very simply, for instance alternate rounds of treble and double crochet can be operated as though they were a 'single' round of double treble, i.e. you work the treble round as though it actually was double treble, then the double crochet round 'straight'—on a one-to-one basis with no increase at all. The flexibility of the stitches permits this.

Central rings: If the fabric is not to start at a central point, plan it in the first place as though it were. Make the starting ring to coincide with one of the rounds on the plan, then you can read off how many chains to make for it and work according to the formula from there. (Make a note of how many rows have been 'missed' at the centre.)

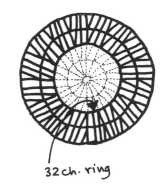

32 ch. ring

If you are working round a curtain ring, it is safer to measure this first and relate it to the general formula. Pot luck will do, if you need to work only one, or a few rounds, but for a more extended fabric, planning is best.

Outside-in: If you need to make the fabric from the outside inwards, plan it from the centre outwards first. It is not normally practical to complete solid shapes right to the centre, because the last round involves working all the remaining stitches together. Instead work these together in, say, two, three, or four clusters and rely on a needle and thread afterwards to make a neat, tight centre.

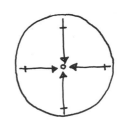

The shapes: If we work circles strictly according to the formula, after a few rounds we notice that the circumference ceases to be a continuous curve and resolves into facets which correspond to the number of increase points (the same as the number of stitches in the first round). In fact a circle in crochet is never really a circle at all, but a polygon. The way to make an intended circle remain as circular as possible is to 'scramble' the increase points, putting them in different relative positions each round (always spacing them equally and keeping the same number as per formula). Conversely the way to make genuine polygons is to start with a suitable number of stitches and concentrate the increase points so as to emphasize the segments and facets.

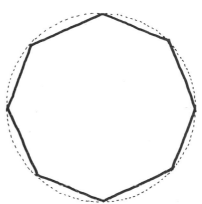

In theory our ability to construct the different shapes with each of the stitches depends upon the proportions of the stitches, and these are usually such that most shapes are impossible. In practice the natural flexibility of crochet stitches comes to our rescue. Within certain limits we can make the number of stitches in the first round an exact multiple of the number of segments required. Then so long as we arrange the increasing to follow the mathematical requirement approximately, the result will be reasonably satisfactory.

There is obviously more than one way to construct each shape, even in its solid form. The examples that follow are useful and effective and will serve until you find ones you prefer. They could be simpler—for instance you could ignore the longer stitches in the corners, or keep to one rate of increase each round when this varies in the diagrams—but only at the expense of rounded-out corners and less convincing fabric tension. To work the shapes outside-in, read the diagrams the other way round.

Ovals: Think of an oval as a circle cut in half with an extra slab slipped in. The central point is stretched into a straight line. The length of this line is the difference between the overall length and width of the final shape.

To start make a base chain of the appropriate length and work completely round it. Along the straights treat it as a linear fabric—along the 'back' straight for the first time round there is only a single loop of each chain left to work into—and into the ends work as though for half of an ordinary circle. Each following round either save all the increasing for the half circles at each end—the basic circle formula will remind you how much to increase—or spread it at one end and narrow it at the other to modify the final shape. More modified shapes still require 'non-parallel' working, particularly in the first round (see Non-parallel, page 113).

Circles

Double Crochet   **Circles**

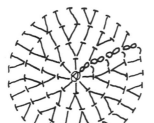

Half Treble

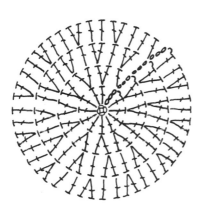

Treble

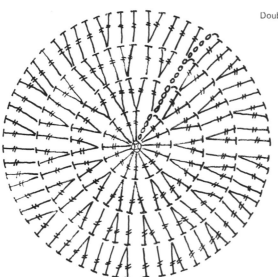

Double Treble

Hexagons

Double Crochet

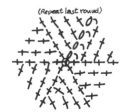

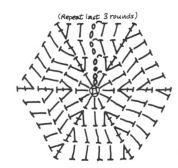

Half Treble

Treble

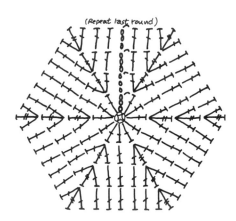

Double Treble

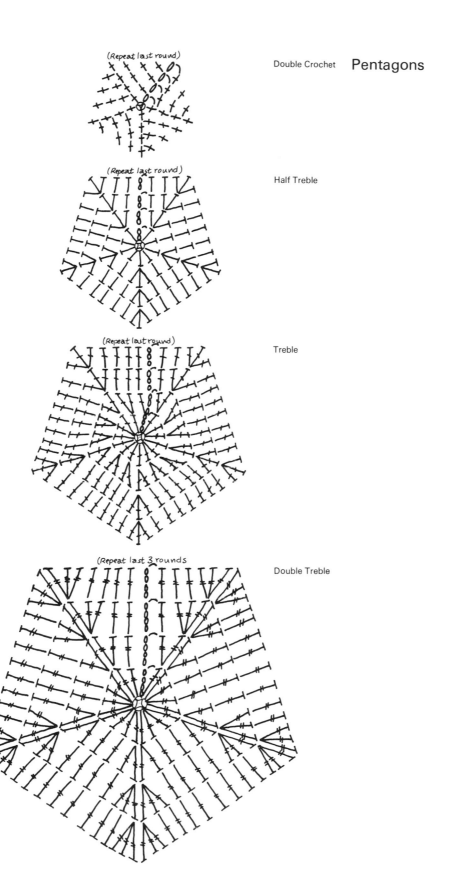

Pentagons

(Repeat last round)

Double Crochet

(Repeat last round)

Half Treble

(Repeat last round)

Treble

(Repeat last 3 rounds

Double Treble

Squares

Double Crochet

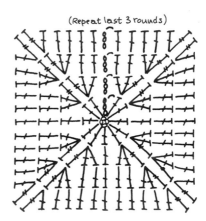

(Repeat last 2 rounds)

Double Crochet Square: Because of its proportions the double crochet does not make a square easily. 4 stitches in round 1 are too few and 8 too many — particularly if you increase 2 stitches every round at the corners, although this may not appear serious for the first few rounds. But in order to avoid 'floating' corners, which do not work on 270° angles, you must contrive to increase 2 stitches at a time — hence the alternate rounds with no increase. The half treble is much more than 41 % longer than the double crochet, so it will not do to work it every round. If the work seems to get progressively more strained round the edge, try working the increase round twice out of three rounds.

Half Treble

(Repeat last round)

Half Treble Square: The treble should be worked into the corners every round, because it is less than 41 % longer than the half treble.

Treble

(Repeat last 3 rounds)

Double Treble

(Repeat last 2 rounds)

Alternative Corner: With the longer stitches it is sometimes necessary to work 8 or more stitches to negotiate a corner. It reduces congestion at the base of these groups to make 'Y' stitches — shorter stitches rooted halfway down the side of a previous long stitch (see page 84).

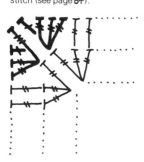

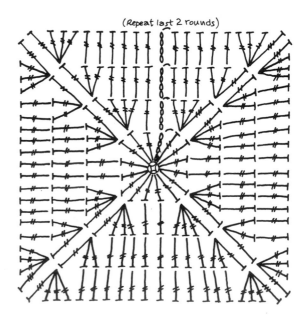

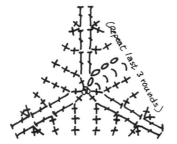

Double Crochet **Triangles**

Half Treble

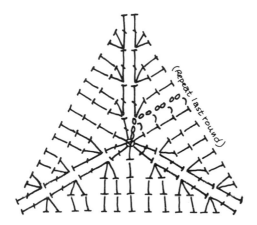

Treble

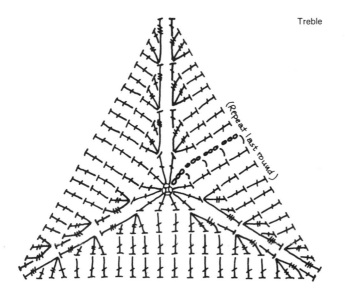

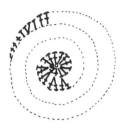

Solid Concentric Spiral Grids (Circular)

Single spiral: The basic single spiral starts just like a circle, except that at the end of round 1, instead of joining into a circle with a slip stitch, you carry directly on, as though you had missed the beginning absentmindedly. Naturally you must increase as you go on a regular basis. The basic circle formula works best, but it is up to you to mark and observe each separate revolution, so you know when to institute the successive changes of gear in increasing (use a thread marker). To finish work a slip stitch into the next stitch and fasten off.

When you use double crochet, that is all there is to it. When you use longer stitches, however, it makes the very beginning and ending smoother if you start and finish with a few graduated shorter stitches.

Multiple Spirals: The secret of keeping a grip on the progress of double/triple/quadruple spirals is to avoid the temptation to work more than the basic half/third/quarter of a round with each of the threads in turn, i.e. when the last segment of each round is completed, do *not* carry straight on with the thread already on the hook to make the first segment of the next round. Stop, remove the hook, go on to the next segment, pick this up and continue. Otherwise you will be quickly lost and have to increase by intuition, to the detriment of the tension and definition of the spiral.

Multiple spirals give rise to the theoretical possiblity of Group 2 patterns (rounds of variable depth), but these are difficult to handle successfully for the reasons mentioned earlier in respect of all Group 2 patterns in the circular format.

In theory also some sort of version of every circular shape is possible in spiral form, although, except in the case of spiral ovals, these would be evidently self-defeating; there is little point in a hexagon or square, for example, if its essential shape is compromised.

Single

Double

Triple

Quadruple

Double Spiral	Triple Spiral	Quadruple Spiral

Solid Eccentric Grids (Circular)

By careful planning the centre (in the constructional sense) of almost any shape in the circular format can be displaced, or made to float.

Displaced

Floating

Displaced   Floating

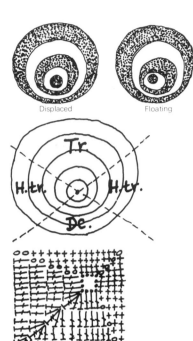

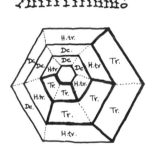

Displaced centre: In shapes where the rounds are continuously curved displacement is achieved by a sequence of graduated stitch depths (see Non-parallel, page 113).

In polygons with straight sides, a different depth of stitch is selected for some or all of the different sectors, although the same depth of stitch is then used throughout any particular sector. At nodes which divide sectors of the same stitch depth, the procedure is the same as for the equivalent concentric figure. At those which divide sectors of different stitch depths, if the angle (outside) is 270° or more, e.g. squares or triangles, it is necessary to improvise a cornering technique. In the example based on treble and double crochet we pretend the depth of a treble is equal to the width of 2 double crochets and the depth of a double crochet is equal to the width of a treble. This is not strictly true (see page 116), but serves for a time before distortion sets in.

Floating centre: This is achieved by working generally as for displaced centres, but by joining each round a little further round the circumference each time (circles, ovals) or at the next node (polygons).

Openwork Grids (Linear)

An openwork pattern is basically a solid one, in which some of the vertical stitches are converted to chain spaces. At the drawing board stage, therefore, the same grid serves for both types of fabric pattern. In practice the more spaces there are, the narrower the fabric will eventually work out, because chain stitches are on the whole narrower than vertical ones. However so long as you are not combining open and solid work in the same fabric (see Mixed Grids below) this makes no difference.

Openwork Grids (Circular)

In view of the smaller width of chain stitches compared with vertical ones, it is usually wrong to assume that a solid, circular grid, which is known to lie flat in practice, will still do so if some of its stitches are converted into chain spaces. A larger total number of stitches will be required from the outset, so fresh experiments and/ or calculations must be made.

Mixed Grids

Even a continuous piece of fabric need not be tied to a single grid throughout. In the linear format particularly, two or more can often be combined, although you must usually expect some problems in mating them. The simplest way to combine grids is to have them alternate in horizontal bands.

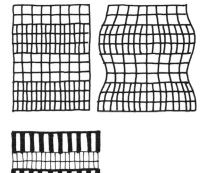

In this example a simple, solid grid alternates with a filet grid. The intention would be to use the same hook and quality of yarn throughout, but in practice the tension in the filet section would probably work out narrower, because the chain spaces would occupy less horizontal space than the vertical stitches. It might therefore be necessary to change to a larger hook for those sections.

In this example the solid grid alternates with one exactly twice as large. The plan clearly requires two different thicknesses of yarn and hook and you would have to experiment with separate test pieces in order to find the ingredients to make it work.

Grids in which the lines of the rows are not straight (oblique, curved, zig-zag, wavy) have very limited usefulness in clothes-making, unless you can find ways of straightening up at least the bottom or the top edge (and preferably both), but, if you can, you can obviously also alternate them with sections of straight grid.

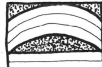

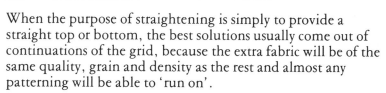

When the purpose of straightening is simply to provide a straight top or bottom, the best solutions usually come out of continuations of the grid, because the extra fabric will be of the same quality, grain and density as the rest and almost any patterning will be able to 'run on'.

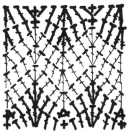

In the context of grid mixing it may be better, however, to construct one or more non-parallel rows (see page 113)—interrupted if necessary—so that, over the transitions, stitches are still always worked into the tops of previous stitches and not into their sides.

Plain openwork networks can often be simple to straighten:

But the more the patterning, the more ingenuity and even invention may be called for:

Complicated mixed grids, i.e. any not limited to arrangements of horizontal bands, are more difficult to work out and much less likely to be practical. And indeed any mixed grid will be harder to shape (edge or dart) than a single one. But remember that unsuccessful experiments in this context could easily alert you to other new possibilities, for instance in the three-dimensional field.

Overlapping Grids

There are two types of fabric obtainable from superimposing two or more grids: single thickness and multiple thickness.

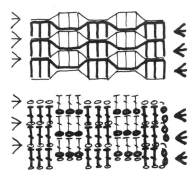

Single thickness (2 grids): In any given row vertical stitches alternate with chain spaces—the vertical stitches being worked always into the tops of the vertical stitches in the previous row but one. (If you find this difficult try picking up the loops first in the barb of the hook, then levering the tip through.) All the odd-numbered rows constitute one grid and all the even numbered ones the other. The main value of this arrangement is the opportunity it affords for deploying colour simply but interestingly (see page 146). Selection of a different colour for each separate whole row leads automatically to either vertical stripes or a multiple chequerboard effect. Neat shaping, however, requires much more careful thought and planning than usual (see page 167).

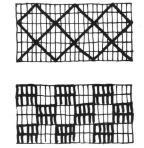

Multiple thickness (2, or more grids): On most occasions when, say, a double thickness fabric is contemplated, it will prove much more practical to make each layer separately and join them afterwards. In all probability both the grid structure and pattern of each will be different. If the two grids are the same, however, and the two thicknesses are worked concurrently, it becomes possible, by working each pair of rows on an interrupted basis, to have them weave in and out of each other. (They will of course be permanently inextricable.)

To form overlapping rose petals, etc. in circular work (the system can also be applied to the linear format) overlapping chain loop networks can be set up and one, or more, rounds of vertical stitches worked into them. The networks may remain independent, or become permanently interleaved (see motifs, page 155).

Proliferating Grids

By working one row into the back loops only and another row into the front loops only, you can double the number of thicknesses in the fabric—every row if required. (You can also reduce them by working one row through two or more thicknesses together.) These multiple thicknesses can then be woven in and out of each other as well.

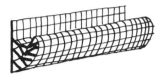 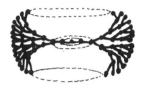

Multi-axial Grids

A grid has only one axis (the purpose of the grid is, amongst other things, to define it), which normally tells you how to operate it. The exception to the rule is the grid representing a fabric made of repeated 'into-the-side' stitches, which must be regarded as multi-axial, or, at the very least, ambiguous, since it turns the general principles of construction on their sides, too.

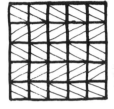

Although the outline grid looks straightforward enough, shaping is now no longer a matter of adding/subtracting stitches—that is the way to adjust the depth of the row—but more akin to adding/subtracting interrupted mini-rows. Any shaping has to be devised and planned for each pattern taking into account its individual structure (see page 167).

Three-dimensional Grids

One way to construct three-dimensional fabrics is to work to a perfectly simple two-dimensional grid pattern, but to use a variety of different yarns and hooks which you know will never be compatible in terms of tension. This approach scores highly in terms of entertainment value, but its results are usually unpredictable and difficult to control.

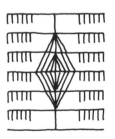

The more formal way is to evolve a three-dimensional grid out of a two-dimensional one, by building in distortions (see Consistency, page 131).

Beyond the Grid

All the grids discussed so far are basic and have some degree of general usefulness. By putting together individual rows of various shapes and repeating them you can devise much more elaborate and specialized ones.

 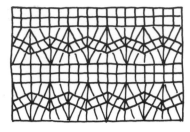 

Still without abandoning the conventional approach to fabric making you can improvise non-repeating grids, sometimes mixing these with regular ones, and then you are almost into free working.

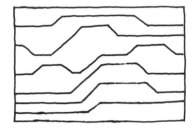 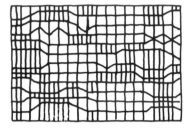 

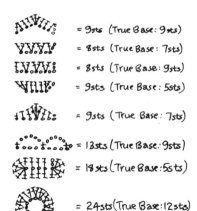

	= 9sts (True Base: 9sts)
	= 8sts (True Base: 7sts)
	= 8sts (True Base: 9sts)
	= 9sts (True Base: 5sts)
	= 9sts (True Base: 7sts)
	= 13sts (True Base: 9sts)
	= 18sts (True Base: 5sts)
	= 24sts (True Base: 12sts)

Individual row construction

The base row: In order to calculate the base chain and so establish the base row accurately in the linear format, it is important to understand the notion of 'true base'—the number of stitches the previous row would have had, if there had been one. This is not necessarily the same as the number of stitches in the real base row.

The base chain itself will need more chains than the true base has stitches, because extra are needed for 'turning'. Add, according to the depth of stitch the turning chain has to represent, as follows: dc: 1ch; h.tr: 1ch; tr: 2ch; d.tr: 3ch; t.tr: 4ch (see also page 69—base chain tension problems, and page 93—planning zig-zag, etc. grids).

If, in openwork, the first stitch(es) after the turning chain are also chains, add these on, too.

Now, even when the true base and base chain have been correctly worked out, you are still not home and dry until you are quite sure into which chain from the hook to work the first vertical stitch. Here is a summary of how to determine all these matters with examples to study. If it all becomes too much for the brain to stand, just work plenty of extra chains to be safe (they can be undone afterwards) and find the most suitable chain to work the first stitch into by trial and error.

1    2    3 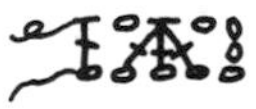   4

5    6    7    8

Base Chain: how many chains?

	True Base	Plus Number of ch.sps between top of t.ch and top of first vertical st. (if any).	Plus For nominal value of t.ch (Dc = 1, H.tr = 1, Tr = 2, D.tr = 3, T.tr = 4, etc.).	Total Chains
1	5	0	2	7
2	5	0	2	7
3	5	1	2	8
4	5	0	0	5
5	7	1	2	10
6	9	0	1	10
7	9	1	3	13
8	7	1	3	11

Base Row: into which chain from hook?

	For nominal value of t.ch (SS = 2nd, Dc = 3rd, H.tr = 3rd, Tr = 4th, D.tr = 5th, T.tr = 6th.)	Plus For ch.sps missed between bottom of t.ch and bottom of first st. (if any).	Plus For chs missed between top of t.ch and top of first vertical st. (if any).	Count from Hook (not including loop on hook).
1	4th	0	0	4th
2	4th	1	0	5th
3	4th	0	1	5th
4	2nd	0	0	2nd
5	4th	2	1	7th
6	3rd	3	0	6th
7	5th	0	1	6th
8	5th	−3	1	3rd

The turning chain: As you become experienced you will find your own ways of adapting and refining your treatment of the turning chain. How many chains? Simple, or turning chain-as-stitch treatment? When your tension is reliable and you are no longer in any danger of confusing yourself, you will do whatever seems neatest or most effective for you in the particular circumstances.

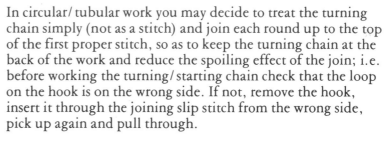

In circular/tubular work you may decide to treat the turning chain simply (not as a stitch) and join each round up to the top of the first proper stitch, so as to keep the turning chain at the back of the work and reduce the spoiling effect of the join; i.e. before working the turning/starting chain check that the loop on the hook is on the wrong side. If not, remove the hook, insert it through the joining slip stitch from the wrong side, pick up again and pull through.

This also enables you to work a puff/bobble/raised or other fancy stitch as the pattern may require in the place of the turning/starting chain, but there is a potential disadvantage: the 'spare' chains form a slight ridge at the back of the fabric.

In filet crochet you may find that the edges look straighter, if an extra chain is missed before you work the last stitch.

You may decide not to work a turning chain in the usual way at all, for instance after a change of yarn (see joining in, third method, page 37) with extended loop stitches (see example e, page 88).

Standard procedures should not be slavishly adhered to, when you can see for yourself when and how they need to be modified. Your solutions are bound to be personal and probably the better for that.

Reversibility/breaking off the supply yarn: We established (see page 27) that the fronts and backs of individual stitches were different and that the front and back of a fabric will therefore be different, too, except when a single—or, to a certain extent, any odd-numbered—row repeat sequence is worked alternately to and fro. In fact by the same token a pattern with any number of rows in the repeat can be made reversible, provided they are all—or the same selection each time—worked first one way and then the other alternately. You are unlikely to go in for this, if it means breaking off the yarn repeatedly, but you should consider what useful patterns emerge (reversible, or not) from working selected rows in unconventional directions without the necessity of breaking off, because you have involved more than one supply ball (of the same, or different shades).

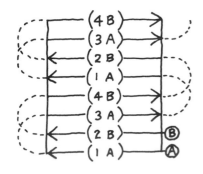

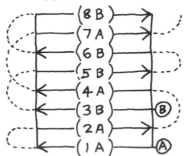

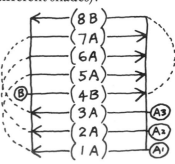

Parallel rows: To make a row parallel to a previous straight one, use the same denomination of vertical stitch and work on a one-for-one stitch basis.

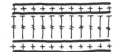

When the previous row is not straight, still keep the same stitch depth, unless there are sudden angles to negotiate, which call for a longer stitch at the nodes (see page 117), and 'shape' so that the stitches are in line with those of the previous row.

NB This one-for-one arrangement as drawn without shaping will not work in practice.

Non-parallel: A solid non-parallel row must involve vertical stitches of differing depths.

An irregular row following a straight one must have more stitches, and a straight row following an irregular one less stitches, than its predecessor.

NB Graduated vertical stitches worked consecutively on a simple one-for-one basis result in a crumpled fabric, rather than irregular rows, unless the graduations are kept small and reversed promptly. Even then the fabric will not lie quite as flat as a simple one does, before pressing.

A rough idea of how many more/less stitches to work can be gauged in much the same way as you plan a zig-zag grid. Mark off on a piece of scrap paper (over the grid drawing, or the test fabric) the estimated length of the non-horizontal section and check it against the genuine horizontal tension.

The whole format of conventional circular work militates against the introduction of irregular row shapes worked on a continuous basis, particularly in solid patterns, but try interruptions. Consider also free-worked circular shapes with interrupted rounds.

Continuous/interrupted: The properties and advantages of the continuous method of row construction are straightforward enough to be taken for granted. Some of the more obvious applications of interruption, grouped into two basic types, are referred to in this book, but it is clear that this approach is underdeveloped, its potential unexploited and its purposes only tentatively defined here. Bear it constantly in mind; see what it can do for you, both as a straight alternative to continuous working and as a tool for substantial innovation.

How to Sketch Stitch Patterns

To analyse or invent crochet patterns you may need to be able to sketch them quickly and realistically. Everyone develops their own personal method of doing this, but here are some guidelines. The most straightforward thing is to represent each stitch with a stroke of the pen. Paper with a printed, squared grid is invaluable for linear patterns and for circular work it is still useful.

Linear Format

On graph paper with a fairly small square it is most convenient to make each vertical line represent one stitch and each horizontal line the depth of one row of double crochet. A half treble row then makes $1\frac{1}{2}$ lines, treble 2 lines, double treble 3 lines, and so on. On arithmetic paper with a larger square it is better to make each vertical line represent every 2nd stitch and each horizontal line one row of treble, with the others in proportion: double crochet $\frac{1}{2}$ line, half treble $\frac{3}{4}$ line, double treble $1\frac{1}{2}$ lines, and so on. In this way you can draw a grid plan of your pattern very much as it will look when you actually make the fabric and lay it down on a table in front of you.

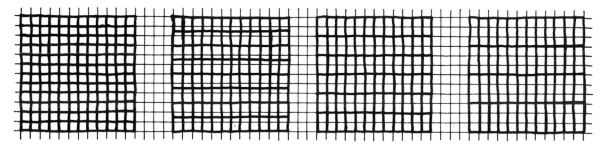

In practice the lines of stitches and rows do not make squares nor are the various depths exact proportions of one another as shown (see page 116), but this is a useful basis for planning and doodling.

Circular Format

For circular work in the shape of a square, graph paper can be used in much the same way. For true circles and even ovals and spirals it can be a useful guide for quick, freehand or compass-drawn rings and curves, but the lines cannot often be made to show automatically where the stitches go—this has to be worked out.

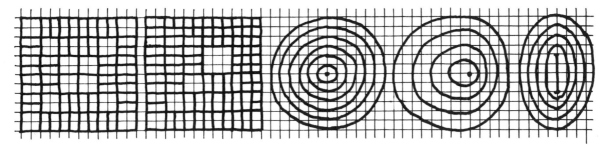

For other shapes—triangles, hexagons, etc.—it is hardly any
help at all and these are best drawn on plain paper, with a
protractor if necessary.

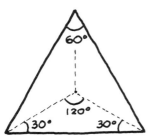
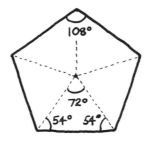

General

To differentiate the standard stitches, more often than not a
simple pen stroke of the appropriate length will be clear. In
complicated patterns containing stitches of several
denominations all at once, to avoid confusion, the system of
crossing the uprights, etc. will help.

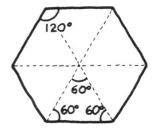

If chains are obvious, or unimportant, they can be left out, e.g.
the base chain of a simple solid pattern can be taken for
granted. If they need to be specified exactly, use a small dot or
circle, or both for clarity. Find an evocative squiggle or blob for
any non-standard stitches.

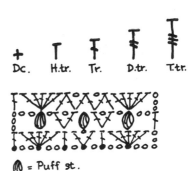

If there is any doubt about the general direction of working or
that of individual rows, put arrows in to remind you.

The main function of the sketch diagram is to reveal the bones
of the structure and it cannot be pressed into specifying,
without additional notes, whether, for example, stitches are
worked into one, two, or three loops, or round the stem, etc.
Other conditions which stretch the system are: reverse side
patterns, multi-thickness fabrics, overlapping, ruching,
crumpling, all three-dimensional and most highly textured

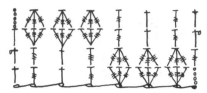

fabrics. To plan the details of ruched or crumpled patterns, it is best to 'squash' them flat, that is, spread out the 'normal' stitches and rows and represent the distorted ones as though they were normal.

When you are trying to unravel the mysteries of somebody else's pattern instructions, first read them through to get some idea of the shape of the basic grid—is it even straight? And be prepared to make a few errors in your trials, before you make visual sense of the text and your sketch. Naturally the more you draw out patterns, the quicker you become familiar with their little ways and the more confident you become in handling them. Try drawing these examples (before looking at the diagrams on page 246):

Example 1
2trs in 3rd ch from hook, * 1tr in each of next 6sts, tr3tog, 1tr in each of next 6sts, 3trs in next st, rep from *.

Example 2
*5ch, miss 3ch, 1dc in next ch, rep from *.

Stitch Proportions

When we draw plans of crochet patterns, it is convenient to depict the various standard stitches in neat proportions to one another. In practice they only approximate to these proportions and the grid of the actual fabric will work out differently. How differently? The size of a stitch depends, apart from individual differences in tension, upon the size of the hook and yarn used. Actually the yarn has surprisingly little effect and the hook plays the major part. Roughly speaking, if a hook is used which fits the yarn most snugly—say 3.00mm with 4 Ply, 4.00mm with double knitting and 6.00mm with triple knitting (chunky)—the proportion of the width of each stitch to its own height in solid patterns will be:

Double Crochet	1:0.79	(1:1)
Half Treble	1:1.23	(1:1.5)
Treble	1:1.66	(1:2)
Double Treble	1:2.44	(1:3)

'Width' here means not the thickness of the main stem, but the horizontal distance between the centres of two consecutive stitches. The figures in brackets are the nominal proportions adopted in grid diagrams. Note that none of the stitches is really as high as it is drawn and that the double crochet is actually wider than it is high.

This chart shows the relative heights of the stitches. In the diagrams 6 rows double crochet, 4 rows half treble, 3 rows treble and 2 rows double treble are all assumed to be exactly equal.

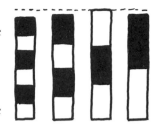

If a larger and larger hook is used with the same yarn, naturally the stitches made will be both higher and wider, in fact by roughly the same amount, which changes the proportions of the stitches—their widths become a larger proportion of their heights. Conversely, if a smaller and smaller hook is used, the stitches will become lower and narrower and their widths will become a smaller proportion of their heights. On the whole, if you use the smallest hook with which it is still possible to work a particular yarn, the height of, say, a treble can be increased in proportion to its width from 1:1.66 to 1:1.75, and if the largest hook is used, it can be reduced to 1:1.45. But the smaller everything is, the bigger the extremes and the more variable the control; with very thin crochet cotton, for instance, and a very small hook a treble may be 1:1.95 and with a very large one 1:1.25.

Squareness

Now this is no reason to throw out the very convenient diagram system in general, but it does mean, for instance, that if, when planning a pattern such as chequerboard, in which square shapes are prominent, we treat it according to those stitches, which look as though they will depict squares on the grid, we shall be in for a disappointment. Luckily most 'square' patterns are perfectly acceptable if they are only approximately square, and so we usually settle for this. Whenever patterns really must work out in squares, however, we need to take more trouble, e.g. when linear squares are made as motifs for a patchwork to fit together on different axes. The only way to be sure of constructing exact squares, or 45° angles, is to make a substantial test piece of the actual fabric with the correct hook and yarn and make careful observations.

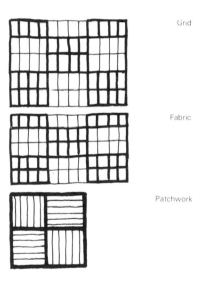

Grid

Fabric

Patchwork

For the same reasons 'squareness', in the sense of the angle between adjacent segments of a continuous row which changes direction, will not be readily obtainable (see Planning Zig-zag Grids, page 93; Concentric Grids (Circular): Squares, page 97; Mixed Grids, page 107). Since the width of the schematic 'square' in the rectangular grid here works out wider than its height, the angle of the corresponding zig-zag grid will not be as sharp as 45°.

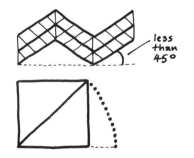

less than 45°

Even if you have forgotten all your mathematics, you will appreciate that the diagonal of any square must be a little longer than one of its sides (by about 41%, in fact, or nearly half as long again). You will notice that, by the same token,

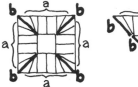

whatever the actual angle whenever a row changes direction, or the edge of a fabric is not at right angles to the line of the rows, the stitches at the centres of the nodes, or at the edges (marked 'b') ought to be longer than the ones along the straight sections (marked 'a')—the sharper the angles, the longer in proportion. Ideally therefore, at least in theory, you would make them so. Yet most people ignore this. The reasons are: crochet stitches are generally sufficiently flexible to absorb the difference; slight rounding of the angles is usually taken for granted; angles exceeding 270° over the peaks (less than 90° in the valleys) are not generally attempted; the basic crochet stitches are mostly more than 41% longer/shorter than their neighbours in the hierarchy. When the change of direction is sharp, however, a better result is often obtainable, either by substituting a longer stitch or artificially lengthening a stitch of the same denomination as the others (slightly extend, or loosen, the lower part of the stitch as you make it).

In the Half Granny Square this factor is emphasized, because the two edges where increasing occurs, form a single straight line—the diagonal of the square. The first specimen was made with a turning chain of 4ch (as 1tr and 1ch.sp) and 1tr for the last stitch—the same as the others in the row. The other has 5ch to turn (as 1d.tr and 1ch.sp) and 1d.tr to end—much more satisfactory.

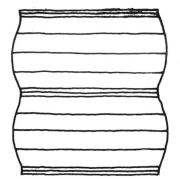

Comparative Horizontal Tension

We assume in grid diagrams that stitches of different heights, when worked with the same hook and yarn, are of the same width. In practice half trebles will be 2–3% wider than double crochets, trebles 6–7% and double trebles 10–11%. In a fabric where one tall row alternates with one short one repeatedly, this makes very little difference, because in their ding-dong battle to determine the overall tension, neither has sufficient chance to dominate. If, on the other hand, a pattern consists of 4 or so consecutive rows of, say, double treble, separated by 2 consecutive rows of, say, double crochet, there will be a pronounced fullness around the middle of the broad band. If this is not wanted, it is worth decreasing by, in this case, 10% (work every 9th and 10th stitch together) on the first of the double treble rows and increasing (work 2 stitches into every 10th stitch) by the same amount on the first of the double crochet rows. Otherwise steer clear of this juxtaposition.

Stitch Lean

Crochet stitches do not in practice stand up exactly at right
angles to the row, nor are they exactly in line with one another,
as is implied in stitch diagrams. They tend to lean forward in
the direction of the next stitch. This tendency varies in degree
from one person's work to another's. In patterns which use the
same stitch for every row, provided the rows are always worked
alternatively to and fro, the overall grid remains square, because
whatever happens on one row is exactly reversed on the next.
Even if all the rows are worked in the same direction the grid
will not necessarily become out of square, because each stitch
never goes into the exact top dead centre of the previous one,
but rather to its right. However if there is any deviation it will
have a cumulative effect and should be watched. Simple
patterns with a two-row repeat, even though they may be
worked to and fro, are highly susceptible to this warping,
because the deeper rows (with more magnified lean) will always
go one way and the shallower ones in the other. You will not be
able to straighten this up by pressing the fabric afterwards, so
you must cure the creeping disease at source: measure the
amount of deviation on a test piece, then compensate for it by
increasing at one side and decreasing at the other—treat the
grid as though it were oblique in fact (see page 91).

You will not be able to emphasize or increase the natural degree
of stitch lean either, except possibly by modifying the
individual stitch-making procedure (see Alternative Standard
Stitches, page 82).

Fabric Profile
Qualities and Characteristics

Weight (Solid/Open)

There was a time when crochet was always assumed to consist of
an open, flowery fabric, imitating lace. In fact it can be
extremely dense and heavy, or so insubstantial and airy as
scarcely to count as a fabric at all.

We started with solid fabrics; one way to open them up is to
work between the stitches, one or two at a time. Three at a time
is not practical on a regular basis. You must count the turning
chain as a stitch here; otherwise in linear work you will lose a
stitch automatically every row.

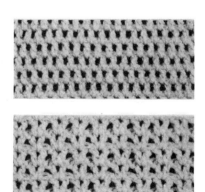

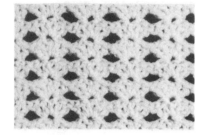

However the two main features of real openwork are true spaces and stitch groupings.

Work several stitches into one place, i.e. make a group and miss a corresponding number of stitches before working the next.

Substitute any stitch or stitches, except the first and/or last by chain spaces (but include enough vertical stitches to hold the fabric together) in a formal or informal arrangement to produce any degree of openness.

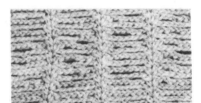

Double crochet and half treble stitches, being shallow, are not usually as useful as treble or double treble, as bread-and-butter stitches in openwork.

The simplest examples of stitches plus space are regular networks with 2 or 3 stitch and 1 or 2 row repeat, usually called Filet Mesh. These networks stand on their own as fabrics or as backgrounds for woven crochet (see page 208), or as the basis for a type of patterning which arises out of the contrast between space and substance.

Filet crochet: The term 'filet' is borrowed from needle lace-making, where it refers to the squared net ground on which stitches are worked. These are the characteristic grids in treble (linear).

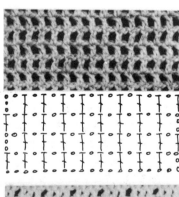

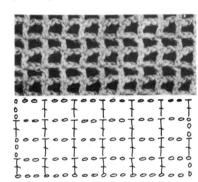

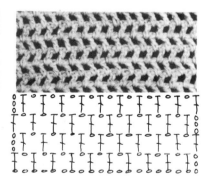

The first two are used very frequently as a basis or ground for block patterning or filet lace, which is normally a matter of filling in the holes, i.e. working trebles instead of some of the chain spaces, or vice versa. Sometimes diagonal loops are included for variety.

The following terms may be found in the context of filet crochet: space—the grid chain space is worked as a chain space; block—trebles are worked instead of grid chain spaces, making solid blocks; bar—chain spaces are worked instead of grid trebles, making double spaces; lacet—a double crochet is worked instead of a grid treble. (Naturally more than the usual number of chains has to be worked either side.)

Pay close attention to how the row endings are worked and see page 169 for how to shape the edges. These patterns are simple to draw and read back from charts (see page 159) with simplified symbols or squares to represent the stitches.

Fine filet crochet also makes a good border or trimming in the traditional style (see page 192), and a very easy-to-work basis for extravagent surface crochet (see page 191). The first and third examples above are suitable for woven crochet (see page 208), when the treble stitches in the first are often worked not under the top 2 loops, but rather under 3 loops of the trebles (see page 83) to make a firmer fabric.

When the filet grounds are adapted to the circular format their flexibility as vehicles for pattern making is reduced, because either the size, or the number, of spaces changes (see below).

By extending either or both elements of the repeat sequence other basic networks can be evolved.

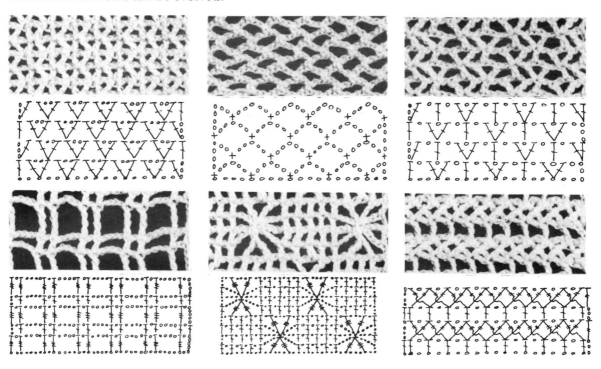

Most of these are capable of embellishment. With rectangular grids in particular the permutations are endless.

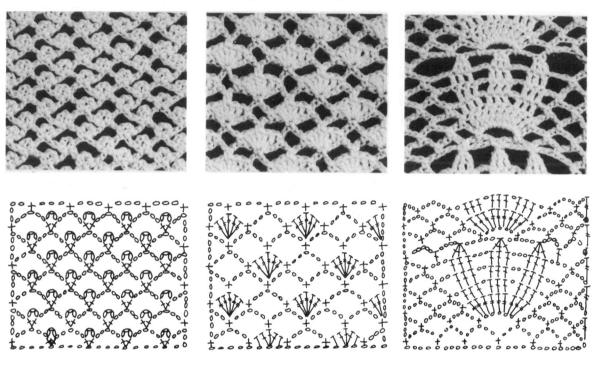

Fewer forms of regular network are possible on other linear grids such as zig-zag. But in any case other types of zig-zag effect can be built into a regular mesh.

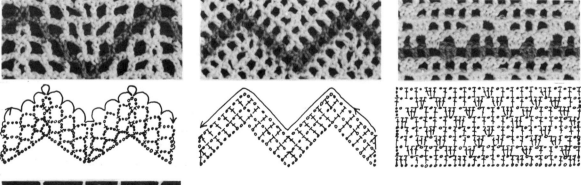

Here are some more specialized networks originally evolved for crochet lace making, but often equally good for larger scale work:

As a complete fabric, or for connecting motifs (see Patchwork, page 233 and Irish Picot, page 129, for how to work the picots).

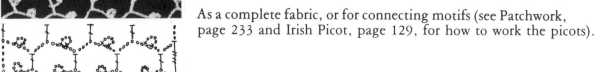

When chain loops are not substantial enough they can be 'upholstered' with double crochet.

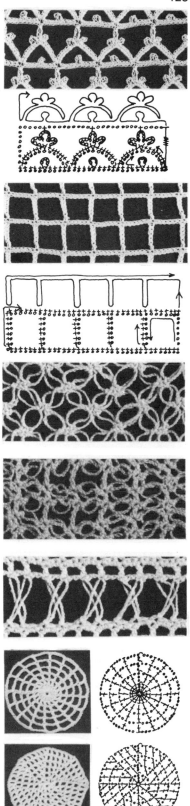

This type of network usually served as a ground for appliqué motifs.

In circumstances where longish chain loops might have been used and no vertical stitches need to be worked into them, the single or double Solomon's Knot makes an attractive alternative.

Extending the last loops of stitches (see page 88) and picking these up on the following row, not necessarily in consecutive order, can make another kind of network suitable for linear and circular work.

There are two basic kinds of circular network: those in which the size of the mesh units remains the same, but their number increases, and those in which their number remains the same, but the size of the individual mesh units changes. In the latter case paradoxically the units in successive rounds may actually have the same number of stitches—at least for a few rounds. In order for the work to lie flat the units become wider and shallower as they recede from the centre (see the last three rounds of the photograph on page 147).

Groups and clusters: The main building blocks in openwork are groups—several stitches worked into the same place so that they appear to fan out from the bottom—and clusters—(the upside-down version of groups) several stitches usually started in different places, but joined together at the top so that they appear to fan out from the top. Stitches started in the same place and joined at the top as well also go under the general title of clusters.

Constructional advice: Double crochet and half treble stitches play only a small part in the formation of groups and clusters, because of their shallowness. The treble is long enough for the smaller ones, but the more elaborate ones require double or triple treble.

The basic constructional considerations are the same for open patterns as for solid ones. Chain stitches tend to occupy slightly less width than others, but this can usually be safely ignored, except in the case of certain mixed grids (see page 107) and extended chain loops (see below).

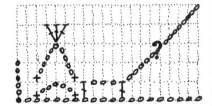

Chain loops: The number of chains required for a chain loop which follows the horizontal (concentric) grid lines is shown automatically by the grid. If it follows the vertical lines, count up on the basis of the number of chains you normally use for the turning chain. Oblique or curved chain loops can be guessed, or even ticked off on a piece of scrap paper over the drawing, which is then aligned with the horizontal grid lines.

Despite the ideals of measurement, in practice the number of chains in a loop must be odd, if, later, the pattern requires a single stitch or group to be worked into its centre point.

Working into chain loops: It is far quicker and easier—all things being equal—to work stitches over a chain loop by inserting the hook underneath the whole chain as in the first round of circular work, rather than insinuating it between the separate threads of each particular chain, as in the base row of linear work. The fabric may often look better for this, or at least remain essentially unaffected either way. However, if there is any possibility of, say, a group splitting up or a single stitch wandering later, you must work into a particular chain.

Working over clusters: The top of a cluster is hardly ever as neat and sharp as the base of a group. If a group is later worked into the top of a cluster, it can open up the top and destroy the shape. In some cases it may help to work more deeply into the body of the cluster, under 3 or even 4 threads. In the case of a single stitch worked over a cluster, it may be better still to insert the hook first before, then after the cluster, picking up the

Groups

Half	Whole	Half

Clusters

Half	Whole	Half

(7) (13) (6+tch)

(7 tog.) (13 tog) (tch+6 tog)

'X' Shapes Crossed Stitches 'Y' Shapes Into-the-side Groups

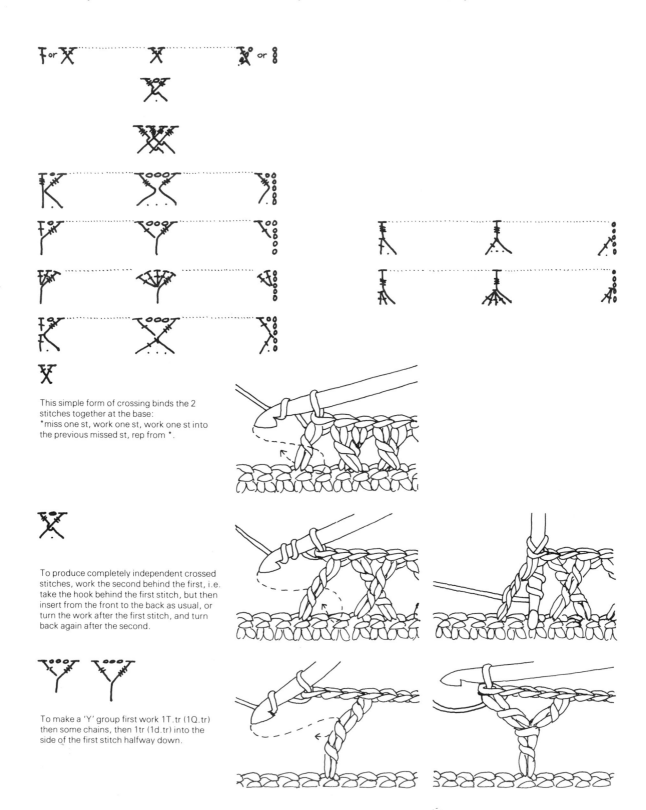

This simple form of crossing binds the 2 stitches together at the base:
*miss one st, work one st, work one st into the previous missed st, rep from *.

To produce completely independent crossed stitches, work the second behind the first, i.e. take the hook behind the first stitch, but then insert from the front to the back as usual, or turn the work after the first stitch, and turn back again after the second.

To make a 'Y' group first work 1T.tr (1Q.tr) then some chains, then 1tr (1d.tr) into the side of the first stitch halfway down.

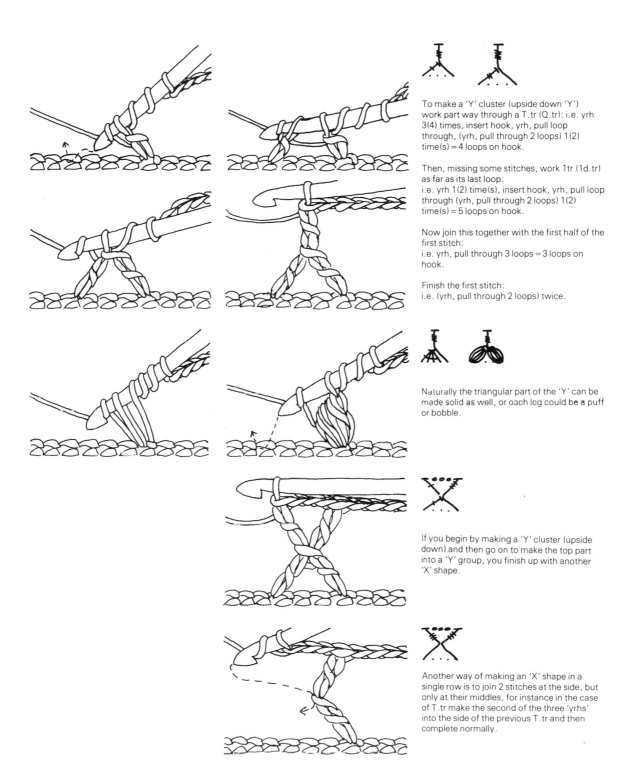

To make a 'Y' cluster (upside down 'Y') work part way through a T.tr (Q.tr): i.e. yrh 3(4) times, insert hook, yrh, pull loop through, (yrh, pull through 2 loops) 1(2) time(s) = 4 loops on hook.

Then, missing some stitches, work 1tr (1d.tr) as far as its last loop:
i.e. yrh 1(2) time(s), insert hook, yrh, pull loop through (yrh, pull through 2 loops) 1(2) time(s) = 5 loops on hook.

Now join this together with the first half of the first stitch:
i.e. yrh, pull through 3 loops = 3 loops on hook.

Finish the first stitch:
i.e. (yrh, pull through 2 loops) twice.

Naturally the triangular part of the 'Y' can be made solid as well, or each leg could be a puff or bobble.

If you begin by making a 'Y' cluster (upside down) and then go on to make the top part into a 'Y' group, you finish up with another 'X' shape.

Another way of making an 'X' shape in a single row is to join 2 stitches at the side, but only at their middles, for instance in the case of T.tr make the second of the three 'yrhs' into the side of the previous T.tr and then complete normally.

supply thread each time (next stage: *yrh, pull through 3 loops*) to pinch the top together, and not into the actual cluster at all.

Half groups and clusters: The logical and usually most practical way to plan patterns is with both the edges (the join in circular work) either exactly between or in the centre of a group or cluster feature.

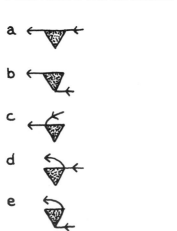

In circular work it is sometimes necessary and desirable to have the join wander.

Whatever the possible variations, it is important to become familiar with and confident in handling the 'half' version of every group and cluster.

At the beginning of a row the second half of a group or cluster is worked starting with what would normally be the centre stitch of the complete figure; the turning chain fulfills this role. At the end the first half is worked, ending with the 'centre' stitch. The centre stitch is thus included in both split halves.

When the group or cluster is a V or Y shape and has a vertical stitch at its centre, the half version is clear; when the centre is a chain space or loop, this must be translated into a vertical stitch of suitable depth.

Puff or bobble clusters are best either included complete or, if problems with a lumpy seam are envisaged, translated into ordinary single stitches of appropriate length.

Planning the route: When you are trying to rough out a complicated pattern, remember there may be more than one way to construct the same, or nearly the same shape. There will in any case be more than one way to approach and leave it.

Alternative Construction

a

b

c

d

e

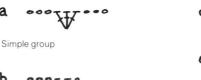

a

Simple group

b

Let a sequence of chains stand for one of the stitches, just as the turning chain does.

c

Let a single long stitch bend over and serve as more than one side of the shape.

d

e

Leave the hook at the beginning rather than the end of the series. (Solid shapes: apply Tunisian Finishing see page **63**. Open shapes: slip stitch backwards.)

Consider the conventional V or shell group (solid or open). You normally approach and leave it along the lines indicated in the first example, but it may well be necessary or convenient to do so in the manner of the others. The principles involved can easily be applied to other shapes and configurations. That of leaving the hook at the beginning, rather than the end of a series enables you to make more subtle, natural, shapes than usual. Combined with the Picot it makes possible double- and triple-decker groups. These are most useful, when the interest in the fabric is to be the contrast between, say, a detailed, lacy device and a strong, solid one, which might be weakened if it had to be built up over several rows. Unlike other forms of interrupted row technique, this need not necessarily make for slow progress.

In the same way that a turning chain is used to fulfill the function of a vertical stitch, consider using a vertical stitch instead of part or the whole of a chain loop, if this makes your route neater or easier.

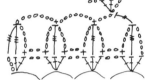

Picots: Picots are normally used for edgings (see page 190), but also, particularly in Irish Crochet, as an embellishment in the fabric, providing more delicacy or prettiness. The principle is usually to make a small detour in the row—a mini-interruption usually without turning the work—returning to the same, or nearly the same place.

Picots

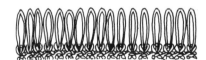

Lace, or Purl Picot: see page 88
e. Extended last loop.

Irish Picot: make a length of chain then, without turning, take the hook to the right back over it and work 1dc (not into any single ch). Going forwards again work, say, 4ch and then 1dc into the loop of the original chain length (not into any single ch.). Withdraw the original chain length to the rear, so that the last two dc.s made are drawn close together and the 4ch loop forms the picot. Continue with, say, 2ch.

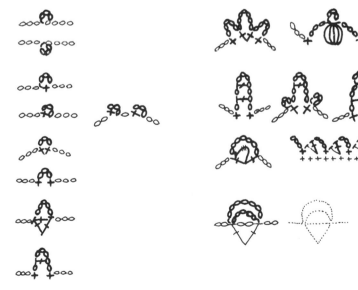

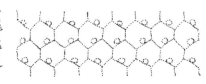

Compounds

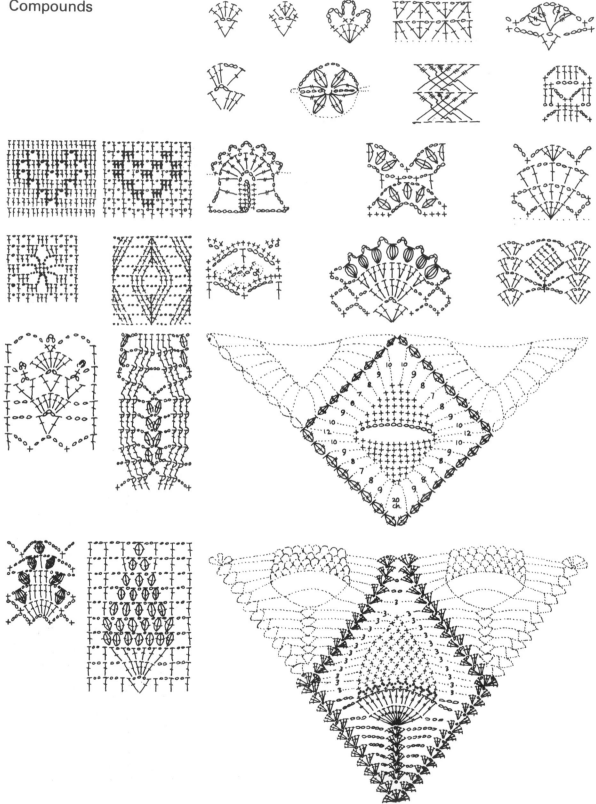

Consistency

It is one of the advantages of crochet that all kinds of variations in fabric consistency are possible. So far we have been preoccupied with identifying the ways of keeping fabrics flat and avoiding accidental undulations. With a thorough understanding of these, it is not difficult to devise controlled distortions.

Crumpling/ruching: Crumpling occurs when long stitches are sandwiched between shorter ones (with the proviso mentioned in connection with non-parallel rows on page 113); ruching when too few or too many stitches for the basic flat grid are included in a row. In the making of bobbles (see page 88) both principles are employed in a single instance, but they can be applied to sequences of stitches and rows, separately or together, to produce various kinds of undulation and bubbling.

When crumpling is used alone, the bubbles tend to project to the back and so alternate from right side to wrong side if you work to and fro. The higher the ratio of long stitches to shorter ones, the more the effect is diluted, finally dissolving into deeper, flat rows.

A straightforward gathering effect is also a method of shaping (see page 164). It involves a decrease, or increase, depending upon the direction of working, usually evenly over a whole row. As the basis of a fabric pattern, it can be reversed and repeated and perhaps confined to specific sections of the row.

Crumpling and ruching used together can produce gentle bubbling. The bubbles will go whichever way they are pushed. In openwork where there are fewer vertical stitches and more space, there are fewer possibilities for small controlled undulations, but gathering and built-in tucks, folds and draped effects are easier.

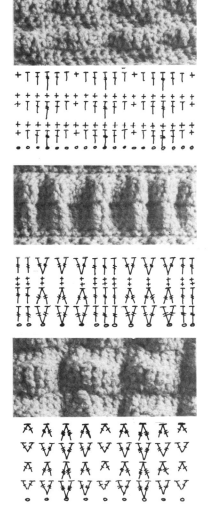

Surface

Crochet is probably at its smoothest when every row is worked with the right side facing and stitches are worked normally into the top two loops. In the first set of examples, variations in the way of working produce differences in the grain. In the second set, which includes raised stitches, deeper, more clearly defined textures are obtained. Raised stitches (see page 84), however, are also the main ingredient of distinct, relief patterning as demonstrated in the third set.

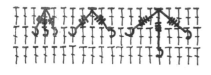

When all the stitches in a row are to be worked round the stem of the stitch immediately below, any denomination from treble upwards can be used. When only some stitches are raised and these are either oblique, i.e. worked round earlier, or later stitches, or vertical, but worked further than one row down, these must naturally be longer than the basic height of the row. Exactly how much longer must be determined by trial and error, but here is a guide.

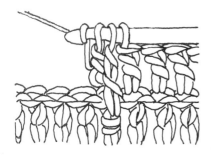

Patterns in which all the stitches in every row are raised (see Basketweave, page 137) will usually be reversible. When the pattern interest comes from a selection of raised stitches making a relief against a background, it is usual (and easier) to restrict the patterning to one side. There is, however, no reason why each raised stitch, or each branch of a raised cluster should not be worked in Siamese-twin pairs on either side of the fabric—the last loop of each twin being left on the hook so they can be joined into one at the final stage.

In patterns of the basketweave type the vertical raised stitches are a complete alternative to the ordinary stitches; in relief patterns, which depend greatly on a solid background for effect, it is often necessary to work the ordinary stitch as well as the raised one(s) to avoid a hole, particularly when the raised stitches are oblique. The ordinary and corresponding raised stitches must then be joined into one at the top in the usual way. According to convenience the ordinary and raised parts can be worked in any order, but stick to the same order when the same feature repeats.

Double Crochet
To and Fro

Front   Back

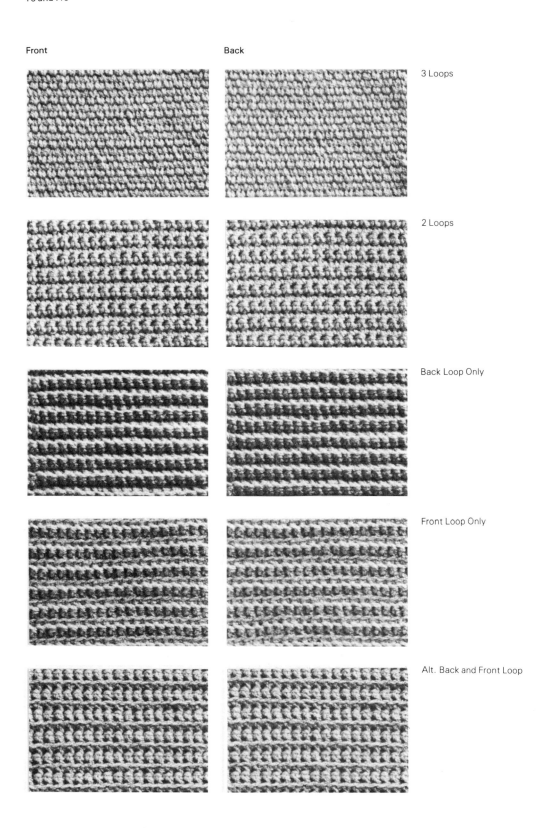

3 Loops

2 Loops

Back Loop Only

Front Loop Only

Alt. Back and Front Loop

Double Crochet
All Rows Right Side Facing

Front

Back

3 Loops

2 Loops

Front Loop Only

Back Loop Only

Alt. Back and Front Loop

To and Fro
2 Loops

All Rows Right Side Facing
Front

Half Treble

Treble

Double Treble

Front Lit

Back Lit

Triple Treble
To and Fro
2 loops

Triple Treble
Joined at the Side
To and Fro
2 Loops

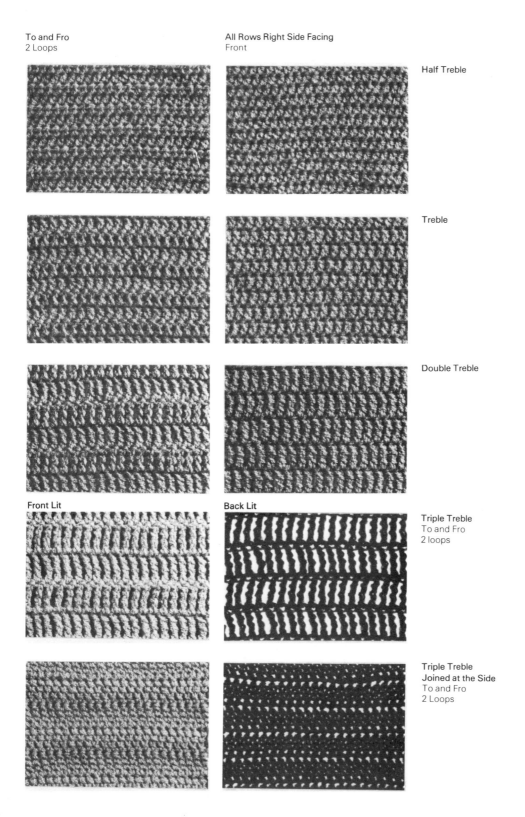

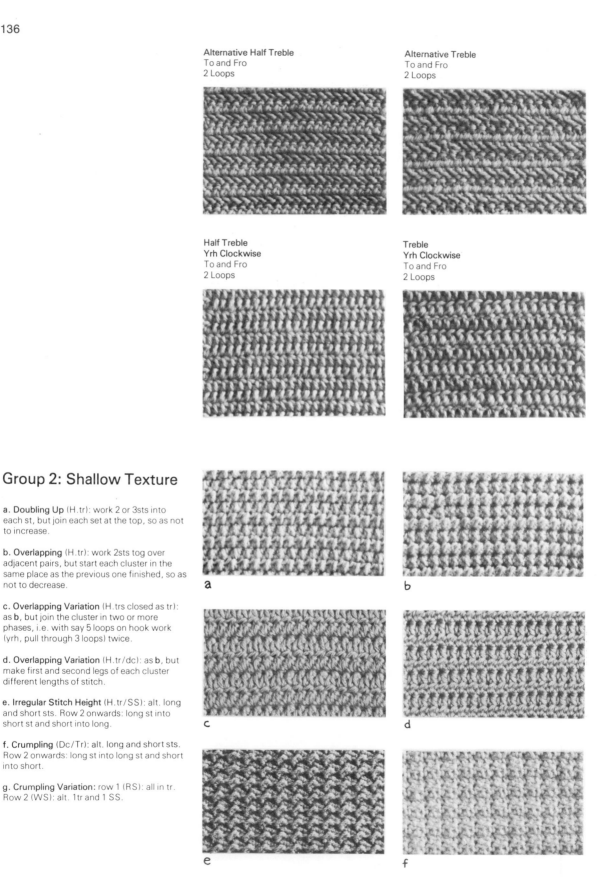

Alternative Half Treble
To and Fro
2 Loops

Alternative Treble
To and Fro
2 Loops

Half Treble
Yrh Clockwise
To and Fro
2 Loops

Treble
Yrh Clockwise
To and Fro
2 Loops

Group 2: Shallow Texture

a. Doubling Up (H.tr): work 2 or 3sts into each st, but join each set at the top, so as not to increase.

b. Overlapping (H.tr): work 2sts tog over adjacent pairs, but start each cluster in the same place as the previous one finished, so as not to decrease.

c. Overlapping Variation (H.trs closed as tr): as **b**, but join the cluster in two or more phases, i.e. with say 5 loops on hook work (yrh, pull through 3 loops) twice.

d. Overlapping Variation (H.tr/dc): as **b**, but make first and second legs of each cluster different lengths of stitch.

e. Irregular Stitch Height (H.tr/SS): alt. long and short sts. Row 2 onwards: long st into short st and short into long.

f. Crumpling (Dc/Tr): alt. long and short sts. Row 2 onwards: long st into long st and short into short.

g. Crumpling Variation: row 1 (RS): all in tr. Row 2 (WS): alt. 1tr and 1 SS.

a

b

c

d

e

f

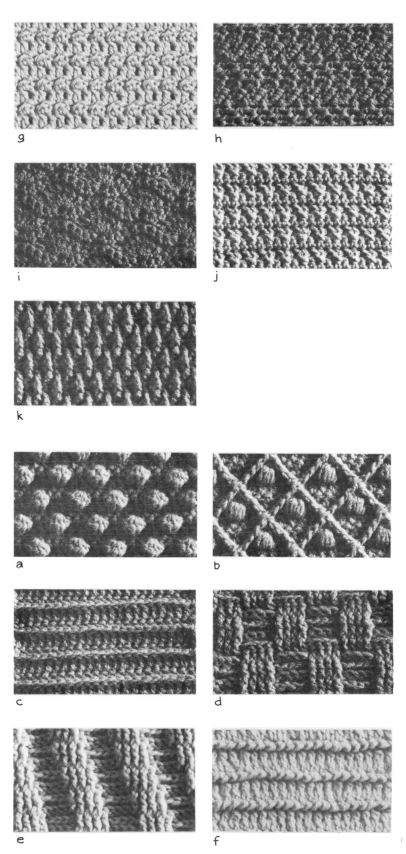

g

h

i

j

k

h. Into-the-Side (Tr groups): work 2ch (plus 3ch for turning at the beginning), *leaving last loop of each st on hook work 2trs into side of last gr. (or t.ch), miss 2sts, insert hook into next st, yrh, pull loop through fabric and next loop on hook, (yrh, pull through 2 loops) until 1 loop remains on hook, rep from *.

i. Wavy Grain: row 1: shell groups. Row 2: all in dc.

j. Crossed Stitches: row 1: crossed pairs of trs. Row 2: all in dc.

k. Raised Stitches: row 1 (RS): all in tr. Row 2: all in dc. Row 3: alt. 1tr and 1 raised d.tr (R.dtr) into tr row below. Rep rows 2 and 3, always working R.dtrs round simple trs and simple trs into R.dtrs of previous RS row.

a

b

c

d

e

f

Group 3: Medium Texture

a. Bobbles (Tr cluster in dc row): see page 88.

b. Raised and Puff Stitches (Tr fabric): see page 84.

c. Raised Stitches (Tr fabric): every st is a raised tr (R.tr) worked round the st immediately below. On RS rows always go in at the back of the work (R.tr/B) and on WS rows at the front (R.tr/F).

d. Raised Stitches Variation (Tr fabric): as **c**, but work, say, 4 R.trs/F then 4 R.trs/B and so on. Maintain the same distribution of F and B for, say, 4 rows then reverse it for 4 rows, etc.

e. Raised Stitches Variation (Tr fabric): as **c**, but shift the distribution one place to the right or left every row, instead of reversing it.

f. Corded Rib (Tr fabric): see page 138.

g. **Spike** (Tr fabric): see page **85**

g

Puffs and bobbles (see page 87) are best reserved for wrong side rows, because they project more away from you as you work and so stand up on the right side. It is advisable to work the ordinary stitch in the row immediately above a puff or bobble round the stem at the top of the bobble. This helps to throw the bobble into greater relief, whilst the stitch above, although 'raised', remains part of the background (unless the stitch above it is in turn worked round the stem).

The next examples are of techniques which supply very deep textures. Remember that they can also be used intermittently and in conjunction with other techniques, not just to make even pile fabrics.

Group 4: Deep Texture

a. Crumpled: row 1: alt. 1tr and 1T.tr. Row 2: all in dc.

b. Loop Stitch (Dc fabric): see page 84.

c. Loop Stitch Cut Variation: as b.

d. Chain Loops: proceed as for Corded Rib (page 138), except instead of working 1dc into each st, make, say, 10ch, then 1 SS into the front loop only of next st to the right.

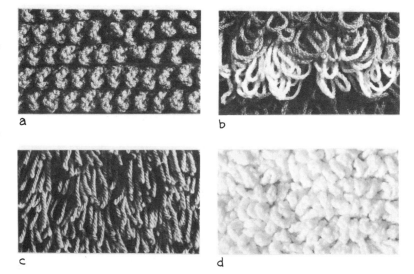

a

b

c

d

Corded rib: At the end of a right side row of any ordinary stitch, without turning, work in double crochet backwards, i.e. from left to right (see page 190), into the front loops only of the row just worked. Again without turning work another ordinary row into the vacant back loops of the previous ordinary row. And so on. This provides a ridge resembling surface crochet (see below).

None of these techniques plays such a large part in openwork fabrics. (Occasionally puffs and bobbles can be desirable; crossed stitches may involve variations in fabric thickness.) On the other hand every openwork fabric is itself arguably a relief pattern, using the object over which it is placed, or the light, if it is viewed in silhouette, as background.

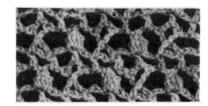

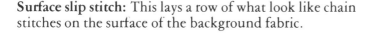

CSG 957

Surface crochet

The various techniques of surface crochet (sometimes called tambour crochet) developed out of the method used in embroidery, where a fabric is stretched over a frame like a shallow drum (tambour) to facilitate the needlework. In the crochet adaptation slip stitches are worked through the fabric with the hook always penetrating from the right side and the supply thread at the back—like the action of a sewing machine. Depending upon where each successive stitch is made any pattern can be traced on the surface of the fabric, either complementing any pattern on the background, or almost completely covering it. When the background fabric is itself crochet work, the frame is usually dispensed with.

Surface slip stitch: This lays a row of what look like chain stitches on the surface of the background fabric.

Surface double crochet: Technique A: This works out very like surface slip stitch except the surface row is a little deeper. Technique B: This results in a surface row of ordinary double crochet stitches, except that it does not stand up square from the background fabric, but leans over one way or the other, depending upon which side of the row the supply yarn is held.

Surface Slip Stitch

Start with the usual slip knot. If you want to begin the surface row somewhere other than the very edge of the background fabric, remove the hook from the slip knot, insert through the fabric from the right side in the required position, pick up the slip knot again and pull through. Otherwise, keeping the supply yarn at the back, work thus: *insert hook one step away as necessary, yrh (at back of work), pull through the background fabric and loop on hook in one movement, rep from *.

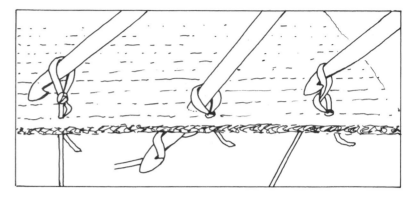

Surface Double Crochet

Technique A: keeping the supply yarn at the back of the fabric begin as for surface slip stitch until the first stitch has been completed. *insert hook in same place as before, yrh, pull through fabric, but not through loop on hook = 2 loops on hook, insert hook in next position, yrh, pull through fabric and through 2 loops on hook, rep from *.

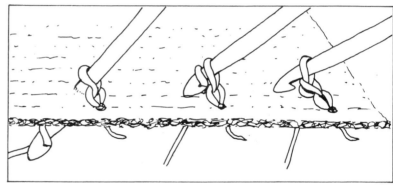

Technique B: keep the hook and supply yarn always on the right side of the background fabric. *Using various threads of the fabric as convenient insert hook in and out again, yrh and make one dc, rep from *. Although it is possible to work from right to left (as you would when making a normal fabric) inserting the hook at right angles to the line of the surface row, working in line ahead inserting the hook parallel to the line of the surface row helps you to see where you are going and to regulate the slant of the surface row thus: if you hold the supply thread to the right of the hook before inserting (normal technique), the surface row will slant to the left. If you hold the supply thread to the left, the surface row will slant to the right. To work a straight line without establishing a slant either way, keep the supply thread to the right and left on alternate stitches.

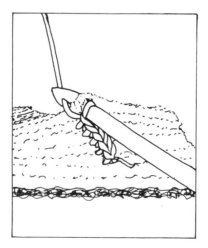
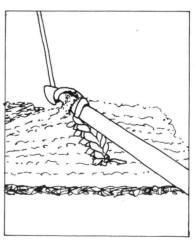

Depending on the nature of the background fabric (maybe an otherwise complete garment) you may find difficulty in handling the whole thing, particularly if you have to twist and turn a good deal—that is to say, in unravelling the yarn from the ball, catching the yarn (which you will not be able to see if it is at the back of the work) without snagging threads you do not want, and simply holding onto everything. You may prefer to keep turning the main fabric so that your next stitch remains dead ahead, or keep this still and change direction with the stitches. It is usually vital not to distort or restrict the eventual elasticity of the background fabric by working too tightly. Personal solutions fortunately develop quite quickly, but most people find it never pays to try and work more than a few stitches at a time before checking tension, and the pattern for accuracy if they are working to a predetermined plan.

The most flexible crochet background purely from the point of view of the surface working is one made entirely of double crochet, because this provides ready-made small steps of roughly equal length both horizontally and vertically. Nevertheless any background can be used—open or solid.

Insert the hook wherever is convenient in the background fabric to make the pattern you want.

If you are using the same thickness of thread for the surface work as for the background, use the same size hook.

Surface rows worked with the yarn at the back of the work can hop over each other, or go under, i.e. you remove the hook from the last loop, insert under the previous surface row back to front, pick up the loop just left and draw through. When the supply yarn is at the front, you can only hop over.

Deeper stitches than double crochet can be worked only with the yarn on the right side. When, say, treble stitches are worked very generously the result can be a deep pile effect (see page 191).

There is no reason why each surface stitch should be attached to the background, if the supply yarn is at the front. Try some chain loops, or picots.

For normal purposes you will try and make each surface stitch a similar length, but interesting effects are to be obtained by varying them.

Surface patterns can themselves be enlarged upon later by inserting the hook under the two top loops of the surface row, this time with both hook and supply yarn always on the right side and working ordinary crochet stitches right to left or left to right as required. For clothes this usually results in an extremely thick fabric and is probably only acceptable if used sparingly.

Surface patterns can be used in conjunction with raised/textured techniques on the background to make, for instance, characteristic Aran patterns.

Colour

More than one colour can be introduced into crochet work in two main ways: after the main fabric pieces have been completed in the form of edgings/ trimmings, etc. (see page 183), surface crochet (see page 139), or woven crochet (see page 208); or during the making of the main fabric.

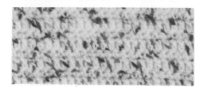

Single multicolour thread: The easiest way to introduce different colours into crochet work is to use a multicolour yarn, of which the main types are:

Heather Mixture: Fibres previously dyed different colours are mixed up together before spinning.

Flecked: Small pinches of fibre dyed a contrasting colour are spun in with the main fibres without the two becoming blended together.

Barber's Pole: Spun threads of different colours are plied together.

'Random' Dye: Complete yarn is wound into skeins, then different parts are dunked into different colours or dyed to a different depth of the same colour.

With any of these you can work in the usual way and the special characteristics of the yarn provide the colour interest. Usually the best results are obtained from solid stitch work, plain or with a low key pattern. The most interesting yarns from the point of view of the pattern effects inherent in their construction are the so-called 'random' dyed yarns. They are in fact far from random, because the colour sequence is always the same and repeats almost exactly after that length of yarn has been used up which corresponds to one circuit of the original skein.

Let us suppose we are making a simple rectangular fabric without shaping in the linear format with a one stitch/ one row repeat and that the end of our row coincides exactly with the end of a repeat sequence in the random yarn. We break off the yarn and start again at the beginning; and so on. Every row will be the same as far as the colour sequence is concerned and the colour will mount up into vertical bands. Even if we work to and fro, in which case the colours will appear to unfold in the opposite order, there will be vertical banding.

Now in practice our row will hardly ever work out exactly like this and, even if it did temporarily, we are likely to be increasing or decreasing sooner or later and throwing the sequence out of phase. Any slight differences will mean that the disposition of the colours will remain on the move, sometimes giving random looking splodges, sometimes amazing interference effects, sometimes formal blocks of colour. It is practically impossible to predict or regulate these effects in detail, since they depend on so many factors: the characteristic colour sequence and length of repeat in the yarn, your tension, the stitch pattern, the format, dimension and shaping of the fabric (and whether any of these change, gradually or suddenly). So within very narrow limits you must take pot luck.

Practical advice about plain stitch patterns: When you join in a new ball, any patterning which has become established by the old ball is likely to be disrupted. It may help to keep it going if you start using the new thread at exactly the same point in the colour repeat sequence as the old ball finished. There may be slight variations in the dye of the new ball, though.

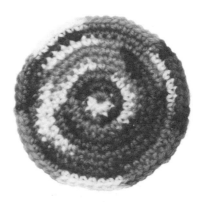

Sudden changes in the shaping of the fabric, e.g. at the armholes of a sweater worked from the lower edge upwards, will similarly disrupt the established patterning. It is sometimes possible to disguise this by breaking off and joining in again at an appropriate point in the yarn repeat sequence.

The circular format guarantees a certain rate of change in phase and therefore of colour formation. Ring construction is usually visually less satisfactory than spiral, because the disposition of colour exposes and draws attention to the join in the former.

If you do not like the colours blocking up into obvious bands or patches and want the fabric to maintain an overall mixed appearance, use a shallow stitch and work each row with a different ball, or rather, to be practical, use three balls so that you can change from one to the other in rotation without having to break off.

Multi-row repeat patterns, non-parallel row construction, etc. affect the overall character of the colour patterning, but hardly ever in a way that you can plan for in any detail.

Random yarn can work very well in conjunction with plain yarn (matching some part of it, or completely contrasting), if it is brought in for specific rows, i.e. stripes (see below) or specific stitches (see Jacquard below), or for sections of interrupted rows.

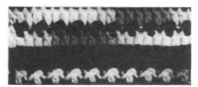 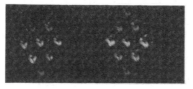

Random yarn may also add interest, according to your taste, to a whole openwork pattern, particularly if it has contrasting solid parts, or a variety of different configurations.

CSG 957

Only if you card, spin and dye your own yarn can you make a more genuinely random effect, or exercise any control over the colours and general specification. This is also the only way of making a controlled variation over a series of balls for a particular article.

Single monochrome thread: A much more controllable way of using colour is to change from one ball to another of a different colour at the end of a row (see page 37) and always to work complete rows with each colour. In its simplest form this naturally makes (horizontal) stripes, but depending on the basic construction of the fabric and the various techniques of stitch formation, quite complicated-looking patterns may emerge, not necessarily resembling stripes at all.

Horizontal Stripes

a. Simple Bands

b. Irregular Bands

a

b

c. Crumpled Bands

d. Simple Zig-zag

e. Eccentric Rings

f. Irregular Bands

Except in the case of overlapping grids, single colours used a whole row at a time cannot be made to appear to run counter to the direction of the rows, but they can be broken up in a number of ways, particularly in solid, raised patterns.

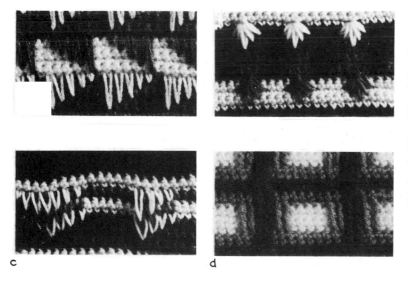

Broken Stripes

a. Graduated Spikes (Dc fabric): the spikes are worked during the first row with each new colour. Work as many rows with each colour as you need spikes.

b. Spike Clusters (Dc fabric): as **a**, but work spikes in clusters.

c. Multiple Spikes (Dc fabric): as **a**, but colour bands are shallow in comparison to depth of spikes, so these overlap.

d. Raised Stitches (Dc fabric): stitches raised at the front of the work mask the horizontal banding.

146

e. Raised Stitches Variation: raised stitches worked in interlocking clusters of three.

f. Raised Stitches Variation: the same pattern as Group 2, **k**, page **137**, but 2 rows only worked with each colour in rotation.

g. Raised Stitches Variation (Tr fabric): a cross between surface crochet and mixed grid construction. On a plain tr fabric worked in M, after every 2nd WS row, leave M, join in C and work *1ch, miss 1st, 1 R.dtr/F round next tr in last RS row. Rep from *. (This row overlaps the last WS row of the background fabric.) Fasten off C, resume M and work next RS row going under (so as to trap) the ch.sps in C, but behind the R.dtrs (so as to leave them free).

h. Raised Stitches Variation (Tr fabric): change colour every row. Row 1: all in tr. Row 2: *1 R.tr/F, 1 R.tr/B, rep from *; reverse distribution of F and B every row.

i. Irregular Rows (Whorls): work 2 rows with each colour.

j. Masked Chain Loops: change colour every row. Work first 2 rows right to left (RS), then turn and work next 2 rows right to left (WS), etc.

k. Overlapping Grid: see page **109**. 2 colours alternating give vertical bands.

l. Overlapping Grid Variation: 3 colours give multicoloured chequerboard effect.

m. Overlapping Grid Variation: the vertical bands make diamond shapes.

n. Interrupted Rows: interruptions in the row can naturally interrupt the distribution of colour.

o. Interrupted Rows Variation: diamond shapes.

p. Masked Chain Loops Variation: the V shapes are clusters, not groups.

Most openwork is at its best in one colour, or sometimes in random dyed yarn. The occasions when several colours are effective in the main fabric are mostly limited to circular work, where they are brought in on either a row-by-row or an interrupted basis. The Jacquard technique (see page 149) is more or less out of the question, because it depends for its success on the ability of the main fabric to conceal threads temporarily not in use.

CSG 957

Multiple threads: Quite distinctive effects, subtle or dramatic, can be achieved if you work with more than one strand simultaneously, perhaps using different thicknesses. Then you may have the option of changing all of them at once, or each one individually, perhaps to a different colour.

Horizontal stripes: When you are working to and fro, the difference between the front and back of the stitches, particularly in double crochet, is emphasized by colour changes. To make plain horizontal stripes with as clean an edge as possible always start each new colour on a right side row and, so as not to have to break off, work a minimum of two rows with each colour. Obtain stripes of different widths by changing the denomination of stitch used.

This difference between front and back can alternatively be used purposely for variety. For example work a 7 row repeat, each row with a different colour. When row 1 comes round again, use an eighth colour for this before going through the colours again in the same sequence as before. It is not until the ninth sequence that the total pattern repeats exactly; if your original plan included a ninth colour it would not be until the nineteenth sequence (the tenth sequence starts on the wrong side). With this sort of arrangement a complete skirt or dress length can be worked before the true repeat comes round even for the second time—and yet there is nothing difficult to remember whilst you are making it, once you have completed the first sequence.

Vertical stripes: To make vertical stripes see Overlapping Grids above, Jacquard work page 149, or simply make a fabric with horizontal bands and turn it sideways. Vertical stripes can also be applied by surface crochet (see page 139).

Breaking off: It is not always necessary to break off each colour at the end of a row in linear work, if you are going to need it again. If the edges of the work are going to be concealed eventually, for instance in a seam, you can carry threads temporarily not in use loosely up the side to the next joining-in point, twisting round the working thread as you pass. This saves some darning in of ends afterwards, but you may need to oversew the edges before making up to hold the threads in place.

Sometimes, however, the colour/row pattern forces you to break off, for instance, to and fro patterns with an even number of rows per repeat and an even number of colours, if only one row is to be worked with each colour. Other combinations are more convenient. As long as there are two or any even number of rows to be worked with each colour, there is no problem.

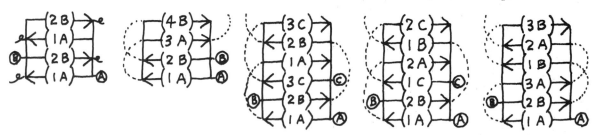

It is usually essential to break off after each round in circular work when you are working concentric rings and changing colour each round. Darn the short ends carefully into a part of the wrong side of the fabric in the same colour; otherwise there is a distinct danger that threads of the wrong colour will show through at inopportune places.

Jacquard crochet: The main difference between Jacquard work and any of the techniques discussed so far is that you introduce more than one thread or combination of threads during the course of a row, so that specific stitches can be picked out. This can be done to colour an existing pattern, but it is normally used to create patterns in their own right—even to 'paint' pictures.

Even complex patterns are easily drafted in the form of charts (see page 159). The best fabrics are those with small stitches, e.g. double crochet, for picture pattern making, but combinations of different stitches may be more appropriate for certain types of formal design. Fabrics must also generally be solid to prevent threads not in use showing through.

Changing yarn: The single loop always on the hook after you have completed every stitch becomes the top of the next stitch. In Jacquard work therefore you must always change to a new colour during the last step of the last stitch in the old colour as follows: *Insert hook, yrh (old col), pull through. Now lead old yarn to wrong side. Yrh (new col), pull through 2 loops.* Try it any other way and you will find threads of the wrong colour creeping into stitches where they are not wanted.

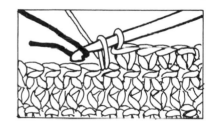

In the case of the longer stitches, work normally until only the last step remains, then change to the new colour to complete.

Do not cut temporarily discarded threads until they are no longer required at all; let them hang down the wrong side until they are picked up again, forming slack loops. For wall hangings, or articles of which the wrong side is never seen, nor subjected to general wear and tear, loops formed in this way may stay exposed. For most garments however they need to be built into the fabric. This involves either working over them or darning in later.

Working over in Jacquard: Never work over spare threads during wrong side rows unless you want them to show through on the right side. During right side rows, however, lay any loops formed during the previous wrong side rows over the top of the stitches in the row ahead (as though you were joining a new ball—see page 37) and work over them as you go. Also work

150

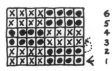

At the end of row 2 we drop ● and pick up
✖, forming a loop of ✖ on the WS, and turn.
At the beginning of row 3 we work 4sts in ✖
and at the same time work over that loop of
✖ and the spare thread of ●, which is
needed for stitch 5. After the change to ● we
do not work over the spare thread of ✖,
because it is already in line with its next pick-
up point on row 4.

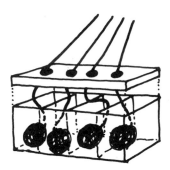

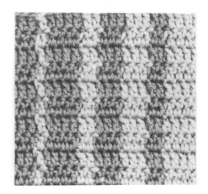

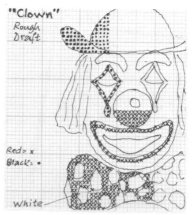

over any threads from the supply balls which will be needed further down the current row, so that these do not have to form loops when picked up again. If such threads will not be needed again until the next row, work over them anyway, if this will lead them to, or towards, their next pick-up point.

Although Jacquard work using many colours is possible, there is obviously a limit, depending upon the size of hook, thickness of yarn, etc. to the number of spare threads and loops which can be worked over at once without detriment to the fabric. Then repeated breaking off may become necessary. When different colours alternate across the row, but fairly wide sections are worked with each, it may be more convenient to use a different ball for each section (divide a single ball if necessary). In this case twist the threads round each other before changing, to prevent gaps developing in the fabric.

Darning in: When it is not practical to work over threads not in use, but unsatisfactory to leave loops, snip them in the middle and darn each end in separately. This amounts to the same thing as breaking off the yarns continually as you make the fabric, but it is much quicker.

There may be many things to cope with simultaneously in Jacquard work: making the colour changes correctly and at the right moment, keeping the spare threads on the wrong side, working over all the spare threads and loops at the right time, keeping all the supply balls from becoming entangled with each other or running about on the floor; you have to be organized and methodical in order to check everything and rearrange supply threads at the end of every row. If things do get out of hand, however, the world will not come to an end; chop off tangled supply threads and join in afresh, or snip loops which have got onto the right side and darn them into the wrong side. You may find a converted shoebox with holes in the lid and compartments inside helps, but most gimmicks become more trouble than they are worth in the long run.

Designing Jacquard picture patterns: Sketch what you want freely in pencil outline on an accurately drawn grid or graph paper (remembering that there will be some distortion since even double crochet stitches are not square—see page 116). Then rationalize the outlines to fit the nearest stitches on the grid. Study the result on a row by row basis for feasibility, and adjust. For your first efforts you will probably find it wise to restrict yourself to a maximum of three colours in any given row, however many you use altogether.

Jacquard patterns in a circular format can be interesting, but they are more difficult both to plan and to work. Abstract patterns are best designed to fit the format and pictures to exploit the special character that the format provides.

Patchwork

A patchwork is the result of joining small pieces into a whole or part of a larger fabric. The pieces may be any shape and all shapes, organized, or higgledy-piggledy. The most practical shapes for general two-dimensional purposes are those which will fit together exactly in a number of different ways and lie flat without leaving any space, e.g. squares, hexagons, equilateral triangles.

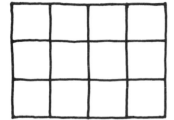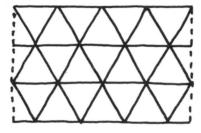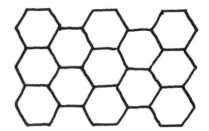

Certain rectangles and other triangles will also do this provided they are orientated in particular ways.

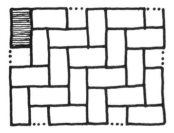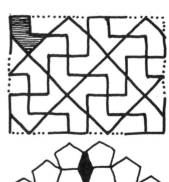

Certain combinations of two or more different shapes will also fit.

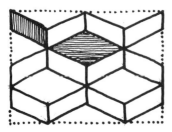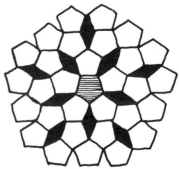

Half shapes may be needed to finish edges.

Other shapes leave some space between, which can be filled with smaller shapes, or further work, when the patchwork has been joined.

 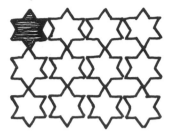 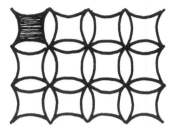

Complete patchwork fabrics have two advantages. In practical terms the piece of work in hand never becomes too large to handle or carry about. The feeling of achievement begins early on and is renewed every time a motif is completed. From the point of view of design, the format gives rise to a range of patterns and patterning not available through any other method.

They also have some disadvantages: all motifs, but particularly ones in the circular format, are far less susceptible to subtle shaping than one-piece fabrics. The final size of the patchwork is difficult to estimate in advance and the technique makes for a lot of work in joining in and darning in ends.

Of the non-motif types of shape linear-made strips are the most useful—they combine most of the practical and design advantages and greatly reduce the disadvantages of patchwork in general.

Patchwork designs: The fact that the fabric is made of pieces joined together gives it a certain interest in itself, even when all the pieces are identical in shape, size, pattern and colour. By varying one or more of these factors, the individual parts can be arranged to make an additional overall design.

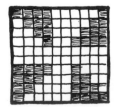 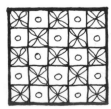   

Some identical motifs, or sets of motifs, can be used as pattern-making tiles.

Or, if the whole fabric is viewed as a single Jacquard chart, any sort of mosaic can be worked with as much or as little variety as you like.

Tile Patterns

Patchwork is also an obvious way to make three-dimensional fabrics. Even certain two-dimensional shapes, instead of lying flat when they are fitted together, naturally become three-dimensional.

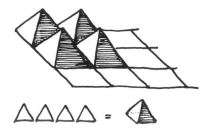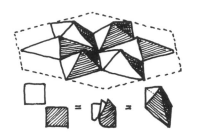

Crochet is an ideal medium for making individual motifs which are themselves three-dimensional anyway.

Often the means of joining the pieces in patchwork can be as important to the design as the pieces themselves. Straightforward edge to edge crochet can make a ridge. Circular made motifs can sometimes be joined progressively during their last round and any intermediate spaces 'filled in' afterwards. Regular shapes may be joined in an elaborate fashion and irregular ones by a specially shaped network. Shapes of any description can be appliquéd onto a background fabric.

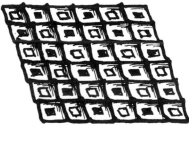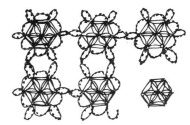

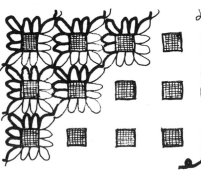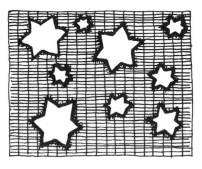

Motifs: From the point of view of construction motifs are just small pieces of ordinary crochet fabric, but because they are small, it is easier even for beginners to carry out ambitious stitch patterns. The examples here have been chosen to demonstrate the widest range of working principles and so at least hint at the infinite possibilities.

Motifs

Format: linear (circular edge).

Profile: solid, smooth, flat, 2 col.

Base chain: 17ch
Work 1st half in D, then 2nd half in L into other side of same base chain.
1st Edging Round (RS facing): change col to match main square.
2nd Edging Round (WS facing): all in D.

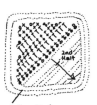

2 Rounds dc.

Format: circular (partly overlapping grid).

Profile: open, textured, (flat), 1 col/multi col.

To form ring: wind yarn 12 times round little finger.
Round 1: 12dc into ring, SS to first dc.
Round 2: 1dc in same place as last SS, *4ch, miss 11dc, 1dc into next dc, rep from * 5 times omitting dc at end of last rep, SS into first dc = 6 loops.
Round 3: into each 4ch loop work (1dc, 1h.tr, 3tr, 1h.tr, 1dc), SS into first dc.
Round 4: *5ch, inserting hook first from back between round 2 and 3 go into next dc of round 2 from front to back and work 1dc, rep from * 5 times, 5ch.
Round 5: into each 5ch loop work (1dc, 1h.tr, 5tr, 1h.tr, 1dc), SS into first dc.
Round 6: *7ch, inserting hook as for round 4 work 1dc in next dc of round 4, rep from * 5 times, 7ch.
Round 7: into each 7ch loop work (1dc, 1h.tr, 7tr, 1h.tr, 1dc), SS into first dc.

Round 8: 1dc in same place as last SS, *4ch, 1dc into 3rd ch from hook (single picot made), 5ch, 1dc into 3rd ch from hook (2nd single picot made), 2ch — picot loop made — 1dc into centre tr of same petal, picot loop, 1dc into first dc of next petal, rep from * omitting last dc at end of last rep, SS into first dc.
Round 9: SS to centre of next picot loop between picots, 1dc into same loop, *8ch, 1dc between picots of next loop, turn, 3ch, 9tr in 8ch loop, turn, 1tr in next dc, turn, 4ch, miss first 2sts, (1tr into next tr, 1ch, miss 1tr) 4 times, 1tr in top of 3ch, 4ch, 1dc into 3rd ch from hook, 2ch, 1dc into same loop as dc after 8ch, (picot loop, 1dc between picots of next loop) twice, rep from * 3 times omitting dc at end of last rep, SS to first dc.
Round 10: SS up side of tr and next 3ch, 1dc into space, *(picot loop, miss next ch.sp, 1dc into next ch.sp) twice, (picot loop, 1dc between picots of next loop) twice, picot loop, 1dc into first space of next block, rep from * 3 times omitting dc at end of last rep, SS to first dc.

Format: circular.

Profile: solid, textured, flat, 1 col.

🌑 Bobble, i.e. tr5tog.
6ch ring.

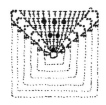

Format: circular.

Profile: open, smooth, flat, 1 col.

4ch ring.

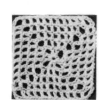

Format: linear (circular edge).

Profile: solid/open, textured, flat, 1 col.

Base chain: 23ch.
Work 2nd (crossed) stitch behind 1st.

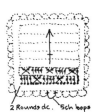

2 Rounds dc.   5ch loops

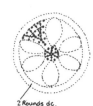

Format: circular.

Profile: solid/open, smooth, ruched, 1 col.

4ch ring.
Petals: round 2: 5tr into 1tr;
round 3: 2tr into each of 5tr;
round 4: 1tr into each of 10tr;
round 5: tr2tog 5 times over 10tr;
round 6: tr5tog over 5tr.

Format: circular (single spiral).

Profile: solid/open, smooth, flat, 1 col.

5ch ring.
Round 1: (6ch, 1dc into ring) 6 times.
Round 2: (4ch, 1dc into next ch loop) 6 times.
Round 3: (4ch, 2dc into next ch loop, 1dc into next dc) 6 times.
Round 4: (4ch, 2dc into next ch loop, 1dc into each of next 2dc) 6 times.
Round 5: (4ch, 2dc into next ch loop, 1dc into each of next dcs except last dc) 6 times.
Cont as for round 5 as required, adding 1ch to each ch loop at 10th and every 10th round.
NB Number of dc per segment is same as number of round.

Format: linear (circular edge).

Profile: solid, textured, flat, 1 col.

Base chain: 17ch.
First Segment: row 1: 1dc into 8th ch from hook, over next 9ch work *1dc, 1h.tr, 1tr, 2trs, 1tr, 2d.tr, 1d.tr, 2T.tr, 1T.tr, do not turn.
Row 2: work Corded Rib, i.e. going into front loop only work 1dc into each st from left to right, do not turn.
Second Segment: 1dc into ch ring, going into back loop only of next 9sts of previous segment rep from *. Complete 10 segments in this way. SS join between first and last segments, SS to tip of last segment.
Edging: round 1: (1dc into tip of segment, 7ch) 10 times, SS to first dc, turn. Round 2: (2dc into dc, 7dc into 7ch loop) 10 times, SS to first dc, fasten off.

Format: circular (interrupted).

Profile: solid, smooth, flat, multi col.

3ch ring.
Round 1: 6dc.
Build up overlapping sections of row with sts of graduated height; inc as necessary to keep work flat.

Format: circular (linear curlicues).

Profile: solid/open, smooth, flat, multi col.

6ch ring.
Round 1: 12dc.
Curlicues: * 12ch, starting into 3rd ch from hook work 5tr into each ch, SS to last dc, SS into each of next 2dc, rep from * 5 times

Format: linear centre, circular edge.

Profile: open, smooth, flat, 1 or 2 col.

Base chain: 14ch (central filet square), work first tr into 6th ch from hook.

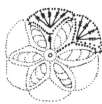

Format: circular.

Profile: open, smooth, flat, 1 or 2 col.

4ch ring.

Format: circular (linear points).

Profile: solid, smooth, flat, 1 col.

4ch ring.
Round 1: 15tr.
Round 2: 30tr.
Complete each point separately ending with single round of edging.

Format: circular.

Profile: solid, textured, flat, 1 col or multi col.

U: Dc loop st.
Unit 16.
4ch ring.
Odd rounds: Tr (inc).
Even rounds: Dc loop st (1:1).

Format: circular.
(Jacquard Star)

Profile: solid, smooth, flat, 2 col.

4ch ring.
Round 1: 15tr. (D).
Round 2: 30tr. (D).

Format: linear.

Profile: solid, smooth, flat, 1 col.

Base chain: 25ch (first dc into 3rd). 4th, 5th and 6th points worked onto main triangle.

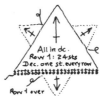

Format: circular.

Profile: open, smooth, flat, 1 or 2 col.

8ch ring.
Round 1: 16 21ch loops.

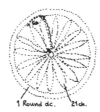

Format: linear centre, circular edge.

Profile: solid, smooth, flat, multi col.

Base chain: 4ch (central square), work first tr into 4th ch from hook.

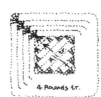

158

Format: circular.

Profile: open, smooth, flat, 1 or multi col.

4ch ring.

Format: circular.

Profile: solid, textured, flat, 1 or multi col.

4ch ring.
Work all raised sts at the front together with the ordinary st in Siamese twin pairs.

Format: circular

Profile: solid, smooth/textured, flat, multi col.

3ch ring.
First 4 rounds – Dc circle: unit 6. Work 6th round spikes between threads of 5th round spikes. ⊕

Format: linear.

Profile: open, smooth, flat, 1 or multi col.

Base chain: 4ch.

Format: circular.

Profile: solid, smooth, 3D, 1 or multi col.

Cone in tr (unit 12).
60ch ring
First 2 rounds: work as for inwards circle, i.e. dec 12 times each round = 36sts.
Next 4 rounds: dec 6sts each round = 12sts.
Next round: work 5tr into each st.
Last round (ws facing): corded edge.

Format: linear (circular).

Profile: solid, smooth/textured, flat, 1 or multi col.

Base chain: as required.
Use for appliqué or as the basis of free working.

Format: as required.

Profile: as required.

Build up spontaneously, mixing all techniques, and maybe make a geometric shape to fit with others into a formal structure.

Charts

In filet, Jacquard and sometimes surface crochet charts are very often used to show working details of patterning which would be exceedingly difficult to follow in text form.

Filet charts: Most often these appear on squared graph paper. The vertical lines represent the treble stitches of the basic open grid. The number of chain spaces, usually one or two, to be worked between grid trebles is specified. The horizontal lines represent the tops of the rows. Whenever a block is to be worked, i.e. the chain(s) between grid trebles is(are) to be turned into treble(s), a square is filled in or cross-hatched. Lacets are drawn in realistically.

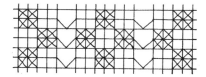

A more explicit form of chart for filet work employs symbols for the various stitches, chains, etc.

Jacquard charts: The most common Jacquard charts are also based on squared graph paper, but here it is the space inside each square which represents each stitch (specified, but usually double crochet). Individual squares are coloured, numbered or given different symbols to indicate different colours. Groups of squares in the same colour may simply be outlined.

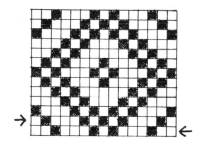

General: With all charts it is always understood that:
1   They represent the final pattern looked at from the right side; the bottom row is worked first and the top row last.
2   Unless otherwise specified the first row is 'read' and worked from right to left and constitutes the right side. In linear work, or whenever the system involves turning between rows the second (and every even numbered) row is 'read' from left to right.

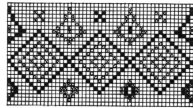

The chart itself may not represent the whole width or depth of the fabric, but frequently only an inset portion. This can be exasperating to follow, so when you are preparing your own charts take them right up to all the edges of the piece of fabric—you then have all the information you need for working on one piece of paper.

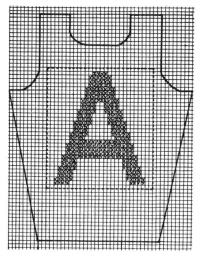

Free Working

The great joy and purpose of free working is to clear the mind of all but the vaguest of formal plans and let the senses take over. It is the intuitive side of your faculties which is most important and so anyone can jump in right from the beginning.

Although true free working is gridless, the gentlest way into it is to extend and exploit the conventional approach. Build up and fill in, in any and every direction; first the significance of the grid will diminish and finally disappear, the notions of 'axis' and 'general direction of working' will disintegrate and the distinction between 'one-piece' and 'patchwork' become blurred.

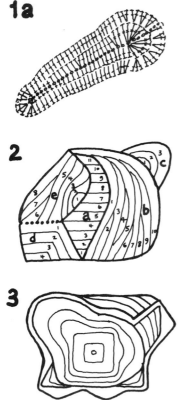

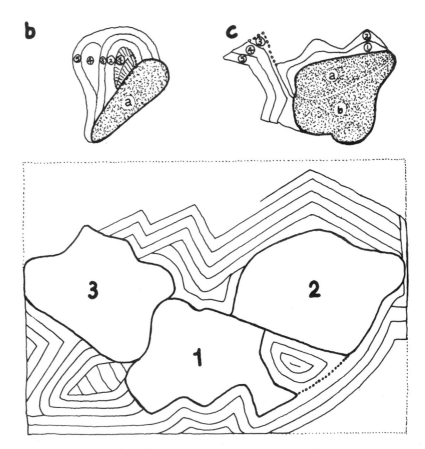

The technical approach is quite straightforward: if you want to and can work details out in advance—well and good. If you cannot (or as a change), try something spontaneously. If this works, leave it. If it does not, see why and then undo it and try again. With openwork the departure from conventional structure can be even more emphatic, including woven elements.

Despite the word 'free' your final fabric usually has to work out to a predetermined shape, for instance for clothes. You can check periodically with a cut-out paper or fabric pattern piece (or a thumbnail sketch with dimensions marked), and still do the actual work meanwhile, sitting in your usual chair, or wherever. In the context of crochet sculpture, however, the shape or interplay of shapes may be very complicated, or parts of the fabric/structure may be intended to be under a particular degree of stress or tension. Then it may be necessary to work partly or entirely on a model. 'Model' here means a dummy figure, frame or template, even a couple of hooks/nails banged in somewhere harmless, the actual armature or fixing points— anything to which the relevant parts of the work can be temporarily, or permanently attached.

Often it is necessary to become quite athletic and devise new ways of holding and manipulating the hook and yarn to manage this way of working, since it may be impossible to twist and turn the fabric at will in the usual way.

Now it is easy to become so involved that your work becomes a way of life, but even if it remains a spare-time activity or a means of relaxation, it has to be to some extent creative, engaging your mind and spirit (not to mention most of your body on occasion) to the greater satisfaction of not only yourself, but those around you.

Finger Crochet

'Finger' crochet means crochet-without-a-hook and includes working with one or more fingers, the hand or arm, or indeed the whole body. When working with stiff, very fat ropes or cables, you have to scramble in, out, over and under the threads dragging a loop with you, as though your structure were a living adventure playground. This is when crochet becomes as much a sport as it is a craft!

Finger crochet can only begin when the scale of the work is large by conventional standards. The sorts of material you are likely to be using can be rough and unsympathetic, so be careful not to damage your nails or wear out your fingers. It may be worth fashioning a hook out of a broom handle or metal rod, if you have the skill, and avoiding using your actual fingers except for loose openwork with soft yarns. When the scale permits, use a glove and maybe an improvised grappling hook; be careful not to graze or 'burn' your arm. On the largest scale, keep a wary eye always on three-dimensional structures—they may decide to collapse or roll over when you are caught up in the threads.

To most people finger crochet will be no more than a fun thing, though large-scale, three-dimensional structures can be rigid enough to serve as the base for more elaborate sculpture made on a conventional scale with a hook, whilst also providing an exciting visual counterpoint.

"Finger Crochet" Cord

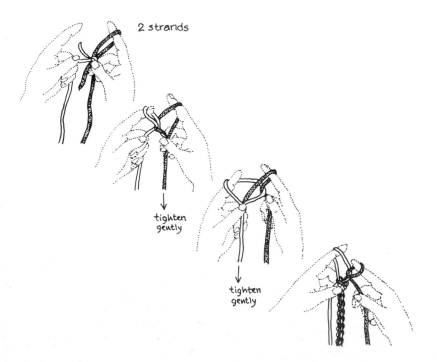

2 strands

tighten gently

tighten gently

Chapter 4
Shaping

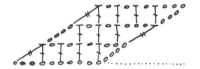

Edge Shaping (Linear)

Chapter 1, page 39 describes general purpose increasing and decreasing in steps and how to avoid these steps when adding or subtracting up to 2 stitches per row in the case of fabrics made of basic stitches and with one stitch/one row repeat sequences.

For the reasons discussed on page 117 (Squareness), if the edge of a fabric follows a line at 45° or more away from the line of the rows for any distance, it may improve the tension if the outside stitch is longer than the rest.

It is useful to be able to add/subtract a third stitch, which can be done from double treble upwards (and sometimes with treble as well), by making one of the branches into a 'Y' group or upside-down 'Y' cluster (see page 127). The examples show double treble in action. Note that when a turning chain is involved, the basic figure receives a commonsense interpretation; in the decrease cluster the turning chain itself loses its independent status as a single edge stitch.

Increase/Decrease
3 Stitches

To increase: 4ch, 1tr in 3rd ch from hook, miss 1ch, 2 d.trs in first proper st, . . .3 d.trs in last st, i.e. top of t.ch, 1tr inserting hook into side of last d.tr, turn.

Notice also how to mitre a corner.

To decrease: 2ch, miss 1st st, 1tr in 2nd st, 1ch, d.tr2tog over 3rd and 4th sts − counts as one decrease cluster,...over last 4sts work together 3 d.trs and 1tr as folls: *(yrh) twice, insert hook, yrh, pull loop through** (yrh, pull through 2 loops) twice, rep from * once in next st and from * to ** in next st = 6 loops on hook, yrh, pull through 2 loops, yrh, insert hook in last st, i.e. t.ch, yrh, pull loop through, yrh, pull through 2 loops = 6 loops on hook, yrh, pull through 3 loops = 4 loops on hook, yrh, pull through all loops.

The 2nd cluster of an inside corner is worked as folls: (yrh) twice, insert hook, yrh, pull loop through, yrh, pull through 2 loops = 3 loops on hook, yrh, insert hook, yrh, pull loop through, yrh, pull through 2 loops = 4 loops on hook, yrh, pull through 2 loops = 2 loops on hook, leaving last loop of each on hook work 1 d.tr in each of next 2sts = 4 loops on hook, yrh, pull through all loops.

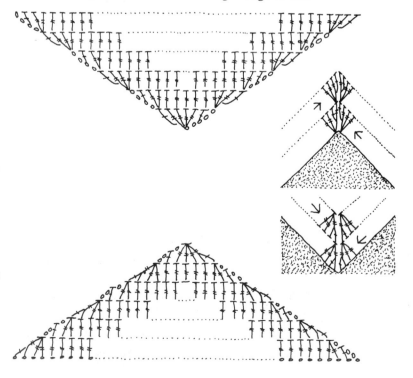

Many more than 3 stitches may be added/subtracted with relative smoothness when the basic stitch is at least double treble, by deploying the shorter stitches in a suitable sequence. When increasing, be prepared to make an extra length of base chains as for step increasing, or work into the side of previous stitches, and, when decreasing, to work in slip stitch back over the shorter stitches to the first genuine pattern stitch, before starting the next row.

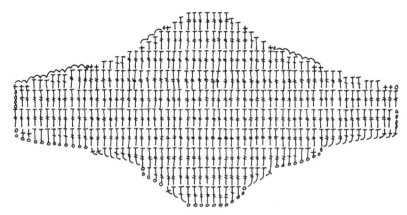

Increase/Decrease Several Stitches

Even solid patterns are not always immediately susceptible to simple edge shaping and discretion must be used to contrive the most satisfactory result in each set of circumstances. With multi-row repeat sequences, whereas the mechanics may still be straightforward, the problem is to increase/decrease the right number of stitches each row to give a straight edge, or even a curve, or, in the last resort, one which wobbles consistently.

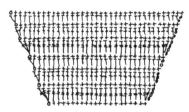

Whenever the pattern includes any fancy, or textured stitches, i.e. puffs, bobbles, doubled-up/overlapped groups and clusters, etc., or built-in ruching—it will not usually be practical to work 'in pattern' over the increase/decrease sequences. Instead work in the corresponding basic stitch and revert to the pattern stitch as soon as possible. You will be avoiding a stepped edge to the fabric, but not to the pattern surface or grain in the fabric.

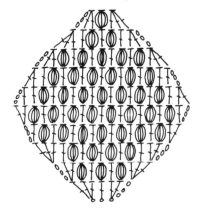
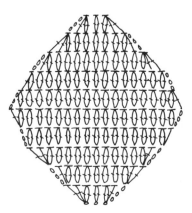
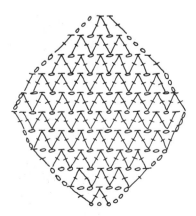

Some innocent-looking 2 stitch repeat patterns can be the graveyard of many people's aspirations! It is vital to be sure whether the basic stitch pattern has a one or two row repeat; otherwise it is very easy, particularly when increasing, to slip inadvertently from one to the other with disastrous effects on the grain. Think and plan very carefully before you begin. Stepwise increasing and decreasing is easiest to carry out and usually quite satisfactory. Make frequent visual checks with the work held away at arm's length, as you work the shaped parts.

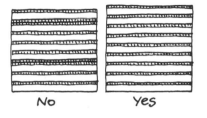

No   Yes

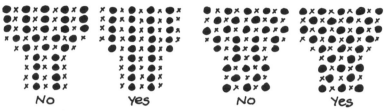

No   yes   No   Yes

The solid stitch configurations which give difficulty are those containing: slip stitches; single stitches, groups, or clusters not parallel to the edges; overlapping grids; or non-paralleled/interrupted row construction.

Some kind of crude, stepwise shaping in whole repeat units is always possible. Ways of achieving more refined shaping, at least at certain angles, may sometimes be discovered through analysis and sketching. Increasing/decreasing by only one or two stitches at a time, or strictly symmetrical shaping may be out of the question. The solutions will be individual in each case, but a study of the examples may prime your thinking.

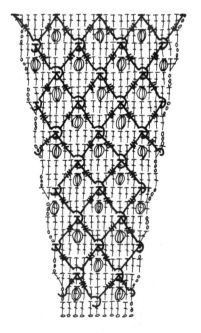

With any form of high key patterning the main problem may not be the physical business of shaping the actual edges so much as maintaining the patterning and running it as near as possible to the new edges. For example in the case of raised stitches in a diamond formation or spikes, when increasing is in progress there may be nowhere to plant the base of some stitch. If this is really unavoidable, you must become resigned to it. But, like the countryman who, when asked the way to some distant town, remarked that if he were going there, he would reckon to start from somewhere else, we could say of stitch patterns that if such and such a degree of shaping were required, it might be better to select a different pattern in the first place, or, if a particular stitch pattern is the prerequisite, it might be a mistake to try and impose a particular degree of shaping on it. The most natural forms of shaping for any stitch pattern are those where one or more complete stitch repeat sequences are added/subtracted over the depth of one row repeat. (Occasionally adding/subtracting a half stitch repeat sequence works as well.) Only careful study of the configuration in sketch form or of a sample of the straight fabric will reveal the characteristics and potential.

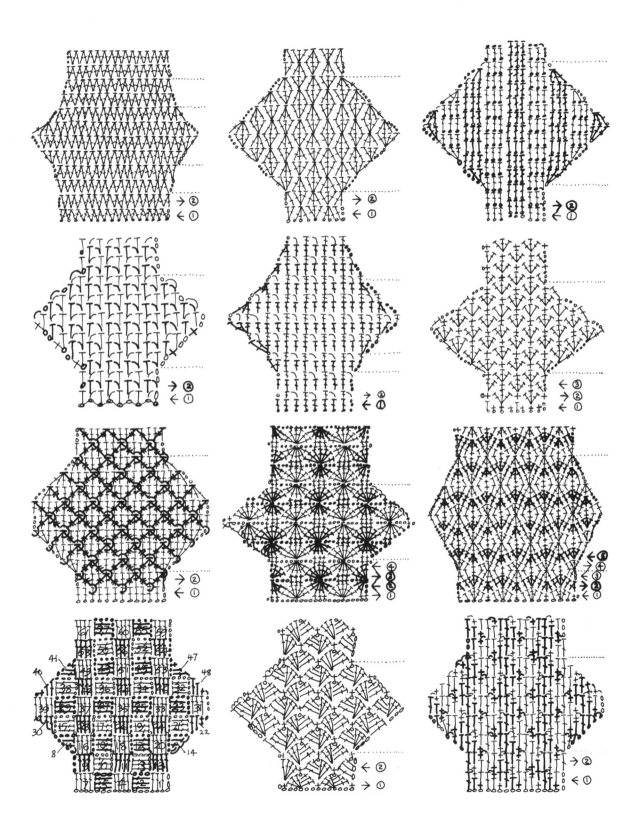

168

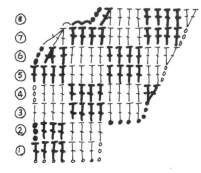

When different coloured yarns are involved, you must remember, in the course of any shaping, to introduce the new colour during the last stage of the previous stitch (see page 36). In this example L is changed to D, for instance, at the end of row 2, so that the new edge stitch (turning chain) in row 3 will be in the correct colour, but D changes back to L on the 7th chain, ready for the 2nd to 4th stitches. At the beginning of row 8 the slip stitch into the 2nd stitch is used to pick up D and the change back to L is effected halfway through the first branch of the decrease cluster. All this is extremely pedantic and you would probably find a less fiddly way of arranging matters in an actual project, but it makes the point that you must think ahead.

Such planning is always necessary in the case of patterns based on oblique, zig-zag or wavy grids (see page 93), where to work straight probably involves increasing/decreasing at the edges and shaping maybe not at all. In fact it ceases to be useful to think of the amount of increasing/decreasing as so many stitches per row, and a specimen of the actual fabric is required before shapes can be planned with any certainty.

Any shaping on these grids which does not follow the lines of the rows, or the direction of the stitches, is complicated.

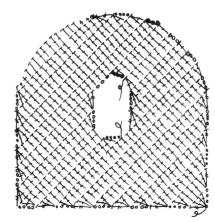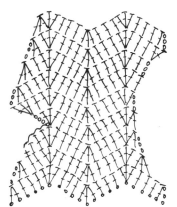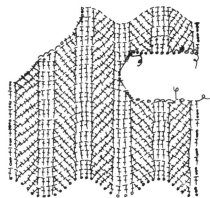

Openwork patterns bring in new considerations in the form of chain spaces and loops. This is made clear even by the examples of simple filet crochet in its various versions. Notice that when, according to the pattern, the edge stitch should be a space you must, for the sake of the construction, break pattern and invent a stitch. The length of this, be it a basic stitch at the end, or the turning chain at the beginning of a row, is determined by common sense and experience, or finally by trial and error in obscure cases.

Watch out for chain loops—in meshes, or with groups—and groups/clusters which are planted neither in the centre nor exactly between previous groups, and large-scale patterning.

Filet Patterns

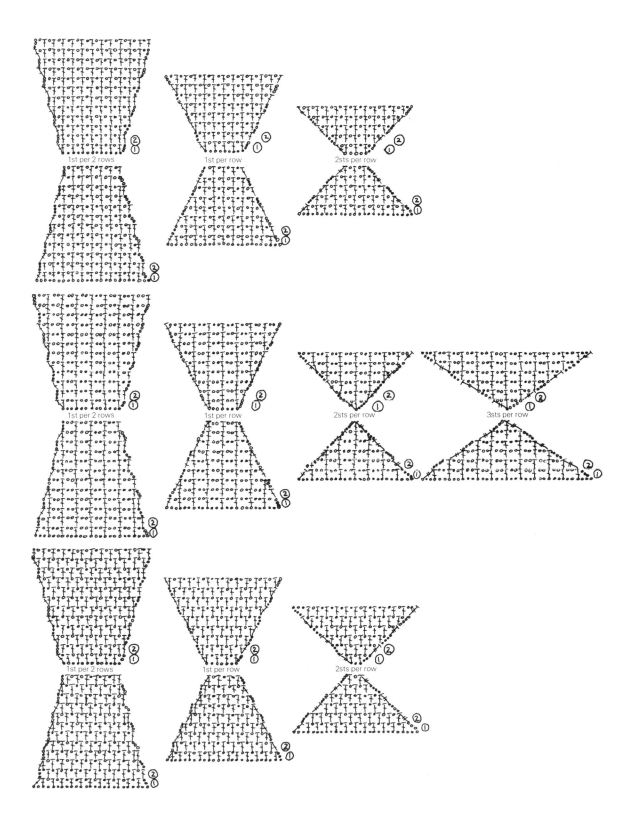

1st per 2 rows   1st per row   2sts per row

1st per 2 rows   1st per row   2sts per row   3sts per row

1st per 2 rows   1st per row   2sts per row

Tricky Open Patterns

Darts

Although covering the body with fabric is a three-dimensional exercise and crochet is an ideal sculptural medium, the traditional approach in clothes making is the same as for ready-made, woven fabric: in the mind we break a garment down into a set of two-dimensional areas of fabric then slice off some of the edges and nick out certain segments (darts), so that, when assembled with a multitude of seams, the whole vaguely conforms to the major shapes of the figure. For obvious technical reasons and because they look good, people also make a lot of crochet clothes with no darts or shaping, but few go in the other direction and make their work much more comprehensively sculptural.

Vertical darts: In crochet we construct darts as the fabric is made, rather than cut them out afterwards, either by dividing the fabric, shaping the space and sewing up afterwards, or by increasing/decreasing (depending upon the direction of working) over the required point. The mechanics of adding/subtracting stitches in the middle of a row are much the same as for edge shaping; and the problems are similar, too—plain, one stitch/one row repeat patterns are most flexible, whereas grain or high key ones tend to impose their own conditions. Darts may be straight—symmetrical, or asymmetrical—or curved, depending upon the arrangement.

Vertical Dart Plans

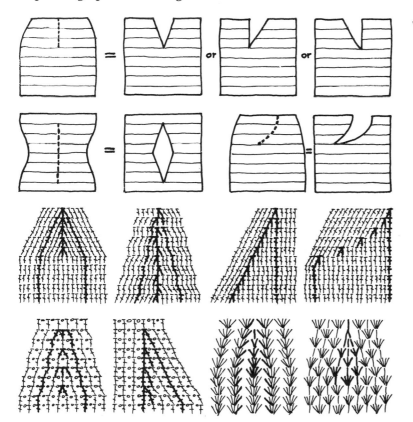

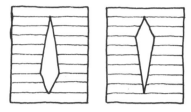

To plan darts you need to know by how much you want the width of the fabric to change overall and the depth over which the change is to take place. Some of the difference may be accounted for in the edge shaping, but the rest is then equally distributed amongst the darts. Closed darts may be required to open more gradually than they close, and vice versa. The exact position and finesse with which the darts are executed may not be critical, in which case it will be sufficient to measure and insert marker threads to indicate their starting points. When they must coincide exactly with a particular phase of a pattern, it may be necessary to draw a chart. (In printed instructions the position of darts is usually pinpointed by counting stitches.) If the practical problems of working darts in continuous rows become too great, divide the fabric as for buttonholes (see page 203), work the fabric between the darts separately and sew up afterwards.

Horizontal darts: Shape the edges continuously, i.e. by working the increasing rows over the decreased ones, or separately to leave a slot which is sewn up afterwards.

Horizontal Dart Plans

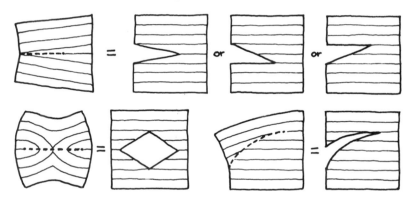

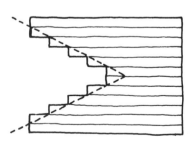

If a stepped effect is unavoidable, do not try to work continuously. Remember when planning that it is not the tips of the steps but the notches which determine the final seam line and hence the dimensions of the dart.

It is hardly ever worth trying to work closed darts continuously; divide and sew up.

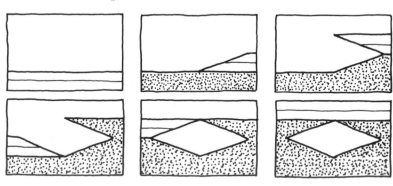

Holes

Single or subdivided holes of any shape compatible with the pattern and your patience may be made in a fabric in the same way as buttonholes (see page 203) or closed darts (which are not sewn up). Some experiment may be needed to judge the final shape which a hole will assume under normal tension.

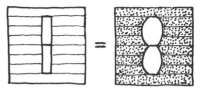

Further crochet work can be added to the edges of a hole, directly or by sewing, as a means of general embellishment or to turn a hole into a solid projection.

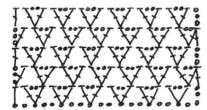

Magnification and Reduction

Sometimes a pattern, usually low key, can be made larger or smaller, so that the fabric dimensions are modified accordingly. The vertical dimension is controlled by selection of basic stitch length and the horizontal by the number of stitches.

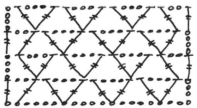

Changing Hook

Alternatively the same stitch pattern may be continued whilst the hook is changed to progressively larger or smaller ones. This affects the tension and therefore the quality and behaviour of the fabric.

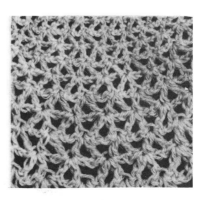

Both the above methods make the working of subsequent edging more difficult to achieve with consistent tension. They will suit only particular patterns and applications and should never be thought of as easy, direct alternatives to the other methods. Fabrics made by magnification/reduction will tend to be more stable, i.e. drop less, but the transitions will be fairly obvious to the eye; those made by changing hooks will change dimensions and character more smoothly and discreetly.

Rescaling

Use of thinner/thicker yarn in conjunction with a thinner/thicker hook can result not only in modified tension (gauge), but in complete rescaling.

Rescaling of the main features of some patterns (openwork) can be achieved by recasting them on a different grid.

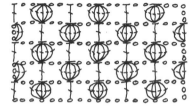 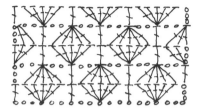 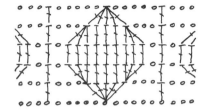

Planning Two-dimensional Shapes

Before you start to turn a shape into an actual piece of fabric, decide which is the best axis and general direction of working. Think carefully how things might work out: will it be more controllable, or mean less unravelling, if things go wrong, to go up, down, or across? Will it be useful to be able to adjust length or width afterwards? (If so, go towards the edge you may wish to alter.) If you are making clothes and do not know what the shapes or dimensions should be, copy an old garment or paper pattern, which you reckon is suitable.

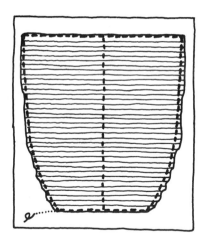

Intuitive approach (look, no maths!): Make a full-size, accurate drawing or cut-out of the shape to use as a pattern. Make a length of base chain which you feel to be comfortably more than adequate for the base row (or make your initial slip knot with a long, spare end, so you can work a few more chains onto the beginning later, if necessary). Start work. Checking frequently with your pattern, shape as best you can, so as to follow the outline. Make sure your increasing/decreasing actually balances on each side, when the piece is shaped symmetrically. If you are making matching pieces to be sewn together later and your shaping tends to be wobbly, make your fabric larger than the pattern piece, so that there is sufficient tolerance to sew a neat seam without reducing the overall dimensions of the article.

Mathematical approach: Make a large test piece of the stitch pattern with the actual yarn and hook you propose to use. If this seems right, measure the horizontal and vertical tension over at least 10cm (4in). Make a full-size or thumbnail outline drawing of the piece and put in all the horizontal and vertical measurements where shaping changes. From the tension of your test piece convert all these measurements into numbers of stitches/rows. Put these in on the drawing. Calculate how many stitches are to be increased/decreased between the various points and how to arrange for this to happen evenly. If necessary, draw detailed stitch diagrams onto the drawing of the shaping so that you need to do no more working out when you come to sit down to the crochet. Check frequently to see that things are working out as they should.

For difficult shapes it may be advisable in the long run either to work a large test piece or to draw up an accurate grid on paper so that you can mark out the edge (with needle and marker thread on the test piece) row by row.

Here we work through a simple example in this way:

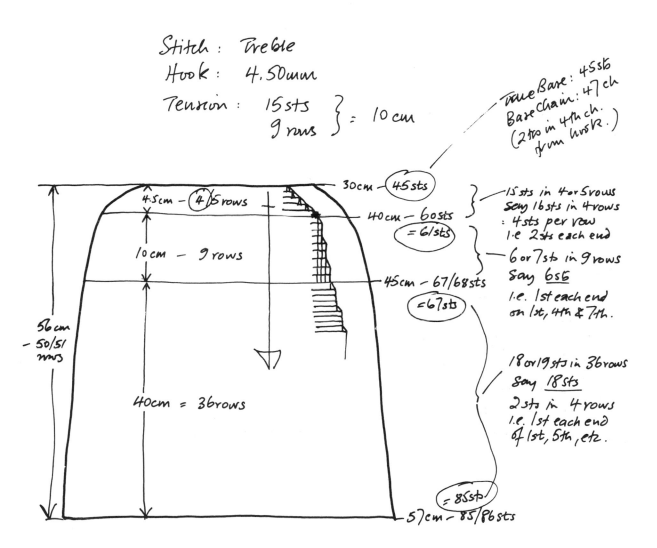

Stitch : Treble
Hook : 4.50mm
Tension : 15 sts
9 rows } = 10 cm

True Base: 45 sts
Base Chain: 47 ch
(2 tro in 4th ch. from hook.)

30cm — (45 sts)

40cm — 60 sts
= 61 sts

45cm — 67/68 sts
= 67 sts

4.5cm — (4)/5 rows

10 cm — 9 rows

56 cm — 50/51 rows

40cm = 36 rows

= 85 sts
57 cm — 85/86 sts

15 sts in 4 or 5 rows
Say 16 sts in 4 rows
: 4 sts per row
i.e. 2 sts each end

6 or 7 sts in 9 rows
Say 6 sts
i.e. 1st each end
on 1st, 4th & 7th.

18 or 19 sts in 36 rows
Say 18 sts
2 sts in 4 rows
i.e. 1st each end
of 1st, 5th, etc.

The circular format: spiral or rings? In general any piece of circular/tubular work can be constructed either in spiral or in concentric rings. If one of your main ambitions is to avoid too much planning, arithmetic, or technical niggles, or your approach is to encourage the work of the fingers to lead the mind, you will probably have more success and satisfaction working in spiral. There will be no join mark, but probably some awkwardness, when the spiral has to end. You will not be able to have closed bands of colour, or reverse the direction of the rows in the normal course of events. If on the other hand you are reasonably happy with the mathematical side of things and like to work to some sort of formal plan, you will probably find it more convenient and flexible to plan primarily in rings, and use spiral construction when its particular characteristics are needed in the design.

When you are confident about the construction and shaping of linear and circular work, the making of any shape is possible. The main thing is to see how far it will be possible to make a shape in one continuous piece, stopping and starting again in different places if necessary, and whether it will be more convenient to plan on a circular or linear grid.

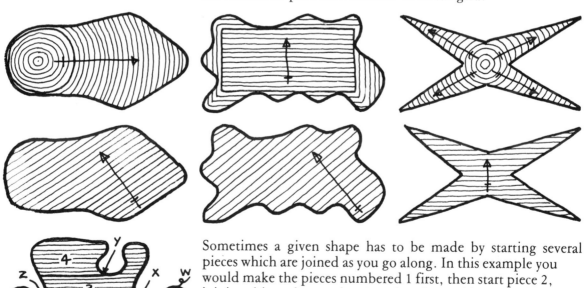

Sometimes a given shape has to be made by starting several pieces which are joined as you go along. In this example you would make the pieces numbered 1 first, then start piece 2, joining this to the number 1 sections by working over them at the appropriate moment and finishing temporarily at W. You would then rejoin at X, Y and Z successively in order to add sections 3, 4 and 5 respectively. In the same way a conventional item of clothing, worked from the shoulders downwards, would require the same sort of approach.

If the fabric is to have a pattern, or the direction of the grain is significant to the design, you might choose what at first glance would be a far from obvious plan.

After a collection of shapes has been made separately and assembled, there may be spaces left to fill in. Common sense will tell you how best to approach this: very small spaces can be filled with a needle and larger ones with more separate shapes worked specially, or with direct crochet in basically circular or linear format. Double crochet stitches provide the greatest flexibility, if there are no other design considerations, but stitches of graduated length may conveniently straighten a wobbly line.

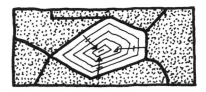
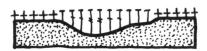

Simple Clothing Shapes

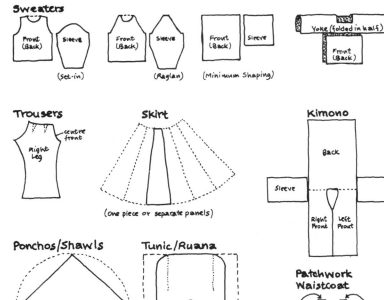

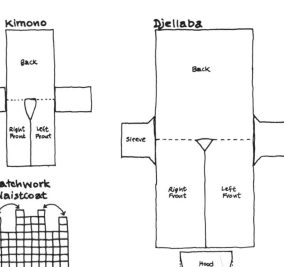

Three-dimensional Shaping

Cones: To make a cone from the point outwards, work as though to make a flat, outwards circle (see page 95), i.e. always increase regularly, but start with too few stitches. A narrow cone requires less frequent increasing than the strict circle formula, but the rate must remain constant. In order to sketch/plan fine detail of a cone, draw it as a circle with a segment missing.

Cylinders (tubes): A straight tube is made without increasing or decreasing, just like a linear rectangle with edges joined together (as you go, or afterwards). You may turn, or not, between rows as required.

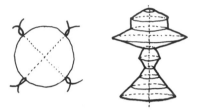

Increasing/decreasing alone will make the tube expand/contract. To do this evenly there must be a minimum of 4 increase/decrease points evenly spaced around the circumference. Increasing/decreasing at all points then takes place during the same row. Straight rows can be worked between increase/decrease rows as necessary.

Tubes can be worked in spiral, but this spiral effect in the tube wall is induced by increasing over one half of each row and decreasing the same amount over the other and phasing this procedure so that the increase and decrease segments rotate by a small, regular amount each row.

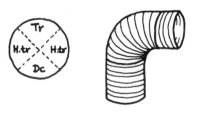

In order to make a cylinder bend or change direction (other than by main force), divide the circumference into equal segments and allocate to the stitches in each, progressively longer, then shorter, stitches over the outward and inward halves of the circle respectively. Work straight in this manner until the desired bend is achieved.

Sharp angles are best made in separate, matching sections, which are sewn together. Keep to the same basic stitch and shape as required.

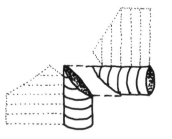

To calculate the shaping for a 90° angle, measure how many rows make the same depth as the diameter of the tube. Divide the number of stitches in the complete cylinder wall by this number of rows and subtract half the result from each edge of the dwindling wall as you work each row.

If you are working flat, use this drawing as a template, scaled up as necessary.

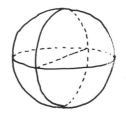

Spheres: To make a hemisphere (cup shape) from the pole towards the equator, start as though to make a flat outwards circle, with the appropriate number of stitches (see page 99), but first gradually, then more frequently, dispense with the increases. For practical reasons it helps to have a coherent plan which is simple to memorize. One way is to adapt the circle formula, i.e. when you increase, do so always by the same number of stitches in the round, but put in first one, then more than one straight round between the increase rounds. Another is to increase every round, but after a few rounds to stop, redivide the circumference into fewer segments (inserting marker threads to remind you) and so make fewer increases in the round. Repeat this after fewer and fewer rounds until at the equator there are no segments and no increases.

Whatever your plan during the outward half, make notes so you can reverse it exactly for the inward half of the complete sphere.

Unit: 12

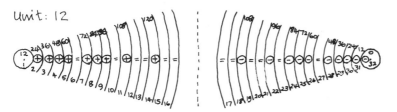

Think of a hemispherical distortion in a linear fabric as a large-scale bubble, caused by ruching and crumpling.

Or build a circular hole into the fabric, make a separate hemisphere in the circular format and stitch together afterwards.

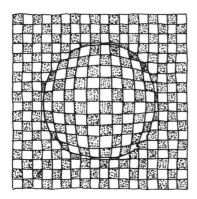

Stitch: Treble
Tension: 16 st = 10cm
10 rows = 11.9cm

Diameter of Sphere:
say 20 rows (23.8 cm)
Circumference:
$23.8 \times \pi$ (i.e. 3.1416)
= 74.8 cm
i.e $74.8 \times \frac{16}{10}$ sts
= 119.6, say 120 sts
AND
$74.8 \times \frac{10}{11.9}$ rows
= 62.86
i.e 15.71, say 16 rounds
in each hemisphere

Planning Three-dimensional Shapes

To make any preconceived shape the main thing is to perceive the underlying geometric structures and, as with two-dimensional planning, to determine the most convenient format, starting points and order of working. Sharp angles between planes are usually best made separately and sewn together.

When you have mastered the basic geometrical shapes, discover the more complex modified ones which result from tampering with the status quo in the usual ways—ruching, crumpling, irregular or biased increasing and decreasing—and from applying surface texture and embellishment.

Modified 3D Shapes

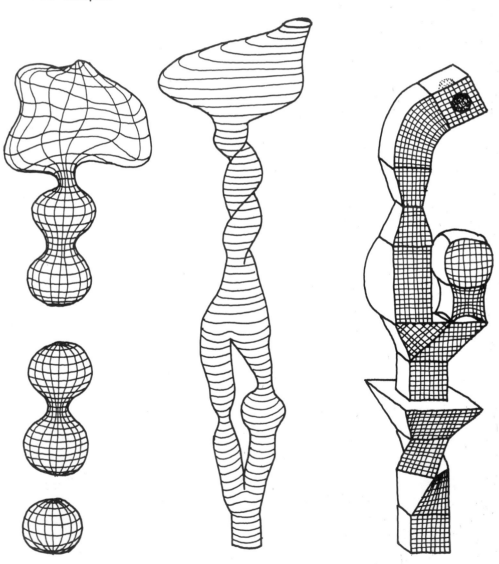

In the context of crochet sculpture experiment also with the effects of distortion by external and internal manipulation with and without physically stretching, compressing or twisting the fabric. Use soft and hard packing material, armatures, templates and tie threads, and sew surfaces together. Try, both separately and in combination, stiff and springy yarns worked with tight and loose tension.

Manipulated 3D Shapes

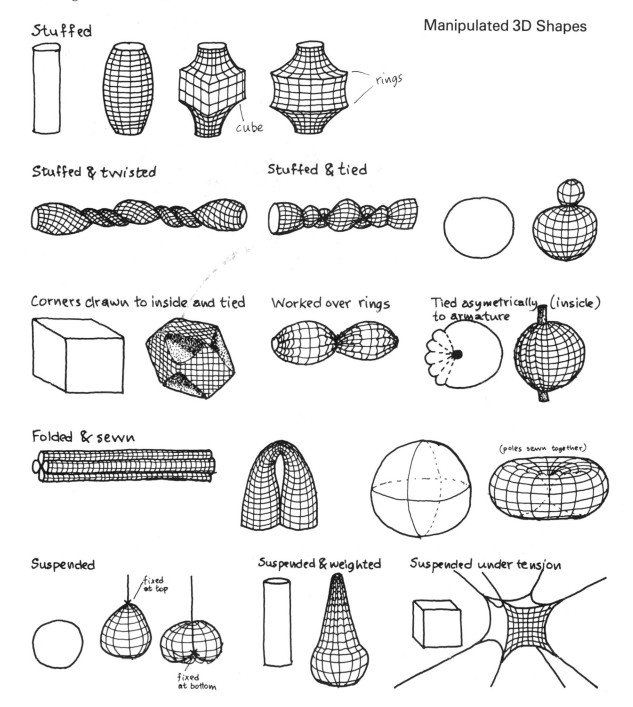

Stuffed

cube

rings

Stuffed & twisted

Stuffed & tied

Corners drawn to inside and tied

Worked over rings

Tied asymetrically (inside) to armature

Folded & sewn

(poles sewn together)

Suspended

fixed at top

fixed at bottom

Suspended & weighted

Suspended under tension

Chapter 5
Decorations

Edgings

Edgings, trimmings, borders, braids and insertions are all ways
of adding to a piece of crochet or any other sort of fabric, either
by crocheting directly or by making separately and sewing on
afterwards. The different terms represent different shades of
meaning in respect of function, application and style, but there
are no clear distinctions as far as their construction is concerned,
and so they are treated here together. The techniques of stitch
pattern and fabric formation discussed throughout this book all
apply. Anything goes. By the same token many embellishments
traditionally reserved for edges can often be applied to any part
of a fabric.

Direct Working
Practical edging: Even though there may be no desire to
decorate or embellish it, it is often necessary to work round the
edges of a piece of crochet fabric for the sake of neatness or
firmness. For firmness alone a single row of slip stitches close to
the edge will do and this may also be followed by several more
worked in the manner of a braid (see page 196), but for general
purposes one or more rows of double crochet is usually found
most satisfactory. The edge will be at its neatest and sharpest if
the first of the edging rows is worked with the right side and the
last with the wrong side of the fabric facing. If only one row is
required, experiment before deciding which way you prefer it.
The edge row may be continuous and join up to its own
beginning, in which case you have the option of turning, or
not, between each round.

Right side facing

Printed patterns tend to give rather meagre instructions for
working along the side of an existing crochet fabric—they may
say: *'work evenly in dc round edge . . .'*—because it is difficult
to be precise or dogmatic about the procedure. Suppose you
have made a piece of linear fabric in solid treble stitches with
straight, parallel edges, and have to work an edging row right
round it. When you go across the top edge, i.e. the last row of
the fabric, insert the hook into the tops of the stitches normally.
When you go across the underside of the original base chain,
insert the hook into each chain where the stitches of the first row

went. If you picked up two threads of each chain on that occasion (the usual procedure) there will be only one left for the edging row, and vice versa. It is usually best nevertheless to settle for that one loop; working between stitches and under all threads of the base chain although easier to do and more secure, distorts the fabric.

Along the other two sides of the fabric you have no clearly defined stitches to go into, but only the sides of the stitches at the row ends, which may sometimes be genuine stitches and sometimes turning chains. Where do you insert the hook and how many stitches must you work per row end, so as to achieve a flat, straight, undistorted edge? Because of individual differences in tension, this must ultimately be up to you, but here are some guidelines:

1   Insert the hook so that the stitches disturb the main fabric least. You should pick up at least two threads, but picking up the whole outside stitch may open up an unwanted gap between it and the next. (This may not matter at all in open fabrics. Sometimes there may be such a gap before you start; this may be closed by picking up one thread from the 2nd stitch together with the whole of the outside stitch.) Pick the best place and go on picking it consistently.

2   There is no simple and obvious relationship between the depth and width of crochet stitches made with the same hook and yarn (see page 116). That is to say it is no good hoping to work say, 1 double crochet per double crochet row end, or 2 double crochets per treble row end—this will usually make too many stitches and a slack, undulating edge. It may however become possible to apply this simple formula if you change to one size smaller hook for the edging rows. This is advisable if firmness is important anyway, and pattern instructions will recommend it. Even so be prepared to 'miss' one stitch, or, better still, work 2 stitches together, occasionally and at regular intervals. Most people rely on instinct plus trial and error to discover the best arrangement, but perfectionists can always work out in advance from their horizontal tension swatch how many stitches need to be worked over a given number of rows. If there is a multiple row repeat sequence, work out how many stitches to put in per repeat, then decide where to put them.

Too many stitches

Too few stitches

When the edging rows are to be in a contrast colour and the effect is to be sharp, it is essential to work the first row right side facing (see Colour, page 147). Better still work one row (right side facing) with the main colour, then start (also right side facing) with the contrast colour (but see Mock Blanket Stitch, page 190).

At corners and around curves it is necessary to increase (outside) or decrease (inside). On your first edging row this means working more stitches than you would have done over the same number of rows along the straight sections, or fewer stitches (or the same number, joining some together).

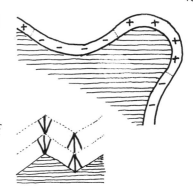

As a general rule it is wisest always to increase or decrease an even number of stitches at a corner, i.e. work an odd number of stitches in the same place, or work an odd number of stitches together, so that there always remains a central stitch in he corner. This is easy to identify next time round and continuously divides the angle between the adjacent straights exactly in half. Otherwise the corner is apt to wander.

Except for stitches longer than treble, which you are unlikely to select for a purely practical edging, this boils down to working 3, or occasionally 5 stitches in the same place, or 3 or 5 stitches together. In double crochet you would need to work 5 stitches in one place only to go round the outside of a corner more than 270°, and this is likely to be impractical if more than one edging row is contemplated. In the opposite situation—going round the inside of a corner less than 90°—the same observation applies, even though, to relieve congestion, rather than work 5 stitches together, you would actually work 3 out of the 5 together, i.e. the 1st, 3rd and 5th, missing the 2nd and 4th.

Mostly, then, the actual angle you want is achieved by working some rows with 3 stitches (3 together) into a corner, interspersed with some straight rows, or some rows with 5 stitches (5 together), interspersed with some with 3 stitches (3 together).

When angles are 270° or more outside, or 90° or less inside, it helps to keep the corner crisp and sharp to work longer stitches than usual into the very corner, i.e. the centre of the group or cluster. (See also solid circular grids, zig-zag and wavy grids, Chapter 3.)

The simplest way to find the appropriate number of stitches to work round the outside or inside of a curve, particularly a short one, is by further trial and error. Otherwise first find the number of stitches you would expect to work over the curved section if it were straight (regard this figure as the number of places the hook is to be inserted along the curve during the first edging row), then find the number of stitches to be added/subtracted, as follows:

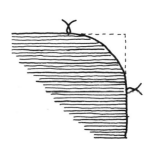

Mark off with contrasting thread the beginning and end of the curved section, measure between the thread markers with a flexible tape following the curve exactly, place this against a previously worked stretch of straight edging, or a fabric of

Double Crochet

Increase 2sts, i.e. 3sts in corner.
Decrease 2sts, i.e. 3sts tog in corner.

± 2sts per row (6sts per 3 rows) i.e. every row
inc/dec 2sts.

± 4sts per 3 rows i.e. 2 rows inc/dec 2sts,
1 row straight.

± 1st per row. (3sts per 3 rows) i.e. 1 row
inc/dec 2sts, 1 row straight.

± 2sts per 3 rows i.e. 1 row inc/dec 2sts,
2 rows straight.

Increase 4sts, i.e. 5sts in corner.
Decrease 4sts, i.e. 5sts tog in corner (actually
worked: 3 out of 5sts tog).

± 4sts per row (12sts per 3 rows) i.e. every
row inc/dec 4sts.

± 10sts per 3 rows i.e. 2 rows inc/dec 4sts,
1 row inc/dec 2sts.

± 6sts per 2 rows (9sts per 3 rows) i.e. 1 row
inc/dec 4sts, 1 row inc/dec 2sts.

± 8sts per 3 rows i.e. 1 row inc/dec 4sts,
2 rows inc/dec 2sts.

Outside   Inside

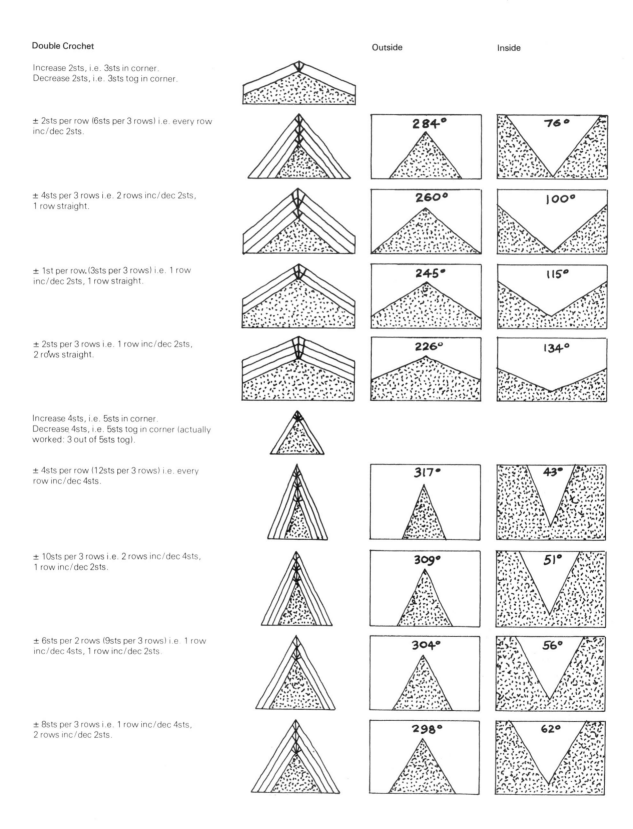

Outside column: 284°, 260°, 245°, 226°, 317°, 309°, 304°, 298°

Inside column: 76°, 100°, 115°, 134°, 43°, 51°, 56°, 62°

Corners/Angles

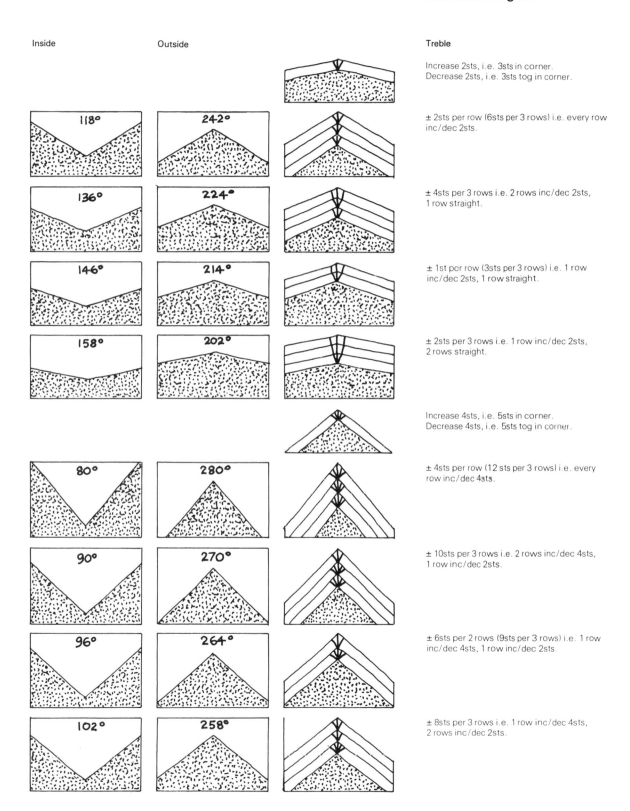

Inside	Outside	Treble

Treble

Increase 2sts, i.e. 3sts in corner.
Decrease 2sts, i.e. 3sts tog in corner.

118° / 242° — ± 2sts per row (6sts per 3 rows) i.e. every row inc/dec 2sts.

136° / 224° — ± 4sts per 3 rows i.e. 2 rows inc/dec 2sts, 1 row straight.

146° / 214° — ± 1st per row (3sts per 3 rows) i.e. 1 row inc/dec 2sts, 1 row straight.

158° / 202° — ± 2sts per 3 rows i.e. 1 row inc/dec 2sts, 2 rows straight.

Increase 4sts, i.e. 5sts in corner.
Decrease 4sts, i.e. 5sts tog in corner.

80° / 280° — ± 4sts per row (12 sts per 3 rows) i.e. every row inc/dec 4sts.

90° / 270° — ± 10sts per 3 rows i.e. 2 rows inc/dec 4sts, 1 row inc/dec 2sts.

96° / 264° — ± 6sts per 2 rows (9sts per 3 rows) i.e. 1 row inc/dec 4sts, 1 row inc/dec 2sts.

102° / 258° — ± 8sts per 3 rows i.e. 1 row inc/dec 4sts, 2 rows inc/dec 2sts.

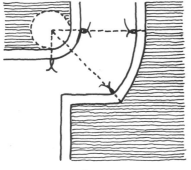

compatible horizontal tension and read off the number of stitches. If the curve is more than a few centimetres insert some equally spaced intermediate marker threads; these will help with the practical business of putting the stitches in evenly later.

A curve making a full circle requires only 5 or 6 stitches to be added/subtracted per round in double crochet (10 to 12 in treble; see page 96). Exactly how many you need over a particular section of curve depends upon what proportion of a circle it turns through and has nothing whatever to do with the length of the section. For instance the long, inside curve here needs 2 decreases per double crochet row, because it runs through roughly 120° or one third of a circle, whereas the short, outside curve needs 3 increases, because it runs through 180° or half a circle.

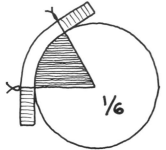

Dc: ± 1st per row   Tr: ± 2sts per row

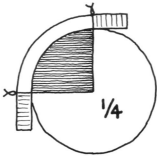

Dc: ± 3sts per 2 rows   Tr: ± 3sts per row

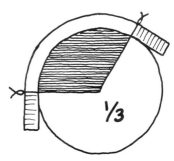

Dc: ± 2sts per row   Tr: ± 4sts per row

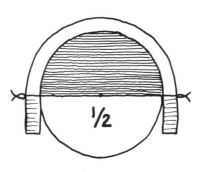

Dc: ± 3sts per row   Tr: ± 6sts per row

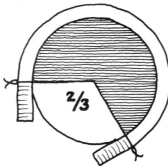

Dc: ± 4sts per row   Tr: ± 8sts per row

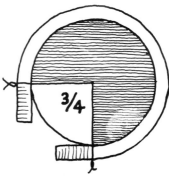

Dc: ±9sts per 2rows   Tr: ± 9sts per row

To make good curves, as opposed to corners or angles, however many stitches are to be added/subtracted each row, work them singly, i.e. 2 stitches into one place, or 2 stitches together, at different points along the full extent of the curved section; on subsequent rows try not to work later ones directly into previous ones.

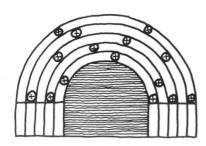

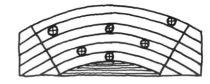

Unless your instincts or your calculations are wide of the mark by a big margin, a simple edging of one or two rows is almost bound to be serviceable. The deeper an edging becomes, however, the more any misjudgements of tension reveal themselves in straining or warping. After a basis has been laid down during the first couple of rows and found wanting, it will not be satisfactory to attempt to correct it by throwing in further additions/subtractions, followed by fierce pressing of the fabric. So, if the edging is deep, take more trouble from the beginning.

Sometimes extra care and accuracy, and therefore forethought, are required in any case. Maybe the base edging row has to contain a particular number of stitches in order to accommodate a special pattern, for example in the case of a circular neck. The larger the neck the more difficult it is to put in exactly the right number of stitches and yet work absolutely evenly all round. Rather than simply travel hopefully, divide up the edge into quarters, or even eighths, with thread markers and work the appropriate number of stitches between each.

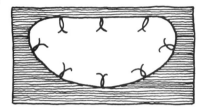

Maybe the number of stitches along, say, the left front of a coat must match exactly those along the right front, particularly if the fastenings are part of the pattern, in which case it may be necessary to preplan the arrangement in great detail and use a great many marker threads.

So far we have assumed that the edging must fit and follow the shapes of the main fabric and lie flat, but sometimes none of these things is at all appropriate. Also we have assumed that direct edging is always worked after the main fabric, but it is often convenient to work the edging first and the main fabric onto this. For a polo neck the edging needs to form a tube which remains the same circumference as the original neck hole, so treat the base row as though it were straight and maintain the same number of stitches all round throughout.

Decorative edging: All the usual ingredients of fabric construction can be employed to devise decorative edgings. Most raw edges benefit from at least one row of double crochet whatever else comes next and this also makes a coherent base row. The simplest patterns are then accomplished in one further row.

Single Row Decorative Edges

Corded Edge: Normally described: 'Work in dc from left to right', i.e. insert the hook into the previous stitch, yrh, pull loop through (but not through the loop on the hook) yrh, pull through 2 loops (see also page 85). There is no need to change your usual handhold or action for normal forwards double crochet.

Corded edge is most effective worked with the right side facing and preferably immediately after a normal double crochet row, also worked with the right side facing.

Chain Loops

Variation: Work a complete slip stitch into the previous stitch, then work 1ch. In both cases working 'backwards' induces the characteristic twist.

Double crochet worked backwards tends to be looser than when it is worked forwards and it can easily be made looser still. Consequently it is not usually necessary to increase round outside corners or curves. To decrease round inside corners and curves (and along straight sections, if necessary) simply miss one stitch occasionally, rather than trying to work stitches together.

Groups

Picots: All kinds of single or multiple Picots can be worked, with or without sequences of ordinary stitches between.

Clusters

Spikes
(Mock Blanket Stitch)

Sprays

Naturally the more rows and/or stitches per pattern repeat, the more complicated it is to make them fit neatly along straight sections and round corners and curves. If you are not a perfectionist patterns with one row (plus base row) and up to 3 stitches per repeat can usually be worked satisfactorily by taking things as they come, modifying the procedure as necessary to negotiate curves and corners. Patterns with more than one row or more than 3 stitches will need planning.

Some patterns with a large number of stitches within the repeat will have to be ruled out if it is impossible to have the necessary number of stitches along each section to accommodate them and still maintain appropriate tension.

Those with several rows will require special modification to turn corners—some will adapt to particular angles more readily than others—but may not be compatible with curves at all.

To help you visualize how your pattern might turn a corner, stand a mirror on a straight specimen of it (drawing or crochet). Depending on where you place the mirror, different solutions will appear. Remember that it may be suitable to introduce a special corner feature; apart from solving the problem, this may be more attractive than the straightforward version in the mirror.

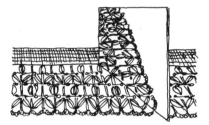

To help you decide what is best, draw out the basic pattern on either side of the corner, leaving the corner segment blank; then see what might fit.

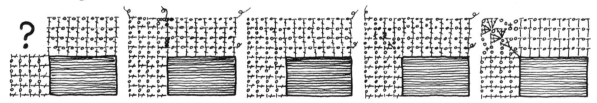

When a gathering effect, which has to be constructed into direct edging, is made full enough, it should be possible to work 'straight' even round a 270° (outside) corner. In fact it is advisable to make sure that this is so.

Provided sufficient planning has been done, directly worked edging rows need not be continuous.

The technique of surface crochet (see page 139) can be used to build up a deep pile. In the example the side and lower border of an otherwise solid treble fabric have been worked as filet crochet (see page 120) with 1 chain space. Afterwards surface trebles, with the yarn on the right side, have been worked over the network of rungs in the directions indicated—5 trebles per rung (chain space or treble stitch).

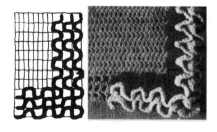

Multiple Row
Decorative Edges

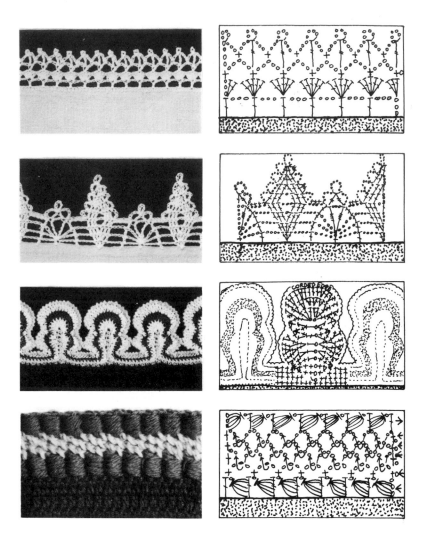

Separate Working

It may not be possible, particularly on a fine woven fabric, to work directly with a crochet hook. For a variety of practical and design reasons it may be more convenient, or even essential, to make an edging or insertion separately and sew it on afterwards. The piece may be constructed in the usual way from a base chain, in which case care must be taken to reconcile tension and accommodation of the pattern with eventual fit (with or without gathering as required).

An advantage of separate construction is that the base row itself need not always be attached to the main fabric.

Nor need the general direction of working of the edge strip be parallel to the edge of the main fabric. It can be constructed on an oblique grid, provided the angle concerned is compatible with any corners in the main fabric, or, on the other axis, at right angles.

In fact no base chain need be required at all. Single row trimmings, or bases for some patterns, may be constructed on a sort of interrupted base chain principle to the length required.

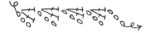

Or the piece can be made of separate motifs, or any combination of these techniques.

If only one side of the article is to be seen, edgings or insertions may be sewn on so as slightly (or completely) to overlap the main fabric; hence the edges need not be strictly parallel to the edge of the main fabric.

When they are not overlapped, however, the relevant edges do need to be parallel.

With a separate edging fabric a gathering effect may be built into the stitch formation, or achieved by physically gathering at the sewing stage.

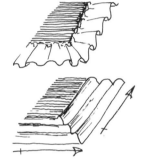

Crumpling (or gathering on the other axis) is best achieved by making the strip in the other direction and building in the gathering.

Edge strip shapes: The diagrams and construction notes show some basic edging shapes for conventional garments, but the principles can be applied, adapted and extended to any purpose. The choice between working directly or separately and possibly the choice of axs in separate work may sometimes be forced on you by the design; otherwise it will be resolved by your personal preferences. Whatever the situation the best results are obtained by planning.

By definition there is only one possible axis in direct edging and one possible general direction of working. In separate work in theory there are always at least two axes, each with two possible directions of working; in practice some of the options are too complicated or unreliable to be really useful. Which you choose may depend upon which part of the strip will benefit most (or suffer least) from the strength and firmness of the base chain, if there is one.

Edging Schemes

Neck Openings

As for flat, inwards circle

Decrease substantially

Work 'straight'

As for outwards circle, but increase substantially

Armhole

Decrease slightly around shoulder seam, if the shoulder is 'shaped'

Decrease as for flat, inwards circle at underarm (between markers)

General Notes: Use a smaller hook to make the edging tighter/firmer than the main fabric.

When circles or tubes are continuous make the join in the least conspicuous place — at a seam or centre back. When they are divided for an opening in the garment, the edges must naturally be aligned with that opening. It is easy to make divided openings overlap (for buttons, links, etc.) by working some extra chains before you start, or at the end of the first row, depending upon which side of the opening the overlap is to occur. (Remember that, for instance, right and left cuffs will be worked in opposite fashion.)

Cuffs/Welts, etc.

 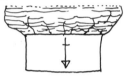 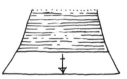

As for 'straight' tube

Decrease on 1st round then work as for a 'straight' tube

Increase regularly so as to maintain line of flare

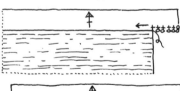

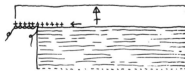

Neck openings: if you have miscalculated and made a neck opening for, say, a polo collar too wide, work the first few rounds as for a flat inwards circle. If you have made the opening too narrow for an intended round neck, work as for a straight tube, so as not to make it tighter still.

Edging/Collars

This sort of collar is best made separately in two halves (which join at centre back of neck) and sewn on ('shaped' edge to garment)

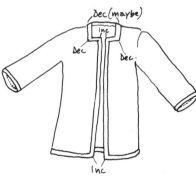

Dec (maybe)

Inc

Dec   Dec

Inc

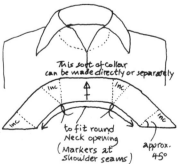

This sort of collar can be made directly or separately

Inc   Inc

Inc   Inc

to fit round neck opening (Markers at shoulder seams)

approx. 45°

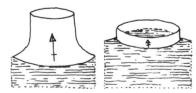

Welts, cuffs and hems: Welts, cuffs and hems can be worked directly, or separately, on the same or the opposite axis to the main fabric, and before or after the main fabric. In the majority of commercial patterns they are worked first and the main fabric is then built on them directly, usually on the same axis. This can be a pity, because the beginner's tension and fluency may not have settled down to consistency right away and the opportunity for final adjustments to depth and tautness, which this part of the job would afford, if left until last, is thrown away. The plainest and most practical welts consist of conventional double crochet worked directly onto the main fabric afterwards, round and round as a tube, either turning between rounds or with the right side always facing.

A much denser, stronger, but less flexible version is made again in double crochet, but inserting the hook not just under the top 2 loops of each stitch, but under 3 loops, i.e. deeper into the body of the stitch between the vertical strands (see page 83).

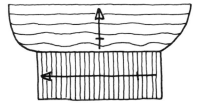

The most flexible ribbed welt is made on the other axis separately and, most conveniently in this case, before the main fabric, by working to and fro in double crochet, always into the back loop only of each stitch. The base row of the main fabric may then be worked as a direct continuation into the side of the welt. Even without changing hook size, a base row worked one stitch per double crochet row end will give an 'increase' of approximately 25% in double crochet (35% in treble), which the welt should stretch out to, when required. This method resembles a knitted welt most closely, visually and in performance.

On account of its characteristic thickness, it is not normally regarded as suitable in crochet to turn the edges of the main fabric in for hems or edging. Away from the field of practical garments, however, all kinds of fold or crease, sewn or crocheted permanently in position, may be called for.

Belts

In constructional terms a belt is merely a long, thin strip or tube of crochet which can be made on either axis, except that if the base chain forms one of the long edges it will cause that edge to behave differently, both in and out of tension, from the opposite one. Consequently, if this can be incorporated in the pattern, lengthwise base chains are best set in the middle.

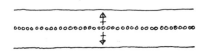

In general unsupported or unstiffened crochet fabrics make poor belts from the practical point of view (Cords may be better) and are not recommended, unless the design demands them.

One exception to this is a fabric made entirely out of single crochet (slip stitches)—sometimes called Bosnian Crochet—which is firm, strong and slightly flexible. The idea is to work successive rows of slip stitches (a) always into the back loop only of each stitch for a smooth finish, or (b) into the back or front loop only of selected stitches for relief patterns. (Plan on a squared chart—see page 159.)

Colour patterns can also be incorporated (see page 149) if you remember always to pick up the new colour in time to pull through the previous stitch. The results resemble woven braid and are fine both for decorative and structural purposes.

If necessary, belt-carriers may be made out of simple lengths of single, double, etc. chain, or cord.

Laces, Cords and Frogging

The simplest lace is a length of chain made, most practically, with the smallest hook compatible with the yarn required. It may not be possible to darn the short ends back into the lace so they must be tightened firmly and snipped off short.

A relatively slim and flat, strong cord or tie can be made by working one row of double crochet into a base chain. This will inevitably have the permanent habit of twisting up, which can be annoying and unattractive. It has the virtues of being stronger and firmer than a double chain and made by a simple, generally understood process and it may be incorporated into edging rows without breaking off the yarn.

A stronger and less stretchy version of this can be made to various thicknesses by working your double crochet over a length of piping or sash cord of predetermined length, instead of into a base chain. As a tie this cord may need to be sewn into place either before or after the stitches are worked over it; as frogging the covering will need to be worked first. When sewing in position, have the tops of the stitches on top or underneath as you wish.

Another slim, flat and textured cord—decorative enough for use as a braid—is made as follows:

Make 2 chains, work 1 dc in first of these, turn.
Work 1 dc in loop formed by 2nd original chain, turn.

*Work 1 dc, inserting hook down through 2 loops at lefthand side of last dc, turn. Repeat from *.

Unlike the double-crochet-into-base-chain cord, this has no tendency to twist, is symmetrical and, being made all at once without a set base chain, is easier to work to a given final measurement.

A twisted cord is difficult to make without two people—a third helps with a long cord. Cut one or more lengths of yarn, depending upon the required thickness, each measuring roughly three times the length of the final cord. Two people each take one end of the strands and, holding them taut throughout, both twist in the same direction as the yarn is spun or plied (usually clockwise) until the whole length of the strands is firmly twisted. The more twist is put in, the stronger and the more consistently they must stretch the cord to prevent twiddles and kinks jumping in, and therefore the harder it becomes both to hold on and to twist. For a better grip it helps to tie the ends of the strands together and insert a stick or pencil.

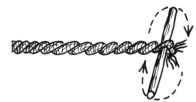

Still keeping the strands taut the twisted cord must now be folded in half (by the third person) and the two ends knotted together. Finally the cord is released from the folded end and

198

stroked downwards from the knotted end as the twist struggles
to readjust itself from a double into a single core of spiralling
threads. The ends of the cord, particularly the knotted end, are
ugly unless finished by discreet thread binding or the addition
of some form of tassel or pom-pom.

Another type of cord with a circular cross section is a very thin
tube worked in double or treble crochet, with perhaps only 4, or
5 stitches in each round. The easy way to work is in a spiral with
the wrong side always facing and going into the back loop only
of each stitch. But if you want to make a pattern in different
coloured rings, you must work in separate rounds. The cord
may be stuffed with either several strands of the same yarn, or
any soft packing, or perhaps semi-rigid polythene tubing,
depending upon the purpose to which the cord is to be put.

Laces or cords of any kind can be plaited (flat or circular), or
crocheted—with the finger if necessary—to make thicker or
more interesting arrangements.

Tassel

Wind the yarn several times, depending upon the bulk of the tassel required, evenly round a piece of card which is about 20–25% deeper than the length of tassel you need. Tie the strands very tightly together at one edge and cut through them at the other. Bind all the threads together just below the knot with another length of yarn, hiding the ends in the body of the tassel. Fluff up and trim.

Fringes

Simple Fringe

To prepare strands, wind the yarn round a book or piece of card approximately 20% wider than the length of the fringe you want. Holding all the strands firmly, say by pressing with the hand nearer the edge of a table, cut through one edge. When all the fibres of all the strands have definitely been severed, fold back the strands and remove the card.

To knot the strands to the main fabric, pick up the tips of as many strands as you need for one tassel in one hand, hold down the remaining strands in the pile with the other, and peel away gently to avoid starting a tangle.

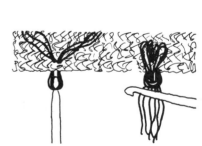

Insert a crochet hook through the edge of the main fabric— from the right or wrong side, depending on how you prefer the final knot to look—double over the strands, pick up and pull halfway through to form a loop. Hook all the short ends through this loop, even up the lengths as far as possible and tighten firmly steadying the knot and not straining against the main fabric.

It is usually necessary to experiment with different lengths of strand, different numbers of strands per tassel and different distances between tassels to find the most pleasing arrangement.

Knotted Fringe

Extra length must be allowed if the tassels are to be knotted once or more.

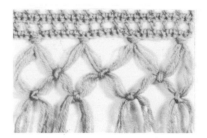

First row of knots: Divide the strands of each tassel in half and tie to half of the adjacent tassel. To ensure an even depth of knots, insert a ruler or strip of card and tie around this, slipping it along as you go.

Following rows of knots: Divide the new tassels in half again and proceed as before. NB The outside half of the edge tassels drops straight.

You must expect to have to trim any cut fringe, if you want an absolutely even edge, but do not assume that a hard line at the base of a fringe is necessarily an improvement.

Loop Stitch Fringe

This is a version of loop stitch (see page 86), which can be made separately or worked directly onto an edge.

To make separately: Make a slip loop on the hook. Take the supply yarn down the front of a strip of card, round and up the back, pick it up again here and draw through the slip loop.
* Lead the supply thread down and round the card from front to back, insert the hook from right to left under this thread at the front of the card, pick it up again at the back and pull through one loop = 2 loops on the hook, † yrh, pull through 2 loops, repeat from *.

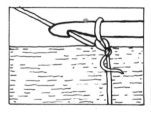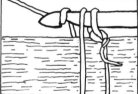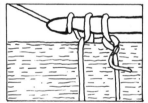

To make directly: Place the main fabric so that you can work along its lower edge and join the supply yarn at the right. Work each loop as for separate working from *, except at † insert the hook through the main fabric edge and pull the final thread through this and all loops in one movement.

Chain Loop Fringe

Work directly, or separately as follows: Into each stitch work 1dc followed by a length of single chains twice as deep as the required fringe, then slip stitch to the same dc. Work the chain loops different lengths, or more or less frequently to vary the density.

Space the chain loops and slip stitch them together at strategic points as you go to make a trellis.

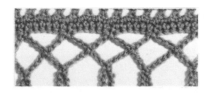

In this version an extended Solomon's Knot stitch (see page 85) is made to the depth of the fringe, and another similar one to return.

Try all kinds of fringe on a zig-zag or wavy as well as straight edge, or include more than one type of fringe feature in the same border. Try varying the colour composition of cut fringes.

Pom-pom

Cut two circles of card slightly larger than the diameter of the pom-pom you want and cut out a round hole in the centre of both. The size of this hole will determine the density of the threads in the pom-pom. Wind the yarn firmly and evenly round the two pieces of card together (several strands together for speed), always going through the centre hole, until this is well filled. You will need to thread the yarn onto a wool needle to make the last few passes.

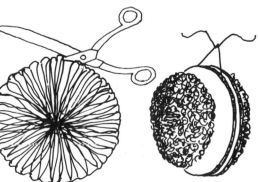

Insert scissors between the two discs and under the wrapped threads, cutting them all round at the outer edge only. Without disturbing the threads tie them up very tightly between the pieces of card, leaving an end for sewing on. Finally remove the cards, cutting away if necessary. Shake and brush the pom-pom into shape and trim.

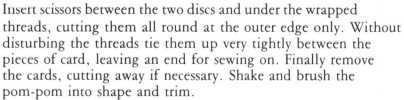

Tuft

A tuft is feasible only with single spun (unplied) yarn.

Make a short tassel as though for a simple cut fringe and attach it to the main fabric. Holding the knot firmly and taking care not to touch the main fabric with the bristles, stroke downwards strongly and repeatedly with a teazle-brush (or one with stiff, wire bristles) until the spin loosens and the separate fibres untwist and mesh together in a single tuft.

Close packed tufts make a fur effect.

Curlicue

Make each one separately, leaving an end for sewing on, or as part of a row of double crochet.

After a length of single chain approximately the same length as the curlicue required, starting into the 3rd chain from the hook work 4 or more trebles into *every* chain. The surfeit of stitches generates the spiral.

Buttons

Bobbles

Make a small, flat, outwards circle in, say, double crochet (see page 99) for as many rows as necessary (work in spiral, if you prefer). Next work one or two rows 'straight', then continue as for an inwards circle, inserting a button for a flattish shape, or a bead or wood ball or soft packing material for a sphere, before the hole closes too much. Finally leave an end for sewing on.

Alternatively the outward half of the button can be worked as a single round of some longer basic stitch, or a combination using basic and/or fancy stitches.

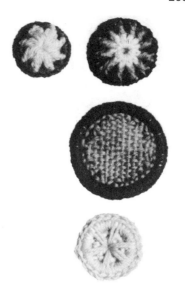

Cover a curtain ring with a round of double crochet. Turn the tops of the stitches inwards, then work a decorative centre with needle and thread by darning, etc.

Or work a crochet centre first to fit inside a curtain ring, then work a final round to cover the ring as well. In this example spikes are worked into the centre during the last, covering round.

Buttonholes

Horizontal

Double crochet: As double crochet is shallow, simply miss the required number of stitches in the appropriate place and work single chains to correspond. On the next row work the same number of double crochet into the chain loop.

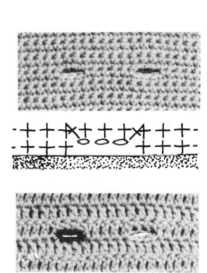

Sometimes it can be neater and firmer to work dc2tog (see page 42) at each end of the hole, but remember to count this as only one stitch each time and put the full number in the buttonhole loop itself.

Half treble, treble, etc.: With the longer stitches, instead of working single chains, which would leave too deep a hole, work half treble, or treble chains as appropriate (see page 29), i.e. work the full stitch normally but insert the hook into the single lefthand thread at the base of the previous stitch in the current row. To close the buttonhole, just before you insert the hook for the next ordinary stitch, pick up the lefthand thread of the previous stitch as before, then into the top 2 loops of the appropriate stitch in the previous row, yrh, pull through the fabric and the odd thread from the previous stitch in one movement. Complete the stitch normally.

Vertical

Double crochet, half treble: To make vertical slots in the main fabric work in separate sections, by fastening off and joining in again, to the depth required, then work a joining row across all sections and continue normally. Take care to work the same

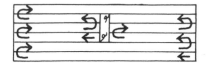

number of rows over each section, to work corresponding rows in the same direction, and not to gain/lose any stitches overall.

Treble, etc.: The deeper stitches may provide a deep enough slot for a buttonhole as they stand. If not, work as for double crochet.

All holes in the main fabric left for buttons, but particularly vertical ones, benefit from a round of buttonhole stitch worked with a needle and thread afterwards for neatness, strength and protection of the main fabric—perhaps sometimes for decoration too.

Circular

Holes can easily be made in the centres of circular motifs or circular features such as flower heads, made in the linear format.

Buttonhole Loops

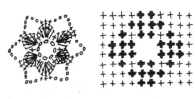

Work a single chain loop as required between stitches during the last edging row.

Or do so during the row before and then, on the final one, work double crochet ad lib. round each loop as you come to it. It may be neater on these occasions to work dc3tog at the beginning and ending of such loops.

Picot loops can be left to form buttonhole loops—and the corresponding ones sewn together to make stems for toggles or buttons.

Beads and Sequins

Whether you intend a formal or informal arrangement, you must do sufficient planning to know how many beads/sequins you will need for each piece of the fabric. If the design uses different colours, it is also necessary to know what order these will be needed in. Before you start thread them all onto the supply yarn—in reverse order, of course. If a wool needle will not pass through them, either stiffen the tip of the yarn with glue or nail varnish or thread a fine needle with sewing cotton and attach this securely to your yarn.

To arrange beads on the front of the work: Work preliminary wrappings of the yarn round the hook (if any), insert the hook into the next stitch from the back through to the front, bring up a bead close to the hook, pick up the supply thread past the bead and pull through, trapping the bead. Flip the bead to the front under the hook, but over the supply thread, and complete the stitch.

To arrange the beads on the back of the work: Work the next stitch up to the last stage. (There will be 2 loops left on the hook, except in the case of half treble, when there will be 3 loops.) Bring a bead up to the hook, pick up the supply thread past the bead to trap it and pull through to complete the stitch.

To set large beads into the depth of the fabric (at the back): Work 1 chain, bring up a bead, work another chain, trapping the bead. Miss 1 or 2 stitches, depending on the size of bead, and continue normally.

Next row: Work 1 stitch into each chain either side of the bead, if you missed 2 stitches; work these stitches together, if you missed only one.

Ribbon

For decorative purposes coloured ribbon can be introduced into rows of solid, basic stitches or filet crochet, by interweaving.

Pockets

An outside, patch pocket consists of a second piece of matching or contrasting fabric, stitched onto the outside of the main fabric.

An inside pocket with access from the outside requires a slot in the main fabric, which can usually be made in the manner of a buttonhole (see page 203). The pocket fabric is then stitched onto the inside of the main fabric behind the slot.

If the slot is diagonal or curved, plan it on a grid and use a combination of the vertical and horizontal methods of buttonholing.

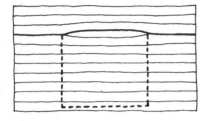

If the slot is straight and horizontal and the garment is worked from the bottom upwards, you may prefer to make the pocket fabric first and, when you reach the required position on the main fabric, instead of working chains, simply switch to working across the top edge of the pocket fabric, missing a corresponding number of stitches of the main fabric before continuing.

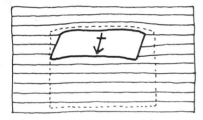

On the other hand, if the pocket is to have a flap, you may wish to work this directly downwards from the top edge of the slot in the main fabric. The flap may otherwise be made separately and sewn on.

Leather, ceramics, wood, stone, etc.

The most convenient way to incorporate hard or semi-hard elements into crochet work is to drill or punch holes at suitable intervals around the edges. Small objects, such as pebbles or sections of mirror, can be enclosed in a network of chain loops and/or vertical stitches.

Pebble

Leather

Chapter 6
Introduction to
Related Techniques

Woven Crochet

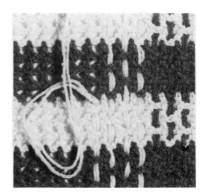

In woven crochet strands of the same or completely different yarn are threaded onto a tapestry needle and woven horizontally, vertically or diagonally into a crocheted background fabric. Traditionally this procedure is used to give a total woven look, so that the finished fabric scarcely resembles crochet at all. Usually a plain treble or filet mesh background is made in repeated sequences of two or more colours, then two or three threads of the same set of colours are woven vertically in a given order. Designs resembling various checks and tartans are obtained in this way.

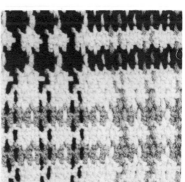

A substantially woven fabric is much firmer and thicker than simple crochet and is therefore most suitable for blankets, bags, cushion covers, etc. or for outer garments. Used sparingly however, a single woven strand in a second colour can add interest to almost any crochet background, sometimes with little suggestion of a woven look about it.

Linear background fabrics are easier to handle, but crochet worked in rings or spirals can also be woven if it is planned with care.

Woven crochet can also be employed as a border or braid.

The Technique

For weaving it is important to use a needle with a large eye and a blunt tip and to pass this cleanly over and under without spearing or splitting any threads of the background fabric (this affects the pattern). Always weave with the right side facing and before making up. Both the beginnings and ends of the woven strands (maybe several threads) must be darned in like ordinary ends. Even with great neatness you will be lucky to avoid bulky edges or seams. To minimize this problem, try and cut strands long enough to weave any consecutive rows of the same colour in one length. Remember that you may be working with double or triple thread and allow approximately an extra one fifth of the length of the woven row per thread per woven row. Never try and join strands in the middle of a row. Sometimes the ends of the woven strands can be knotted and allowed to hang in fringes or tassels, or even crocheted into an additional border.

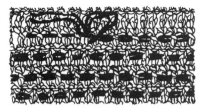

A guide for tension in weaving is to leave the background fabric undistorted and the same size as before weaving. There will inevitably be some 'shrinkage'—possibly up to 10%—and this should be allowed for at the design stage. It is a good idea to note the exact dimensions of the background fabric before weaving and to check during weaving, teasing out the fabric if necessary. Weave rather more loosely than you would expect and take special care not to pull in the edges at the beginning of each row.

For strength and firmness filet mesh backgrounds are usually made by inserting the hook under the top 3 threads of each treble (see page 83).

Weaving, perhaps several sets of strands alternately up and down the same 'channels', can be a way of closing up open background fabrics.

Designing fitting garments is difficult with woven fabrics, because of 'shrinkage'. Estimating the total amount of yarn required in advance is also difficult because so much depends upon the economy with which the woven strands are cut.

Tunisian Crochet

Tunisian Crochet is made with a longer hook than usual; this has a uniform diameter and preferably a knob at the end. Although only one hook is used, the technique resembles that of knitting.

The first (outward) row from right to left consists of working each stitch as though you were preparing to work every stitch together at the end, i.e. you leave a loop of each on the hook. During the second (inward) row from left to right—you do not turn the work—you then repeatedly take the supply yarn round the hook and pull through, say, 2 loops, effectively 'casting off' the stitches in turn and so returning to square one, but with some substance added to the fabric. The groups described on page 83 are tiny examples of Tunisian technique.

The description below shows the basic procedure, which can be repeated to form a plain fabric on its own or used as the foundation of other types of pattern. This basic procedure provides a thick fabric suitable for blankets, but even slight variations to the procedure for outward or inward rows (or both) result in very different density and elasticity, grain and texture. Shaping at the edges and internally and by swapping hooks is quite manageable. The true circular format is obviously not, although circular fabrics can be engineered by programmed shaping. There is much scope for interesting colour changes, too. Provided you have compatible hooks, you can make continuous fabrics in which Tunisian and conventional techniques are alternated.

Basic Tunisian Technique

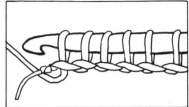
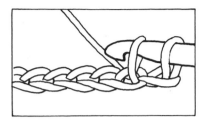

Make a length of chain containing the same number of chains as stitches required.

Row 1 (outward): Insert the hook into the 2nd chain from the hook, *yrh, draw loop through* = 2 loops on hook.

Going into each chain repeat from * to *, leaving all the new loops on the hook. Do not turn the work.

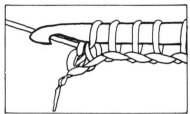
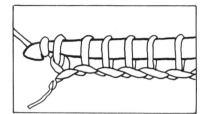

Row 2 (Inward): Yrh, draw through 1 loop, *yrh.

Draw through 2 loops.

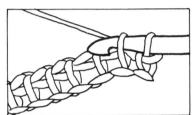
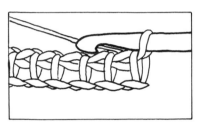

Repeat from * to the end of the row. Do not turn.

Row 3 (Outward): Work 1 chain as the first stitch, then, starting at the 2nd stitch and inserting the hook from right to left behind the single, vertical thread at the front of each stitch, work as for row 1.

Basic Tunisian

Colour: basic tunisian with random dyed yarn.

Colour: basic tunisian with 2 cols and Jacquard technique (4sts with each col reversing after 6 rows).

Texture (WS facing): Make an odd number of chs.
Base Row 1 & 2: basic tunisian.
Patt Row 1 (outward): miss 1st vertical thread, *in next thread work tr3tog, in next thread work basic st, rep from * ending basic st in thread at edge.
Patt Row 2 (inward): basic.
Patt Row 3: as patt row 1, but alternate positions of basic sts and tr3tog clusters.
Patt Row 4: basic.
Rep patt rows 1–4.

Openwork
Make a length of chain which is a multiple of 4 plus 1.
Row 1 (outward): starting into 2nd ch from hook work basic st, *miss 1ch, basic st in next ch, rep from * ending basic st in last ch.
Row 2 (inward): 2ch, yrh, pull through 3 loops, *3ch, yrh, pull through 3 loops, rep from * until 2 loops remain, 1ch, yrh, pull through 2 loops.
Row 3: basic st in next ch, *basic st over 1st and 3rd chs of next 3ch loop, rep from * ending basic st into each of last 2chs.
Row 4: yrh, pull through 2 loops, *3ch, yrh, pull through 3 loops, rep from * to end.
Row 5: *basic st in 1st and 3rd chs of next 3 ch loop, rep from * ending basic st into thread at edge.
Rep from row 2–5.

Hexagon: basic tunisian shaped to make wedge segments, which accumulate into a circle.

Make 13chs. *First Segment: work each outward row to the end (row 1 = 13sts), but the inward rows only over a gradually increasing number of sts as folls: row 2:2sts, row 4:3sts, row 6:4sts, row 8:5sts, row 10:6sts, row 12:8sts, row 14:9sts, row 16:10sts, row 18:11sts, row 20:12sts, row 22:13sts, rep from * 5 times = 6 segments. Sew up the join.

Colour: basic tunisian worked with 3 plain cols as folls: lower half: 1 row with each col, upper half: 2 rows with each col. Try and work out why there is no real difference.

Hairpin

Hairpin crochet is worked with the usual hook, but with the assistance of a hairpin or frame of thin, parallel steel pins. Basically as the description shows, the supply yarn is repeatedly wrapped around the frame (by revolving it) and some sort of basic stitch, say double crochet, is worked in the centre to lock the loops so formed.

Strips of fabric are made in this way and crocheted together directly, or with some decorative embellishment. The main interest emerges from the delicate loops and the ways the strips are joined, rather than from the construction of each individual strip, where any variations in hook technique make but slight differences.

The shapes hairpin strips are required to conform to are best kept simple, unless you are determined to be ingenious. The critical factors in your calculations are obviously the width of the strip, determined by the distance between the pins, and the tension (length) of the central core of the strip. Hairpin strips can be used alone or in combination with conventional crochet, or used as insertions or appliqué embellishments.

The open-ended, U-shaped hairpin may be easier to handle than an adjustable, frame type, but its width will be fixed and it will not be possible to slip the first loops off the bottom end of the pins, as is necessary to make a long strip. (In this case remove them all and replace the last few.) To prevent the loops twiddling up when they are released from either type, thread them onto a length of contrasting thread (each side) and tie loosely into a circle.

In general, any kind of wire which can be bent reasonably easily into a U shape will prove useless as a Hairpin, because the prongs will bend inwards under normal working tension and so your loops will not be of equal length. In the absence of a purpose-made Hairpin you need to find some metal rod and do some woodwork.

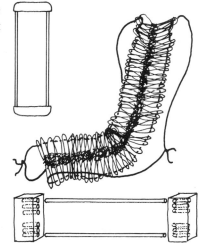

Basic Hairpin Technique

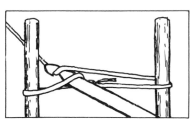
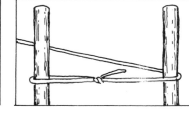

Make a slip knot in the usual way and place over the righthand pin. Adjust the actual knot so it sits midway between the pins.

Revolve the pins half a turn clockwise as viewed from above.

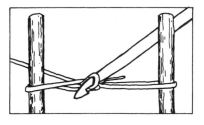
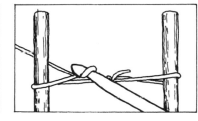

Insert the hook in the slip knot.

Yrh, pull through.

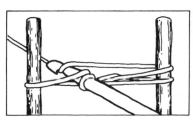
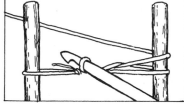

*Without dislodging the loop on the hook manoeuvre the handle of the hook to the rear of the righthand pin.

Revolve the pins half a turn clockwise.

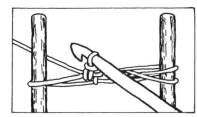

Insert the hook under the front thread of the last loop made on the lefthand pin,

and work 1 double crochet.

Repeat from *.

Joins:

1 A single loop from one band is hooked through the corresponding loop of the adjacent band then the next loop of that band is hooked through this loop and so on.

2 The same procedure as 1, but 3 loops are taken together at a time.

3 The loops of one band are laid over the corresponding loops of an adjacent band. The join is made with some fresh yarn in the manner of surface slip stitch (see page 140).

4 The loops of each band are first edged separately, in this case as folls: *picking up 3 loops work 1dc, 3ch, rep from *. Then the bands are joined: SS into first dc of first band, 5ch, SS into first dc of second band, **5ch, SS into next dc of opposite band, rep from **

Edges

1 Row 1 (RS): 1dc in each loop. Do not turn. Row 2: Corded Edge (see page 190).

2 Row 1 (RS): *miss 3 loops, pick up next 3 loops, 1dc, 5ch, pick up 3 missed loops, 1dc, rep from *. Turn at end. Row 2: 5ch, *in centre ch of next loop work (1dc, 3ch, 1dc), 5ch, rep from * omitting 5ch at end of last rep and working 2ch, 1tr in last dc.

Circular: Make 1st Band to form the centre with 50 to 60 loops each side and join the central spine into a ring with a slip stitch. Thread some yarn through the inside loops, gather and fasten off. Make the 2nd Band with twice as many loops and join in ratio 1:2. Make 3rd, 4th, etc. bands with 3, 4, etc. times as many loops as the first band and join in ratio 2:3, 3:4, etc.

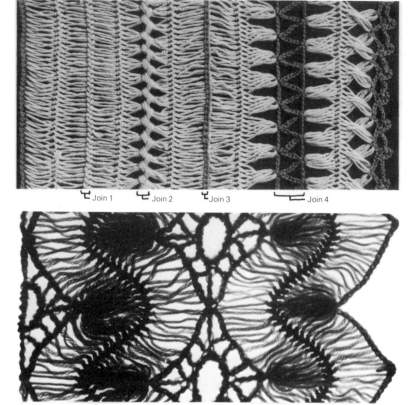

Join 1   Join 2   Join 3   Join 4

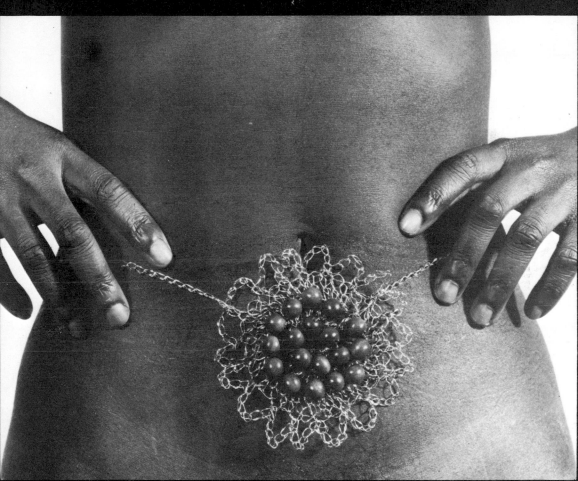

Chapter 7
Yarns

Fibres

For the purposes of crochet sculpture and wall-hangings the things which matter about a yarn to the individual artist are generally superficial and revealed simply by look and feel. For the making of clothes and other practical articles, however less obvious characteristics must be appreciated and taken into account.

Wool

Wool is the most plentiful and popular animal fibre. It is very beautiful, warm and soft, yet reasonably hard wearing. A garment made of wool will absorb an amazing proportion of its own weight in water before the wearer begins to feel cold. The disadvantages are that natural wool requires special care in washing and drying to avoid felting, shrinking or generally losing its shape and it is vulnerable to moth damage. Wool yarn is now available which has been specially treated by the manufacturer to permit washing in a machine and to resist moth attack, but it is naturally relatively expensive.

Other Animal Fibres

The fibres of other animals, such as mohair and cashmere (goat), alpaca (llama), angora (rabbit), vicuna, camel, reindeer and silk each have special qualities of either fineness, softness, warmth, lightness or colour which make them desirable. They are always expensive and their availability, usually rather limited, fluctuates with fashion and economic conditions.

Natural Plant Fibres

With wool the most widely used natural fibre is cotton. It is also beautiful and sympathetic to the touch. In view of its fineness and lack of bulk, it is particularly suitable for fine lace work in crochet. Linen (flax) is perhaps not so soft as cotton, but hard wearing. Other fibres from plant sources such as raffia, manila, hemp, jute and sisal are usually coarse and tough and provide excellent texture and rigidity.

Synthetic Fibres

Synthetic yarns have been developed because they are more convenient, and therefore on the whole cheaper, to produce and manufacture. In general they are harder wearing and easier to care for than those made of natural fibres, which makes them popular, although garments made from them seem to become dirty more quickly and feel less sympathetic. The main types are acrylic ('Acrilan', 'Courtelle', 'Orlon'), nylon ('Bri-Nylon', 'Tendrelle') and polyester ('Dacron', 'Terylene', 'Trevira'). Very many mixtures of both natural and synthetic fibres are attempted, in order to combine the best characteristics of each. Yarns of each type of fibre, pure or mixed, must be handled and cared for in different ways (see page 271).

Selection of yarns for aesthetic reasons is ultimately a personal matter, but here are some general guidelines about teaming yarns with stitch patterns:

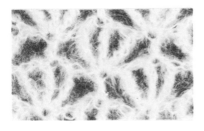

Good: Plain, crisp and even yarns with elaborate, lacy fabric patterns.

Exception: Light, fuzzy yarns can make an effective, misty lace impression, although the detail of the stitch configuration may be lost.

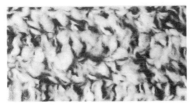

Good: Elaborate, fancy yarns with plain (solid) fabric patterns. Let the slubs, nubs, flecks, bouclé, glitter, etc. provide the interest.

Exception: Consider these two fabrics worked with a glitter effect yarn—one in a plain, solid pattern and the other in an elaborate openwork pattern. When they are viewed in direct light, the fleck kills the patterns and makes them practically indistinguishable. When they are lit from behind, however, a substantial difference reveals itself. This combination of yarn plus openwork pattern might have some point if the fabric were intended for a lampshade. Otherwise it would be useless to expect 'openness' to contribute anything more than a lightening of the fabric, in which case a simpler pattern would be equally effective.

Front Lit Front Lit

Back Lit Back Lit

Bad: Fuzzy yarns with subtly textured fabric patterns.

Bad: Very dark yarns when texture or stitch detail is important.

Yarn: Construction

Single Spun

Z twist

Slub

Nub

Plied

2 Ply / equal

2 Ply / 2 colour

Despite some standardization the term 'ply' does not denote the thickness, but simply the number of single spun threads combined in the yarn.

2 Ply / thick and thin

Bouclé

Navajo

One thread traverses up and down the other during plying.

Chenille

Machine chained

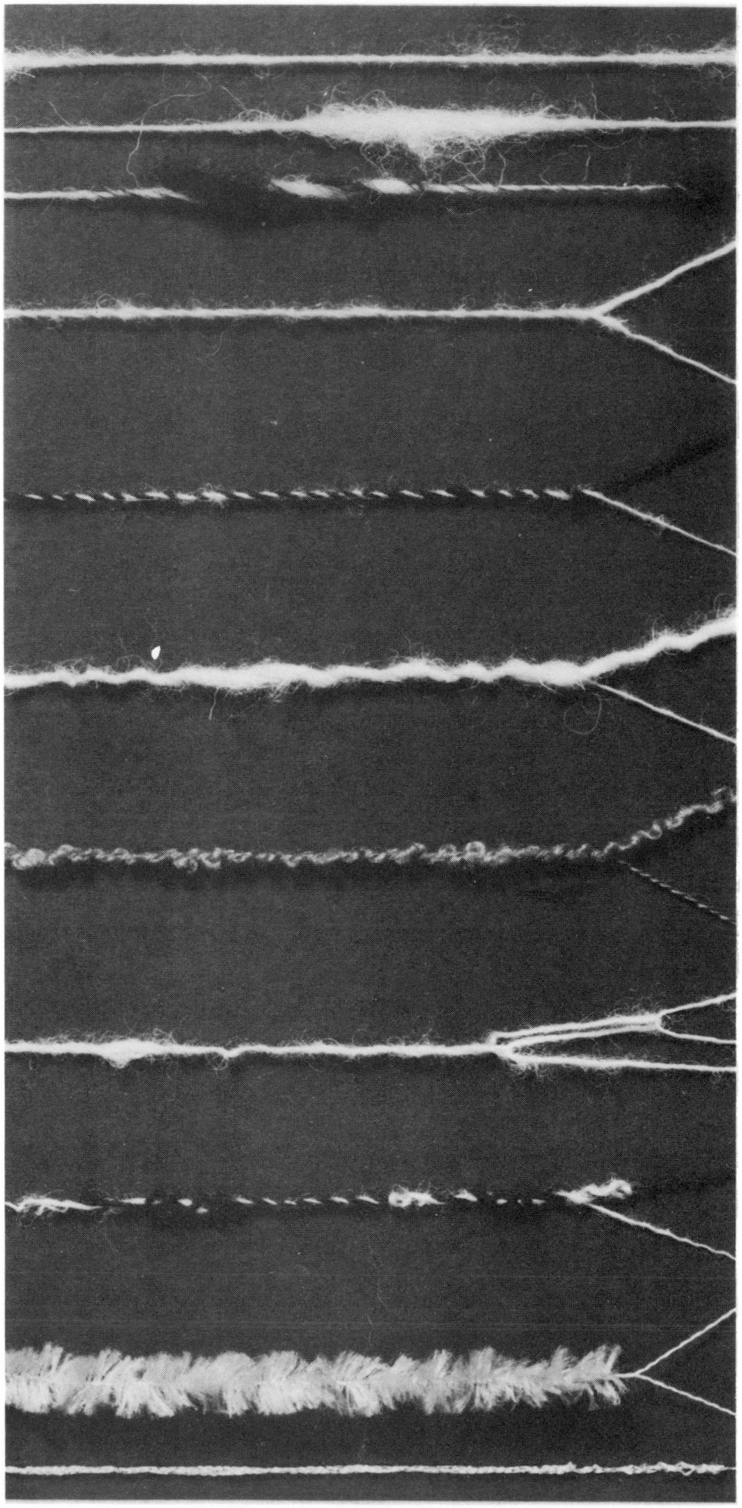

Yarn: Common Types

3 Ply

Cotton Qualities

4 Ply

Double Knitting

Triple Knitting

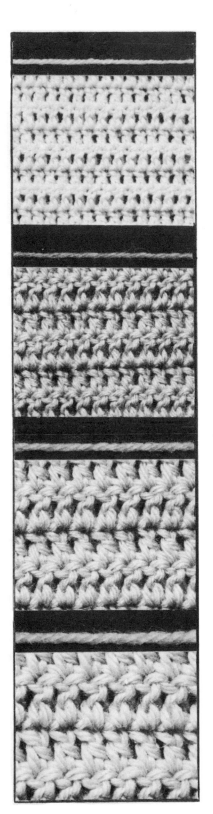
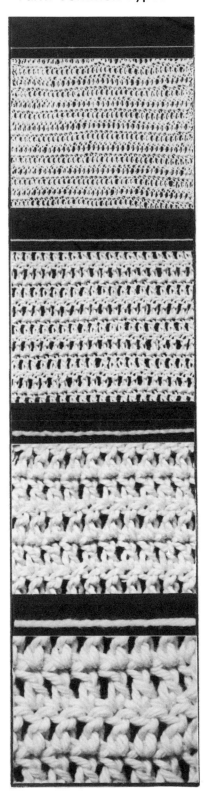

220

Mohair

Previously hand
chained yarn

Glitter

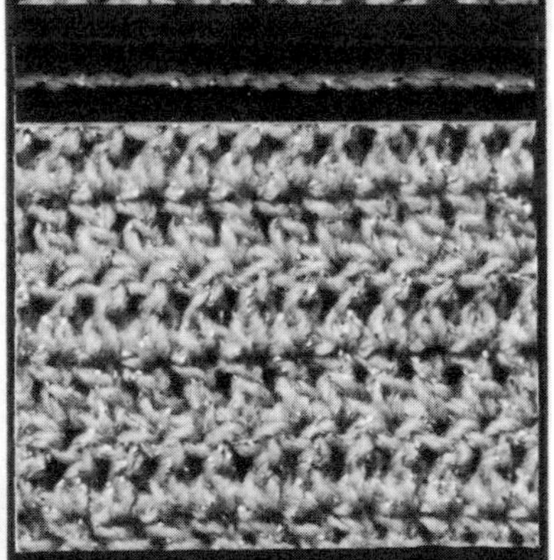

Metallic

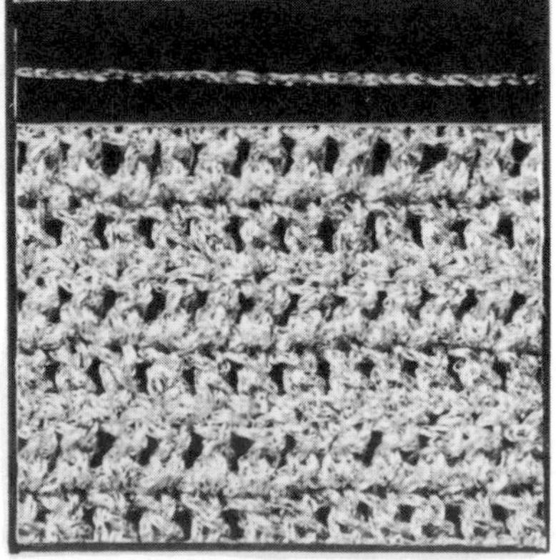

Bouclé

Crepe

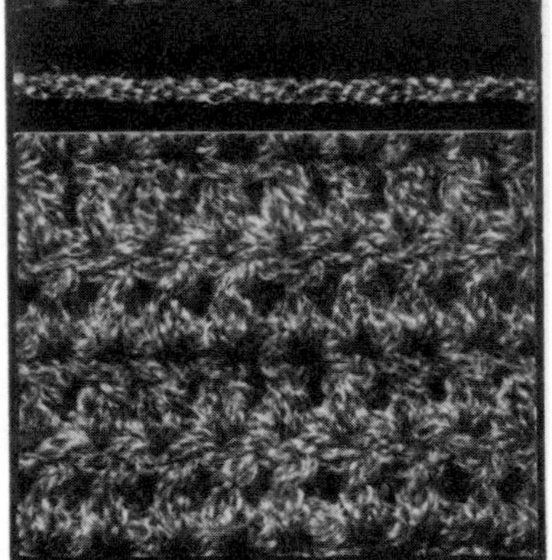

Slub

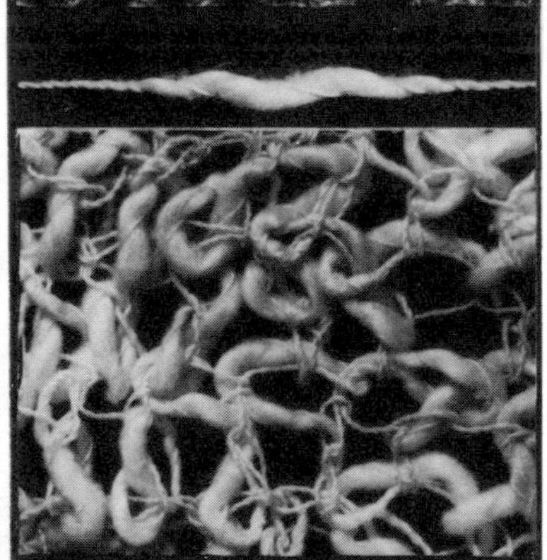

Rayon (tubular)

Commercially made machine spun yarns have the advantage that they are easy to obtain and require no preparation by the crochet worker. Anyone whose practical needs and aspirations are entirely satisfied by commercial pattern instructions will probably find that they will be happy with commercial yarns. Remember, however, that the whole nature of any piece of crochet work is determined as much, if not more, by the design of the yarn, as by the configuration of the stitches. Since the only yarns in the market place intended for crochet are, by definition, those which can be manufactured efficiently and cheaply and sold in huge quantities, the creative worker cannot expect to make anything at all individual using them alone. He will need to experiment with a much wider range of materials and become involved in the preparation of his own yarn.

Handspinning and Dyeing

Machine spun yarns are characteristically regular in quality and colour. If you spin by hand you can exploit all the natural variations which the manufacturer would exclude, and, when you are skilful, make completely individual yarns for particular projects, which change their colour and general character over short or long spans. Most plant fibres (including nettles!), animal fibres—particularly wool, but why not try the coat of your own dog or cat?—and synthetic fibres, for use on their own, or for blending, should be reasonably easy to obtain.

For dyeing natural fibres, which are often quite beautiful colours themselves anyway, try natural materials—berries, leaves, roots, bark, flowers. The wholesome, but subtle, results are quite unlike the simplified, flat and often crude synthetic colours we are used to now. Whether the colours you want are natural or synthetic, you will need to make your own.

Miscellaneous Materials

Ribbon

Unspun filament

Suede (strip)

Fusewire

Acetate (strip)

Rubber bands (linked)

Raffia

Jute

Miscellaneous Synthetics

Other Materials

The quest for suitable yarns is endless. Try materials not primarily intended for crochet: examine stocks of weaving yarns, visit rope and string makers. Many materials will not be suitable for clothes, but for sculpture and for some domestic articles fibreglass, plastic, polyethylene, polypropylene, all kinds of ribbon, leather and suede, bootlaces, cable and wire, straw, acetate and paper strip (twisted), linked rubber bands and flexible tubing all give variations in weight, bulk, flexibility, texture and colour and in the way they take the light.

Chapter 8
Making Up, Finishing and After Care

Darning In

Normally any loose ends of yarn which have accrued during the making of each piece of fabric should be darned in before any pressing or making up. Occasionally however it can be convenient deliberately to leave an extra long piece to use for sewing a seam.

To darn in short ends first make sure they are projecting on the wrong side of the fabric. Thread them individually onto a blunt, wool needle and darn neatly and inconspicuously into the wrong side. If they are too short to thread, darn in the needle first, bringing the eye up to the base of the thread, then thread and pull through. If there are two ends together and they are very short, darn each first through the base of the other, then into the fabric. Before finally snipping off any loose ends after darning, ease the fabric slightly along the direction of the darned thread to relax the tension in it.

Some types of yarn are so slippery that they give the greatest difficulty in joining, fastening off and darning in. In some cases, maddeningly, a tightly made reef knot will pull quietly apart like a hot wire through butter. On these occasions you must use whatever ingenious means you can to keep the ends in place.

Yarn Treatment

Conventional crochet yarns may be made of natural or synthetic fibres, or mixtures of both. In each case different treatment is required for pressing, washing and/or dry-cleaning. Some yarns indeed must not be pressed or washed at all; some require special attention in dry-cleaning. Application of the wrong procedure at any stage can easily prove fatal, so it is extremely important to know what the material is and what the manufacturers recommend. In the case of branded yarns all the relevant information will be printed on the ball band, which should be kept safely.

In order to be prepared for the occasions when you buy unbranded yarn, perhaps in the hank, and no information is supplied, it is a good plan to collect a 'library' of clearly labelled left-overs from balls whose constitution you definitely do know. Take a scrap of your new, unmarked yarn and (exercising all due care!) set light to it briefly. If it forms a brittle blob, the fibre must be predominantly synthetic. Do the same to your synthetic library specimens in turn, comparing the smells, until you find the one which matches. (Polypropylene smells rather like candles.)

Pressing

Here is a general guide to pressing procedures, but always follow the exact specifications of the manufacturer, where these differ.

Material	Iron	Cloth	Manner
Pure Wool	Warm	Damp	Light-firm
Cotton	Hot	Damp	Firm
Mohair	Warm	Damp	Very light
Nylon	Cool	Dry	Light
Acrylic	Do not iron		
Glitter			

Even though your materials may technically permit pressing, in crochet it is by no means always prudent. So many kinds of fabric and texture are spoiled, even by the discreet attentions of the iron, that it is almost better to say never press, unless you are personally convinced that the process will definitely improve your result. Most fine lacework needs firm and comprehensive pressing before it will lie flat or fall beautifully. On the other hand a fabric made predominantly of raised stitches, knobbles or ridges can scarcely afford to be steamed. Your main object in pressing at all is to set the fabric into its appropriate shape and plane by resolving some of the myriad stresses in the thread, but without causing the thread to fuse or the individual stitches to merge and lose their identity. Indeed if you find you prefer a fabric in this condition it may be that you are working in the wrong medium.

General Technique for Two-dimensional Work

You need a firm but padded horizontal surface—for instance an old table covered by at least a double thickness of old blanket with, for protection, a thick spread of old newspapers underneath, and, for convenience, an old sheet stretched on top. A conventional ironing board is hardly ever large enough. You also need an iron with a controllable heat output, a large number of pins (preferably rustless) and pressing cloths as large as you may need and capable of being used wet or dry.

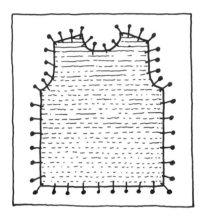

Blocking: Place the fabric right side down. Pin it to the pad all round the edges to the correct dimensions and shape, starting with the corners, patting and coaxing into place. Check frequently with your tape measure. Make sure the parts which should be straight or curved are really straight or appropriately curved; that edges which are supposed to match other edges do so; that parallels are really parallel and right angles really 90°. It is often useful to have a large enough area to be able to pin out several pieces of fabric side by side, but failing that pin down corresponding pieces right sides together and press them together, or fold a single piece in half right sides together and remember not to press near the fold itself.

Never skimp on pins; always pin each picot separately. You have probably put in many hours of careful work; do you propose to ruin it all in the course of the next few minutes?

If you have no iron, or prefer not to use it, leave the well-damped fabric pinned out in this way to begin with under damp cloth (and, may be, some weight); let it dry completely before you unpin.

Pressing: When the iron has reached the correct working temperature, lay the pressing cloth carefully over the work (damp or dry as indicated) and apply the iron (firmly, gently, just touching or held above) in a series of downward-upward movements across the cloth. Never sweep sideways in contact with the cloth, as you might when ironing normally. Wait until any steam has subsided and the fabric has cooled before removing the pins, then lay it aside on a flat surface in shape until you are ready to join the pieces.

Three-dimensional Work

In the case of three-dimensional work your intentions are the same, except that the last thing you want is to press the fabric flat. A selection of soft but firmly padded shapes, which you must make yourself, is most useful. Pinning and anything other than very slight pressure are often out of the question. In crochet sculpture frequently there is no alternative to pressing or rather steaming the right side of the fabric. Fortunately stuffed shapes should require no pressing, but, if they do, take care that the stuffing material is not of a kind to react unfavourably to the heat of the iron.

Seams and Sewing

Seams may be sewn by hand or machine, or sometimes crocheted. The strongest hand sewn seam is made by backstitching. This method has the advantage that stepped edges may be straightened or angles curved, but it always leaves a ridge. This ridge is usually made on the wrong side and reduced by pressing, but it can occasionally make a design feature on the right side. Or, if the stitch pattern is fairly solid and the fabric not too thick, it can be enclosed in an overlapping seam by a second row of topstitching.

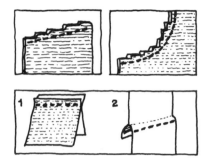

The flat, woven seam is ideal when it is important to avoid any extra bulk, for instance in openwork, or for sewn-on bands, but it cannot be used unless the edges in question are straight or at least interlocking.

Overcast stitching is useful for turning up hems and attaching ribbon, petersham, appliqué motifs or patch pockets. It is normally easy enough to attach the straight edge of a second piece of fabric so that it aligns horizontally with a particular row of the main fabric, but to help align it vertically, try weaving in a thin knitting needle or some contrasting thread along the appropriate line of stitches first.

Herringbone stitch is a convenient method of securing elastic.

Buttonhole stitch, besides being a practical finish for actual buttonholes, is useful for decorative work.

Needle and thread: For machining you will select a matching thread of material compatible with that of the main fabric. For hand sewing the main yarn itself is best. If it is too thick, try splitting off a single ply; otherwise find a matching yarn in a thinner quality. Use a wool needle with a blunt point and large hole. Secure the yarn by making two or three small backstitches on top of one another at the beginning and darning in the end in the usual way.

Hand Stitching

Backstitch

Flat Woven

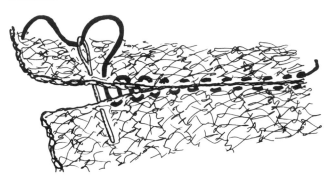

Overcast

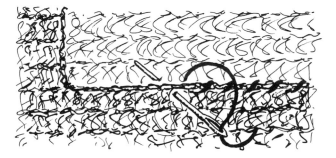

Herringbone

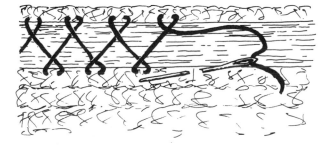

Buttonhole

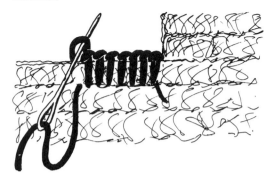

If pieces of two different colours are to be joined, it is usually
better to use the darker coloured thread. When bands of colour
run across a seam the perfectionist may wish to vary the seam
thread accordingly, in which case it is more convenient when
making the fabric in the first place to fasten off after each band,
leaving enough over for sewing up that particular band, rather
than to carry the yarns unbroken up the side of the work.

Side seams between two similar fabrics should be carefully
matched row for row. In the case of a flat seam this is easy
because you can arrange to see the same side of each piece. In
backstitching on the other hand this is deceptive and you
should work with care and, if you are inexperienced, make
constant visual checks with the fabric unfolded flat. Seams
should be sewn neither too tightly nor too loosely. It is usually
easy to see whether either of these things is happening,
provided you check frequently. The order for sewing seams is
usually stated in pattern instructions; otherwise use common
sense—perhaps saving yourself breaking off and rejoining by
sewing, say, side and sleeve seams in one.

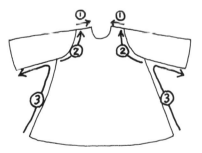

The direction of sewing a particular seam may not be important
so long as any corresponding seam is sewn in the corresponding
direction.

Backstitch seams normally involve placing the two pieces to be
joined right sides together and with their edges aligned. Some
exceptions are: 1 when you want the ridge on the right side;
2 collars; 3 overlapping seams.

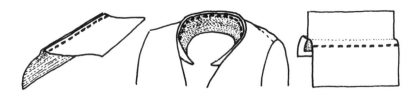

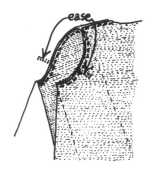

Preliminary pinning or tacking may not always be necessary, but, when it is, do not skimp. Gathering which has not been constructed into the pattern of the fabric is easier to control if a temporary draw thread is woven through first.

Setting in sleeves: To set in a sleeve first sew the shoulder seam. It is then most convenient to turn the main garment wrong side out, keep the sleeve right side out and slip it between the front and bck sections of the main garment, so as to bring the top edge into line with the armhole. Make sure that the centre of the sleeve is aligned with the top of the shoulder (usually a seam), that the underarm curved sections each side are fitted smoothly and that any ease is taken up evenly over the top of the shoulder. After setting in, if the sleeve and side seams have not already been sewn separately, it will be possible to draw the sleeve through and sew them 'in one'.

So that you will have some spare yarn at a later stage for minor mending in the same colour and condition as the article, weave some with your needle down any backstitched seam.

Seam strengthening: Some seams, for instance the shoulder seams of a heavy jacket, can benefit from the additional strength of a firm strip of ribbon or binding.

Crochet Joins

Slip stitch and double crochet: In circumstances where you would otherwise sew a backstitch seam with a needle, it will usually be possible to work a row of slip stitches with a crochet hook instead. The resulting seam will tend to be more bulky. Similarly double crochet may be used (see also Edging, page 183). This creates its own neat ridge on the right side when the wrong sides of the pieces are put together and can therefore be more suitable than other methods when the seam has a decorative value, for instance in patchwork. Regulation of tension and of row alignment may be more awkward with crocheted seams, but unravelling—should this ever become necessary—much easier.

In patchwork pieces can be joined with some form of decorative work, which complements the design of the main pieces.

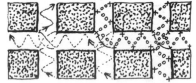

Motifs constructed on the circular format can often be designed so as to join to others during the last round. Characteristically chain loops or picots are interrupted halfway, whilst a slip stitch is worked into the centre of a corresponding loop.

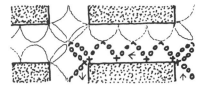

Any intermediate spaces may be filled in by on-the-spot crochet after the pieces have been joined.

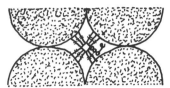

As in some forms of crochet lace individual shapes and motifs can be basted onto a backing sheet, e.g. a tracing of a design, and a complete background network made to fit by trial and error between and around them, connecting them into a fabric (see page 122).

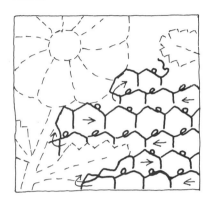

In appliqué work a complete fabric is made first and motifs, etc. are sewn neatly onto it with invisible or decorative stitches. Sometimes when the main fabric is a network, or liable to distortion, or the motifs are to fit a particular design, it is advisable to baste the main fabric onto a tracing first.

Whatever method of joining is used, it is vital to take great care assembling the pieces of a patchwork fabric. Not only will it matter that each piece is in the right place in relation to its neighbours and the overall design, but that the correct side of each piece is facing, and possibly also that it is rotated to a particular angle. Since the mechanics of joining may involve placing pieces together two at a time, face to face, upside down and the wrong way round, there is plenty of opportunity for error. A way of reducing part of the problem is to assemble all the pieces in their final positions on a flat surface whilst they are still separate and leave them there until actually required for joining.

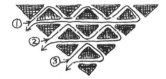

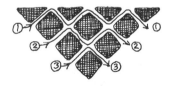

The simplest way to join formal arrangements of identical shapes is first to make rows and then join these. Schemes using fewer continuous seams are possible and they will be quicker to complete—provided they do not nudge you into mistakes!

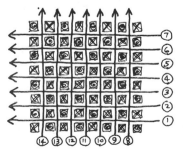

Elastic

First cut the required length and sew into a circle. Then stretch to fit the dimensions of the fabric and pin in at least four (if not eight, or even sixteen) evenly spaced places. Then at the sewing stage—using herringbone casing—you need concentrate on stretching out only a few centimetres at a time between your fingers to ensure even distribution. It does not seem to be important whether you actually catch the elastic with the needle, or simply encase it.

Zip Fasteners

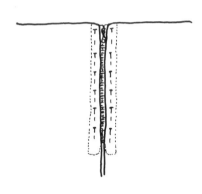

A zip fastener should be closed and placed underneath the fabric (i.e. with its own right side against the wrong side of the fabric) and then pinned to both sides of the opening so that the rows of the fabric match in the usual way. (The fastener may be opened later to facilitate the actual sewing.) Be careful not to stretch or gather the fabric along the length of the zip whilst pinning. If the yarn of the main fabric is not too hairy, it should be possible to have the edges meet over the zipper teeth and so conceal them; otherwise take the edges as near to the teeth as possible. Starting at the top on one side and with the right side facing, work in neat backstitch down to the bottom. Then, unless the zip is open ended, make a few strengthening stitches across the bottom and continue up the other side.

Velcro

Provided it is sewn on firmly and manipulated carefully velcro can be useful for semi-permanent joins, for instance for multi-purpose garments having, say, a detachable collar, or an optional mid/full length skirt. As a normal fastening it is dangerous, because in practice the wearer will strain the garment in his repeated efforts to separate the surfaces, or damage the crochet fabric accidentally by enmeshing it with the hooked surface.

Buttons and Buttonhole Edging

Edgings where there are buttons and buttonholes will be strengthened if you sew a strip of ribbon or non-stretch fabric on the wrong side. A slit will then have to be made for each buttonhole and the openings circled with buttonhole stitch. Some people like to sew their buttons, not onto the fabric but onto second buttons at the back of the work.

Lining

There is a great deal of disagreement about the feasibility and effectiveness of lining crochet garments, whether this be to help preserve the shape and life of the garment, improve the hang of the fabric, provide the extra substance, elegance and richness some people look for, or simply to preserve the modesty of the wearer when the fabric is semi-transparent. Experience is apt only to reinforce any prejudices one started off with. If you are an expert dressmaker and have the experience and sensitivity to select an appropriate material which will support the flexible crochet fabric without fighting with it, you may well find lining is worthwhile. The less gifted are advised not to try. An iron-on type of fabric which adheres to the wrong side all over may provide excellent support for, say, a heavy jacket and, if it does not inhibit the way the crochet hangs and moves, contribute usefully to the overall effect. More often than not, however, the behaviour of a conventional lining material will not be compatible with that of crochet fabric. In the case of a dress, blouse or skirt, it is better to have the wearer invest in a suitable, separate underslip, or, if an integral lining is absolutely necessary, to attach it to the garment at a minimum of strategic points, for instance at the waistband only of a skirt.

It may be that the traditional approach to lining represents a complete misconception of the medium of crochet. Perhaps as a general rule the best types and styles of garments are those which derive directly from the nature of the materials and their construction and maybe these are entirely at odds with any notions of lining in the usual sense, imported wholesale from other disciplines as they tend to be. Solid crochet fabrics have a special way of clinging, hanging and swirling; some openwork ones demand to be seen as two or more thicknesses moving independently behind one another. The most genuine case for a so-called lining is one in which the design has been conceived from the outset as a series of two or more separate layers; even this is a far cry from the conventional slip, intended as a neutral barrier.

Cleaning

Washing
Always follow the exact specifications of the manufacturer. If in any doubt, wash by hand.

Handwashing: Wash briefly and frequently, using a solution of well dissolved soap or detergent specially designed for knitwear. Wash by gently massaging and squeezing so that the lather permeates the fibres. Rinse extremely well in tepid water by squeezing against the side of the bowl whilst the water runs away, changing the water several times until all traces of the soap have gone. If you add fabric conditioner for the last rinse (this works by neutralizing the electrical charge in the fibres) always immerse the whole batch in the water at one time rather than one item after another, because the ingredients, irrespective of how much you have put in, are likely to spend themselves on the first article and promptly lose their effectiveness.

Finally squeeze out as much water as you can, carry the article carefully to a flat surface which you have covered with a clean towel and lay out, patting into shape. You may be able to remove more moisture by placing a second towel on top, rolling up, squeezing and unrolling. Alternatively give the article a brief spell in a spin-drier, say, until the main rush of water subsides. Leave to dry flat away from direct heat or sunlight. If you must use a clothes horse, do not let any part of the fabric hang down unsupported. *Never:* leave in soak; use very hot water; rub, wring, twist, or use aggressive movements; let the weight of water put stress on the fabric; hang up (even damp dry); or power dry. If you starch the article, leave to dry pinned out to the exact shape.

For washing and drying in the hank see Re-using Yarn below.

Dry Cleaning
Some manmade materials should not be dry cleaned at all; others only in certain solvents. Symbols to this effect are now

usually printed on the ball bands; always inform the dry cleaner of them and of the composition of the material.

After Care

Store crocheted articles flat, not hanging up.

'Pills' can sometimes be removed from a smooth fabric by laying it out flat and shaving carefully with a safety razor, or by dabbing with clear adhesive tape, or stroking with a proprietary 'cat's tongue' brush.

A fluffy surface can be restored by stroking with teazles or the hooked surface of a velcro strip.

Unravelling

Crochet unravels easily backwards, but not forwards.

Forwards: Of course it is actually possible to unravel from the beginning of the thread, if you have the patience, by hooking the whole thread right through each and every loop one at a time. A few chains are easily dispatched in this way, but otherwise it is never worth the effort.

Backwards: Feathery yarns, and sometimes knobbly ones, too, can often be difficult to unravel even in the way they are supposed to, because stray fibres become meshed. (They can take longer to unravel than to crochet up in the first place!) Never pull indiscriminately and impatiently. At the first signs of reluctance stop pulling, so as to avoid strangling the loops, and look carefully for the offending fibres. If you cannot see them, gently coax undone the stitch *behind* the snagged point—it will then be easier to find the snag, which may come undone of its own accord at that stage anyway.

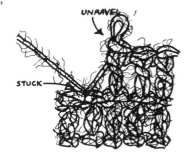

Shortening

If you need to remove some of the first rows of a fabric, leaving the rest intact, for instance to shorten a skirt which was made upwards, you have to cut. Before that, however, secure the lower edge of your new 'first' row with a fresh base chain as follows:

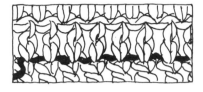

1   With a wool needle and some contrasting thread pick up neatly all the threads at the base of each stitch right across the row. Take care not to miss any, not to split them and not to catch any threads of the stitches in the previous row. Tie the thread marker into a loose ring.

2   Cut through the yarn at the base of the last stitch at the end of the previous row. Unravel that stitch and darn in the short end. Pull the other end to unravel the rest of the row and the superfluous material will fall away.

3   Work one row of slip stitches into each stitch to simulate a base chain. Cut and pull out the marker thread.

Lengthening

To lengthen at the 'wrong' end, prepare in much the same way as for shortening, i.e. slip a marker thread into the bases of the first row of stitches so you can remove the base chain. Then make the extra fabric separately, until it is one row shorter than required. Making sure the old fabric is orientated correctly, in order to maintain the continuity in the direction of working each row, work the final row onto the new fabric, at the same time joining to the old fabric as follows:

Work 1 chain less than the usual turning chain, remove the hook from the last loop, insert the hook in reverse direction through the base of the first stitch of the old fabric, pick up the loop just left and pull it through, yrh, pull through, *remove the hook from the last loop, insert the hook in reverse direction through the base of the next stitch (old fabric), pick up the loop just left and pull it through, work the next stitch into the new fabric normally, repeat from * to the end of the row. Darn in ends. Cut and pull out the marker thread.

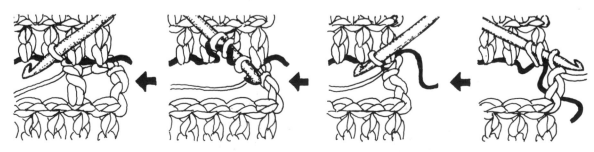

Re-using Yarn

Unpick all seams carefully without snipping any threads in the
main fabric. Unravel the yarn directly into hanks, either round
your forearm or a chair back. Secure the hanks with a loose
figure of eight tie in at least four places with pieces of
contrasting yarn and wash as you would the made up article.
Hang the hanks up to dry away from direct heat with just
sufficient weight to remove the kinks. An old plastic bottle
filled as required with water makes a convenient and adjustable
weight. Finally wind loosely into balls again.

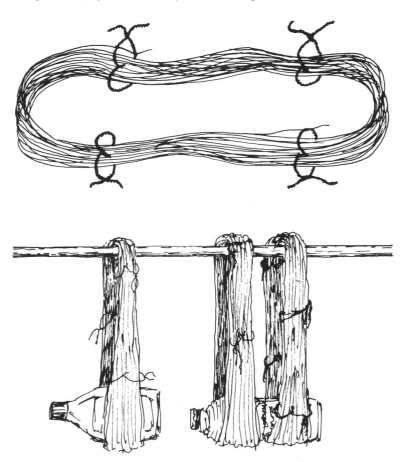

Appendices

Useful Formulae

$2\pi r$
Circumference of a circle, where r is the radius. ($\pi = \frac{22}{7}$ or 3.1416)

πr^2
Area of a circle

2n–4 right angles
Total of angles inside a regular polygon, where n is the number of sides

Equipment

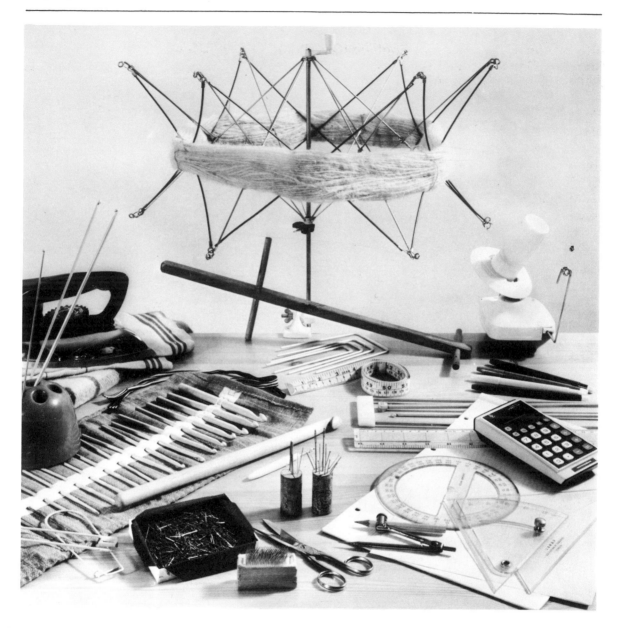

Storage
Workstand, bags, boxes.

Crochet
Range of ordinary and Tunisian hooks; stitch holders (safety pins); hairpin(s); (row counter).

Measurement
Non-stretch tape measure; 30cm (12in) transparent ruler.

Cutting
Scissors, stitch-ripper.

Sewing Up
Wool needle, sewing needle, bodkin; rustless pins, thimble.

Pressing
Iron (steam);
pressing surface – a large, old table (conventional ironing boards are seldom large enough) covered with newspaper and an old blanket;
pressing cloths – 1 metre or 1 yard square fine cotton/muslin;
sleeve board – padded cotton material;
selection of padded shapes for 3D work.

General
Notebook, pencil, coloured pens, graph paper, protractor, set square, pair of compasses;
small, tie-on labels for identifying crochet specimens/test pieces/yarns;
skein winder, ball winder;
niddy-noddy – for winding loose or balled yarn into skeins.

Hook Sizes

International Standard Range (ISR) Figs=diameter of hook in mm	England (Old Nos.)			USA	
	Wool	Cotton Aero	Milwards		
10.00					
9.50					
9.00	000			15	
8.50	00			13	
8.00	0			12	
7.50	1			11	
7.00	2			$10\frac{1}{2}$	K
6.50	3			10	J
6.00	4			9	I
5.50	5			8	H
5.00	6			7	
4.50	7			6	G
4.00	8			5	F
3.50	9			4	E
3.25	10			3	D
3.00	10/11	3/0	3/0	2	C
2.75	11			2	
2.50	12	0	2/0	1	B
2.25	13		1/0	0	
2.00	14	$1\frac{1}{2}$	1		
			$1\frac{1}{2}$		
1.75	15	$2\frac{1}{2}$	2		
1.50	16	$3\frac{1}{2}$	$2\frac{1}{2}$		
1.25		$4\frac{1}{2}$	3		
			$3\frac{1}{2}$		
1.00		$5\frac{1}{2}$	4		
			$4\frac{1}{2}$		
0.75		$6\frac{1}{2}$	5		
			$5\frac{1}{2}$		
0.60		7	6		
			$6\frac{1}{2}$		
			7		
			8		

Terms/Abbreviations/Symbols

English		Symbol	American Equivalent	
St(s)	Stitch(es)		St(s)	Stitch(es)
Ch(s)	Chain(s)	o oo●oo	Ch(s)	Chain(s)
Sp(s)	Space(s)		Sp(s)	Space(s)
T.ch	Turning Chain		T.ch	Turning Chain
St.ch	Starting Chain		St.ch	Starting Chain
SS(Sl.st)	Slip Stitch (Single Crochet)	⌒	Sl.st	Slip Stitch
Dc	Double Crochet	+	Sc	Single Crochet
H.tr(Hlf.tr)	Half Treble (Yrh once)	T	H.dc	Half Double Crochet
Tr	Treble (Yrh once)	f	Dc	Double Crochet
D.tr(Dbl.tr)	Double Treble (Yrh twice)	‡	Tr	Treble
T.Tr(Trip.tr)	Triple Treble (Yrh 3 times)		D.tr	Double Treble
Qd.Tr(Quad.tr)	Quadruple Treble (Yrh 4 times)		T.tr	Triple Treble
Qn.Tr(Quin.tr)	Quintuple Treble (Yrh 5 times)		Qd.tr	Quadruple Treble

Bl (Blk)	Block	R	Raised (prefix to vertical stitches hence R.tr = raised treble)	
Cl	Cluster			
	Bar			
Gr (Gp)	Group	R.tr/F	Treble raised at the front	
	Lacet	R.tr./B	Treble raised at the back	
Lp	Loop		Solomon's Knot	
	Bobble	Tog	Together	
P	Picot	Yrh	Yarn round hook (also: Yo. Yoh. Wo. Woh. Wrh. etc.)	
Pc	Popcorn			
P.st	Puff Stitch			

A,B,C, etc.	Yarn shades	Mult	Multiple
Alt	Alternate	No(s)	Number(s)
Approx	Approximate(ly)	Patt	Pattern
B	Back	Oz	Ounce(s)
Beg	Beginning	Rem	Remaining
C (Con)	Contrast shade	Rep	Repeat
Cm	Centimetre(s)	Rnd	Round
Col	Colour	RS	Right side
Cont	Continue	WS	Wrong side
Dec	Decrease	1st	First (may also mean 'one stitch', but see context.)
Excl	Excluding		
F	Front		Stitch (tr) worked into the front loop only
Folls	Follows		
In	Inch(es)		Stitch (tr) worked into the back loop only
Inc	Increase		
Incl	Including		General direction of working
lb	Pound(s)		Direction of individual row
M	Main shade		Markers
L, D	Light, dark shades		Ends of thread

Conversion Tables

In	cm		Cm	In	
$\frac{1}{8}$	0.32		1	$\frac{3}{8}$	(0.39)
$\frac{1}{4}$	0.64		2	$\frac{3}{4}$	(0.79)
$\frac{3}{8}$	0.95		2.5	1	(0.98)
$\frac{1}{2}$	1.27		3	$1\frac{1}{8}$	(1.18)
$\frac{5}{8}$	1.59		4	$1\frac{1}{2}$	(1.57)
$\frac{3}{4}$	1.91		5	2	(1.97)
$\frac{7}{8}$	2.22		6	$2\frac{3}{8}$	(2.36)
1	2.5 (2.54)		7	$2\frac{3}{4}$	(2.75)
2	5.0 (5.1)		8	$3\frac{1}{8}$	(3.15)
3	7.5 (7.6)		9	$3\frac{1}{2}$	(3.54)
4	10.0 (10.2)		10	4	(3.93)
5	12.5 (12.7)		12.5	5	(4.91)
6	15.0 (15.3)		15	6	(5.90)
7	17.5 (17.8)		17.5	$6\frac{7}{8}$	(6.88)
8	20.0 (20.4)		20	$7\frac{7}{8}$	(7.87)
9	22.5 (22.9)		22.5	$8\frac{7}{8}$	(8.85)
10	25.0 (25.5)		25	$9\frac{7}{8}$	(9.83)
11	28.0		27.5	$10\frac{7}{8}$	(10.81)
12	30.5 (30.6)		30	$11\frac{7}{8}$	(11.80)
13	33.0 (33.1)		32.5	$12\frac{7}{8}$	(12.78)
14	35.5 (35.7)		35	$13\frac{3}{4}$	(13.76)
15	38.0 (38.2)		37.5	$14\frac{3}{4}$	(14.74)
16	40.5 (40.7)		40	$15\frac{3}{4}$	(15.73)
17	43.0 (43.3)		42.5	$16\frac{3}{4}$	(16.71)
18	45.5 (45.8)		45	$17\frac{3}{4}$	(17.69)
19	48.0 (48.4)		47.5	$18\frac{3}{4}$	(18.67)
20	50.5 (50.9)		50	$19\frac{3}{4}$	(19.67)
21	53.0 (53.4)		52.5	$20\frac{3}{8}$	(20.65)
22	55.5 (55.9)		55	$21\frac{5}{8}$	(21.63)
23	58.5 (58.5)		57.5	$22\frac{5}{8}$	(22.61)
24	61.0		60	$23\frac{5}{8}$	(23.61)
25	63.5 (63.6)		62.5	$24\frac{5}{8}$	(24.59)
26	66.0 (66.1)		65	$25\frac{5}{8}$	(25.57)
27	68.5 (68.7)		67.5	$26\frac{5}{8}$	(26.55)
28	71.0 (71.2)		70	$27\frac{7}{8}$	(27.54)
29	73.5 (73.7)		72.5	$28\frac{1}{2}$	(28.52)
30	76.0 (76.3)		75	$29\frac{1}{2}$	(29.50)
31	78.5 (78.8)		77.5	$30\frac{1}{2}$	(30.48)
32	81.0 (81.4)		80	$31\frac{1}{2}$	(31.48)
33	83.5 (83.9)		82.5	$32\frac{1}{2}$	(32.46)
34	86.0 (86.4)		85	$33\frac{1}{2}$	(33.44)
35	88.5 (88.9)		87.5	$34\frac{1}{2}$	(34.42)
36	91.5		90	$35\frac{1}{2}$	(35.41)
37	94.0		92.5	$36\frac{3}{8}$	(36.39)
38	96.5 (96.6)		95	$37\frac{3}{8}$	(37.37)
39	99.0 (99.1)		97.5	$38\frac{3}{8}$	(38.35)
40	101.5 (101.7)		100	$39\frac{3}{8}$	(39.34)

Grams	Oz/lb
1	0.035 oz
5	0.176
10	0.353
20	0.705
30	1.058
40	1.41
50	1.76
100	3.53
200	7.05
227	8.0
300	10.58
400	14.11
454	16.0
500	17.65
1000	2.2 lb
2000	4.4

Oz	Grams
1	28.35
2	56.7
3	85.05
4	113.4
5	141.75
6	170.1
7	198.45
8	226.8
9	255.15
10	283.5
11	311.85
12	340.2
13	368.55
14	396.9
15	425.25
16	453.6

Answers to Puzzles

Beginners' Project: Mistakes

(see page 72)
Read anticlockwise.

Round 1:
1. 2dc instead of 1dc.

Round 2:
2. Dc instead of h.tr.

Round 3:
3. 3rd tr in ch loop.
4. Only 2trs in group.
5. No 5th ch in loop.

Round 4:
6. Sts not worked together properly.
7. Cluster worked under ch loop instead of into specific chs.

Round 5:
8. 3rd st of group is tr instead of d.tr.
9. Joining SS in wrong ch.

Round 6:
10. Extra T.tr in first group.
11. 2nd T.tr worked over first.
12. Only 3ch in loop.

Round 7:
13. Part of group missing.
14. No ch loop.
15. Extra tr in group.

Round 8:
16. Dc in wrong place.
17. Only 3ch in loop.

Round 9
18. 3rd loop missing.
19. Cluster worked under ch loop instead of into centre ch.
20. Dc worked instead of SS to join.

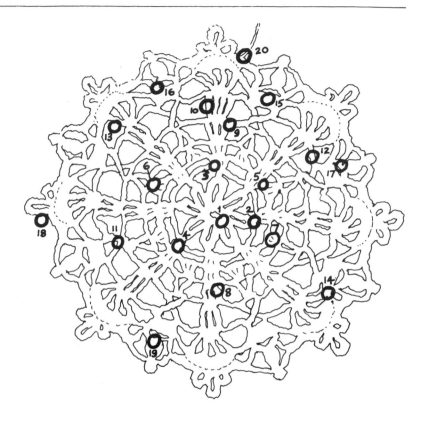

Naturally if you had had the fabric itself your examination would have been more realistic. Partly because of the photograph you have probably not found all the mistakes listed, but think you have detected others instead. How hard did you look? How many mistakes would you have spotted, if you had not been specifically encouraged to do so? Would you normally look at your own work quite as hard? Do mistakes matter anyway? If so, when?

Stitch Diagram Exercise

(see page 116)

Example 1

Example 2

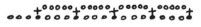

Punctuation

(see page 62)

Jones, where Brown had had 'had', had had 'had had'. 'Had had' had had the examiner's approval.

Index